RETHINKING THE LABOR PROCESS

SUNY series, The New Inequalities
A. Gary Dworkin, editor

Rethinking the Labor Process

Edited by
Mark Wardell,
Thomas L. Steiger,
and Peter Meiksins

STATE UNIVERSITY OF NEW YORK PRESS

Published by
State University of New York Press, Albany

© 1999 State University of New York

For information, address State University of New York Press,
State University Plaza, Albany, N.Y., 12246

Production by Cathleen Collins
Marketing by Fran Keneston

Library of Congress Cataloging in Publication Data

Rethinking the labor process / edited by Mark Wardell, Thomas L.
Steiger, and Peter Meiksins.
   p. cm. — (SUNY series, the new inequalities)
   Includes bibliographical references and index.
   ISBN 0-7914-4281-0 (alk. paper). — ISBN 0-7914-4282-9 (pbk. :
alk. paper)
   1. Braverman, Harry. 2. Industrial sociology. 3. Division of labor.
4. Employees—Effect of technological innovations on. 5. Industrial relations.
6. Sex role in the work environment. 7. Management. 8. Social conflict.
9. Equality. 10. Organizational change. I. Wardell, Mark L., 1946- II. Steiger,
Thomas L., 1958-   III. Meiksins, Peter, 1953-   IV. Series.
   HD6955 .R47 1999
   331—dc21   98-51013
                                       CIP

10 9 8 7 6 5 4 3 2 1

Contents

Preface

Twenty-five years ago, Harry Braverman (1974) published *Labor and Monopoly Capital*. Almost immediately, the book and Braverman received a great deal of scrutiny, much of it favorable and much of it unfavorable. In large part, the focus of this scrutiny centered on the subtitle of the book, *The Degradation of Work in the Twentieth Century*. This subtitle triggered what has come to be known as the "deskilling debate," involving questions such as what Braverman meant by degradation, whether an absolute degradation of work occurred in the twentieth century, and if so, what that meant for workers themselves. Still others criticized Braverman's work for its grounding in Marx's *Capital*, whereas others defended this influence as the strength of Braverman's work. Numerous other debates emerged as well.

While much debate has occurred since Braverman's book appeared, and in a variety of disciplines (education, management, economics, and sociology) in the United States and Europe, few observers would deny the impact of his work. It focused on a prominent intellectual agenda in the study of work and inequality throughout the late 1970s and 1980s. As years passed, observers began assessing the theoretical mileage gained from the various debates and from the major concept central to Braverman's work, namely, the labor process.

The purpose of this collected volume is not to retrace the history of the debates or to reassess Braverman's reasoning for a particular emphasis, or lack of emphasis, he gave to specific concepts, such as subjectivity, gender, Taylorism, control, and resistance. Rather, the purpose is to move beyond Braverman, his book, and the subsequent debates by showing how the labor process remains an important unit of analysis for understanding the changes transforming workplaces and the implications for the people involved. Indeed, the significance of Braverman's work in the long run is not whether his conclusions about degradation of work in the twentieth century were right or wrong, but in his drawing attention to labor processes as a key unit of analysis by which to gain insights into the hidden abode of workplaces.

Toward this end, we have assembled a variety of authors, attempting to rethink the labor process perspective and to show how it can extend the understanding of today's world of work and the inequalities produced and reproduced in the workplace. We begin with a chapter that sets out the theoretical parameters of a labor process perspective. While some recapitulation of the debates will be necessary, the first chapter is an attempt to reach beyond the focus of any subsequent chapter in the volume. Nevertheless, it represents only one possibility for rethinking the labor process.

The chapters that follow contain various analyses in which the authors rethink the labor process but in different ways and on a different scale than the first chapter. In many ways, this collection represents a compendium of possibilities for future labor process research. Chapters 2 and 3 address recent trends in management orientations and their relation to the way workplaces have been reorganized in the past twenty-five years. Teamwork, computer technologies, and the flexible distribution of workers are of particular interest. Chapters 4 and 5 likewise look at flexibility and changes in the workplace with a particular concern for how these changes result in different labor processes, leading in certain instances to a devaluation of women's work. Chapters 6 and 7 reach for new ways of relating management orientations with the conventional labor process themes of control and resistance. The authors analyze influences that lie beyond the shopfloor and ultimately impact the organization of and experiences within labor processes. Chapters 8 and 9 turn to a theme deeply embedded in labor process thinking; the value of labor. The former looks at workers' earnings by gender and occupation, while the latter concentrates on labor's share by industry. Finally, the book ends with a statement from two British colleagues as they relate recent developments in labor process thinking in their country; in doing so, they provide a capstone to the entire volume.

Importantly, this collection of papers is jointly sponsored by the Society for the Study of Social Problems and its Division of Labor Studies. Braverman won the 1975 C. W. Mills Award of the Society for the Study of Social Problems for *Labor and Monopoly Capital*. And, all but two of the contributors to this collection have been active participants in the annual meetings of this society. Additionally, the Division of Labor Studies annually recognizes a graduate student paper with the "Harry Braverman Award." Jackie Krasas Rogers and Larry Christiansen are past recipients of that award. Phil Kraft, Peter Meiksins, Tom Steiger, and Mark Wardell have all chaired the Braverman Award Committee in the past, while Larry Isaac, Phil Kraft, Peter Meiksins, and Mark Wardell have chaired the Division of Labor Studies at various points. James Geschwender was the 1990–91 president of the Society for the Study of Social Problems.

Equally important, Chris Smith and Paul Thompson have been active participants and organizers of the Annual Labour Process Conference held in England. Likewise, several of the contributors from the United States have participated at those conferences and have had their papers included in various collections of the conference papers published in the Labour Process Series (published by The Macmillan Press LTD and Routledge; edited by David Knights, Hugh Willmott, Chris Smith, and others). Thus, the contributors to this volume are no strangers to the labor process arena and the history of debate surrounding it, which largely accounts for their consensual view that a labor process perspective has a meaningful role to play in analyses of work and workplaces today and into the future.

We owe Tara Habasevich a great deal of thanks for her responsible assistance.

Mark Wardell
Thomas L. Steiger
Peter Meiksins

1

Labor Processes

Moving Beyond Braverman and the Deskilling Debate

MARK WARDELL

In the decades immediately following World War II, many workers in the United States, Canada, and western Europe enjoyed routine wage increases, job stability, and health and pension coverage, much of which was collectively bargained by their trade union representatives. While blue-collar workers were not getting rich, they and their families could live relatively comfortably. Nevertheless, in 1974 Harry Braverman published his classic *Labor and Monopoly Capital: The Degradation of Work in the Twentieth Century*. Braverman maintained that work increasingly was being fragmented into discrete functions, while workers increasingly were dissatisfied with the organization and conditions of their jobs. For the latter observation, Braverman relied on the Special Task Force for the Secretary of Health, Education, and Welfare (1973:13), which concluded workers increasingly were dissatisfied with their jobs because of " . . . constant supervision and coercion, lack of variety, monotony, meaningless tasks, and isolation."

Braverman's work became the main source for a stream of social scientific research that emerged about labor processes. This research area, however, was not entirely homogeneous (cf. Meiksins 1994 and V. Smith 1994 for overviews). To a casual observer it might have appeared as if, for every researcher who attempted to follow in Braverman's footsteps, another researcher attempted to challenge, if not discredit, Braverman's work.

Many of the challengers were inspired in large part by another 1973 publication, Daniel Bell's *The Coming of the Post-Industrial Society*. In an obvious attempt to extend the "industrialism and industrial man" thesis of Kerr et al. (1960), Bell envisioned a decline in the percentage of workers engaged in repetitive motion jobs, such as routine assembly, and an increase in the percentage of workers engaged in knowledge manipulation tasks. Importantly, Bell used much the same type of data as Braverman, yet he forecasted a very different transformation in the way work was done, a transformation many researchers inferred would require enhanced skills from workers. As a result of the challenges to Braverman's work, a long debate ensued about the changes in the skill levels of workers (Zimbalist 1979; Wood 1982; Spenner 1983; Attewell 1990; Keefe 1991), and it has continued (Steiger and Wardell 1992; Osterman 1995; Cappelli 1996; Vallas and Beck 1996). Braverman's work helped to launch other long-term research efforts. In particular, his (Braverman 1974:27) self-proclaimed emphasis on structure at the expense of subjectivity was a source for a broad-ranging debate in Great Britain, as well as for much of the impetus behind the annual Conference of the Labour Process sponsored by the Universities of Aston and Manchester.

To be sure, Braverman had his followers and not all of his challengers were critical of the basic political-economic framework he propounded (Friedman 1977; Burawoy 1979; Walby 1989; Littler 1990). The purpose of this chapter is to summarize the main features of Braverman's work and some of the debates surrounding it, and then to set the stage for rethinking the labor process perspective.

BRAVERMAN'S PERSPECTIVE ON WORK

Braverman was not an academic. Rather, he worked at various skilled metal trades for many years before assuming editorial duties at two different publishing houses (C. Smith 1996a). Hence, the attention drawn to his book perhaps revealed more about the historical moment in which it was published and its content than in Braverman's scholastic credentials. For example, in the United States his book came at a time when different groups (e.g., women; minorities; antiwar protestors) were voicing their criticisms about the organization of everyday life, and in particular how that organization disadvantaged them. The book itself represented a significant deviation from the conventional sociological approach to work, an approach Braverman criticized because he saw the organization of work and the workplace as analytically essential for understanding the organization of everyday life. For Braverman, the workplace contained the key social forces that produce and reproduce class inequality.

In Great Britain, Braverman's work attracted possibly more attention than in the United States, a situation described as an "over-reaction" by Wood (1982:12). There, his work came at a time when sociologists were focused squarely on the relation between subjectivity and objectivity in a variety of contexts, while, similar to the United States, a conventional British emphasis on the division of labor and its relation to job content had not been challenged seriously. Braverman's book was a catalyst in bringing the subject–object debate into the discussion of job content (Knights and Willmott 1989).

In both countries, conventional sociological studies of work, workers, and their workplaces typically began with a notion that work involves human effort in making goods or services valued by others.[1] For example, Udy (1970:3) defined work as " . . . both physical and social at the same time . . . [and] . . . as any purposive human effort to modify man's physical environment." Also typical of conventional sociological approaches to work is the distinction among a job, an occupation, and a career, where a job represents a set of acts associated with a type of paid work or occupation, while the cumulation of jobs over a period of time by a person represents a career with distinctive outcomes in terms of income, job satisfaction, and status. Furthermore, conventional approaches typically allow for the analytical separation of occupations and career patterns from the particular organization of and activities in the workplace, implying that career patterns, for instance, are not related necessarily to job designs, technological implementations, and the formal and informal social networks within an organization. Finally, conventional studies of work typically take for granted that a person must be employed in order to have a job, that is, they generally do not question the influence of the employment relationship on employees' behaviors inside or outside the workplace. In sum, conventional approaches to work, workers, and their workplaces tend to reflect a micro-analytical perspective, emphasizing the fit between individual characteristics and characteristics of jobs, occupations, or careers.

Not having been steeped in the traditions of the sociological discipline, Braverman was not constrained by the conventional approach to work. Rather, he could assume employment and its outcomes for individuals were uncertain because employment (1) itself is not guaranteed, and (2) does not guarantee a living wage, a particular career path, or comparable work settings for similar occupations. His analysis, therefore, did not start at the level of individual workers and their work context. While Braverman, too, defined work as "purposive action" involving the production of goods and services having value for others, he adopted a broader perspective by which work, the workplace, and the people involved were located in the political-economic context of the capitalist employment relationship.

Seen from this vantage point, employers and employees do not establish a relationship at will. Employers hire workers in order to expand their capital base, while employees seek employment because they have no viable alternative by which to sustain their lives and those of their families (Braverman 1974:52–53). Employers and employees, then, are linked in an interdependent relationship, albeit asymmetrical, where employers have far more flexibility in whom they hire than employees have in choosing their employer. Braverman's explicit recognition of the employment relationship's importance enabled him to mark the parameters within which to understand the organization of work and the behaviors of the people involved. Conventional sociological studies, by contrast, frequently start with characteristics of workers, jobs, occupations, or professions without the explicit analytical recognition that individual workers and their families are more dependent on employers for their survival than the latter are dependent on individual workers for theirs.

From this general level, Braverman moved his analysis to the detailed divisions of labor in the workplace. His analytical unit of analysis for this level of investigation was the labor process, " . . . that is to say, the separation of the work of production into its constituent elements" (Braverman 1974:75). Essentially, a labor process is a means by which objects, people, tools, knowledge, and tasks are organized so that they are transformed into different objects or services having some value for others. Nevertheless, the very combination of technologies and job designs affects where and how people work (Braverman 1974:Chapter 10). The introduction of new technology, for instance, often combines tasks previously performed by several classifications of workers, making some workers redundant while requiring new classifications for other workers. In this way, new skills could be required of some, though the question would remain if the workers with enhanced skills also would have enhanced their value to an employer. Thus, occupations, careers, and individual well-being generally are intricately related to the particular labor processes people experience.

The key to organizing labor processes within capitalist workplaces, Braverman reasoned, was yet another constituent element—managerial control. Prior to the onset of capitalism, the regulation of workplace activity was much less centralized, in part because of the reliance on contractors and subcontractors who performed their jobs in accordance with particular trade skills (Wardell 1992). Braverman (1974:65–67) maintained, however, that a principal signifier of capitalist work organizations was the drive by managers to gain more direct control over the performance of hired workers. Like Karl Marx, Braverman believed capitalist managers are motivated to wring out effort from workers in the pursuit of profits, concentrating on workers' flexible potential to labor, which can be intensified by changing the social and technical means of production.

In developing this argument, Braverman identified Frederick Winslow Taylor's principles of scientific management as the management method most exemplary of the history of U.S. capitalism. In Taylor's notions and practices of scientific management, Braverman saw one recurring theme: to directly influence the effort of workers while maintaining control over the intended purpose of their activities. In Braverman's terminology, the recurring theme is one of finding ways to separate the conception of a task from the execution of the task, thereby transferring knowledge and power to management. The addition of new technology, the introduction of new work rules, changes in the wage formulas as well as the level of direct supervision result from management's recurring effort to control the physical and mental effort of employees. From Braverman's perspective, then, labor processes have changed over time though the direction of that change, dictated by the intent of management, has led to a degradation of work, with the average job reduced to mindless physical activities and the overall worth of the average worker devalued.

From his integrated perspective, which included the constituent elements of production as well as the surrounding political-economic context of the employment relationship, Braverman thought he saw a historical trend of jobs becoming increasingly subdivided into smaller fragments without workers necessarily seeing this as a degradation of work in general. As a result, he thought workers had no way to understand the organizational context for the job dissatisfaction they might feel. Indeed, job dissatisfaction, while relative for Braverman, was relative from a historical perspective more so than from the perspective of one job to another within the same political-economic setting. Braverman's (1974:45–49) historical referent, however, tended to be more of an ideal-type craftworker based on a philosophical anthropology, where conception and execution are not separated by social and technical relations introduced from a central authority, than any specific historical form of a classical craftworker.

MAJOR CRITICISMS

Braverman's work has drawn a variety of criticisms. At one level, many of the criticisms can be seen as challenging his preoccupation with explaining why labor processes within capitalism are what they are, rather than analyzing the details of how they work. The term "labor process" suggests motion or fluidity, rather than a static state, but Braverman's work can be read as if he focused almost exclusively on class relations and took the "processes" of production for granted.

At a more substantive level, the major criticisms can be summarized into seven basic categories. First, while presenting his analysis, he discussed the degradation of work in terms of a decline in craft skills. Many researchers have questioned if skill levels simply declined in the absolute sense, or whether new skills were created as others were lost or declined in importance. Second, since Braverman set this decline against an ideal-typical model of a craftworker, numerous critics viewed his work as romanticizing the craftworker. Third, because Braverman presented the history of work

within capitalism as characterized by a steady degradation process, critics
countered that this was a linear and deterministic model that did not allow the
possibility for a transformed labor process where workers were challenged to
expand their skills and move toward a recoupling of conception and execution.
Fourth, Braverman (1974:27) explicitly stated he would address only the structural or objective features of the labor process, and not include the subjective
aspects, but this too became a point of contention. Specific issues include the
shaping of workers' consciousness as a means of managerial control and the
formation of a critical workers' consciousness as a basis for resisting that control. Fifth, Braverman's portrayal of Taylorism as the primary management
method leading to a degradation of work has been questioned as giving scientific management too much credit for the emergence of the contemporary
workplace. Indeed, some argued Braverman's analysis credited management in
general as being far too rational and successful in their initiatives to wring
more effort from workers. Sixth, coupled with the rationality criticism was an
argument that Braverman concentrated too heavily on matters related to the
shopfloor, or the points of physical production, at the expense of other constituent elements, such as managerial strategies, markets, or governmental
regulations. Finally, Braverman was criticized for discussing labor processes as
if only one general form existed such that its characteristics could be found in
a variety of settings, regardless of the workers involved, the type of work performed, or the national setting. This criticism has been coupled with the
notions that race and gender make a difference within the same job and workplace, resulting in very different labor processes for women and men, and for
people of color and whites. Similar arguments have been made regarding professional and technical labor processes versus assembly work and other forms
of repetitive motion jobs.

   Of the seven criticisms, two seem less serious. The criticism that
Braverman's analysis relied on a romantic notion, or an ideal-type craftworker,
seems of little consequence in the long run. First, use of ideal-types for comparative purposes has a long tradition within sociology. Max Weber (1947)
viewed such constructions as essential to sound sociological analysis. Second,
Braverman drew from anthropological findings for part of his conceptualization of a craftworker, suggesting that, while he did not portray the "natural"
worker, he at least portrayed a form of worker not subjected to the various
contingent factors that have been constructed in the past 150 years. Third,
sociological studies frequently include a critical dimension. In the United
States Albion Small, the Lynds, and C. W. Mills are among the more historically notable in this tradition. In that light, the ideal craftworker outlined by
Braverman represents a call for a more humane workplace, and he has thus
provided an important reminder that analyses of the workplace should include
a critical human dimension.

The criticism that Braverman's analysis inappropriately portrayed scientific management as a central feature of capitalistic work relations might not be sustainable, at least in the United States. There, Taylor directly influenced the development of management (or cost) accounting (Miller and O'Leary 1987), and management accounting data continue to play a central role in developing organizational strategies, as well as maintaining employee accountability, within firms. Moreover, Taylor's influence continues in a new generation of management practices as Western countries increasingly adopt variations of the Japanese Total Quality Management (TQM) scheme, a direct descendant from Taylor's writings on scientific management (Warner 1994). Coupled with the adoption of Just-in-Time (JIT) inventory, Statistical Process Control (SPC) techniques, and the striving for ISO 9000 certification, TQM in many instances appears to represent an updated form of scientific management.

This trend appears no less true in Great Britain than in the United States (Hill 1991; Applebaum and Batt 1994). Indeed, Webb (1996:269) concluded from her case study of three British-based manufacturers that "in all cases TQM resulted in a more pronounced division between 'conception' and 'execution', focusing conception more clearly at corporate level with the consequent loss of discretion at middle-management and technical levels." Furthermore, in the 1980s and early 1990s literally millions of workers in the United States witnessed eroding job stability, declining real incomes, and deteriorating health and benefit packages. For many others their jobs were expanded and intensified (Houseman 1995), a pattern replicated in Great Britain (Edwards and Whitston 1991) and in many other parts of the world (Córdova 1986). Employment and working conditions in the 1980s and early 1990s overall indicate Taylorist elements remain in managerial approaches to workplace reorganization.

The remaining five criticisms (deskilling, a linear degradation of work, the absence of the subjective in Braverman's work, a narrow focus on shop-floor activities, and the formulation of a labor process as representative of all labor processes) more directly challenge the analytical substance of the labor process perspective. Specifically, they question using the labor process as the unit of analysis for understanding the detailed division of labor in the production of goods and services. Indeed, these criticisms point to omissions or simplifications in Braverman's discussion. While assuming that various constituent elements comprise the detailed division of labor, he took a very broad approach to analyzing relations and conditions in the workplace and did not elaborate the substantive arenas in which constituent elements are organized, changed, and challenged.

Recognizing this weakness, Littler (1990) suggested any analysis of the labor process should focus on (1) the technical division of labor and commensurate design of associated tasks, (2) the control structure, and (3) the employment relationship as specified by the political-economic context. However, Littler's formulation remains sufficiently vague, especially regarding the meaning and dimensions of the control structure. Plus, the foci he identified have overlapping properties. For example, technology and the technical division of labor arguably can be seen as part of the control structure (R. Edwards 1979; Wajcman 1991). Still, Littler's basic point reflects a common concern that Braverman's work focused too heavily on management's attempts to gain direct control over the flow of human effort in the work process.

Brief mention of two earlier attempts to address this weakness in Braverman's perspective further illustrate the importance of elaborating the substantive arenas in which constituent elements of labor processes are organized. First, A. Friedman (1977) distinguished responsible autonomy from direct control. In the former, management retains the principal influence over the organization of human effort but in ways other than by direct surveillance and supervisory pressure. In direct control situations the immediate supervisor is responsible for the pace and direction of human effort, whereas in responsible autonomy situations workers themselves assume some of the supervisory functions. Second, Burawoy (1979) went further, maintaining workers can and do develop a workplace subculture, in which they assert a form of autonomy from the formal lines of managerial commands that effectively produces results in keeping with management's interests. Minimally, then, control in and over the labor process appears much more complex and convoluted than as represented in Braverman's discussion about work. Importantly, Burawoy and Friedman addressed the weakness in Braverman's perspective over a decade before Littler's attempt, and yet little headway can be seen in advancing beyond Braverman's discussion (cf. P. K. Edwards 1990; A. Friedman 1990; and P. Thompson 1990 for similar points).

Elaborating the notion of control remains an important project in rethinking the labor process perspective. Missing from Braverman's approach to the labor process is any systematic acknowledgment that the organization and outcomes of a labor process might well be problematic for employers and employees. A linear projection of Braverman's model would suggest the proportions of the working class being relegated to mindless repetitive physical activity will increase over time, while the opportunities will further diminish for them to become involved in decision making regarding the conditions of their employment and work. Alienation and conflict seem inevitable from this perspective, because the capitalist employment relationship presumably has the same or very similar effects on the conditions of work regardless of mediating factors, such as the presence and strength of unions, training programs, or internal labor markets. Yet, we know, for example, that the levels of conflict versus cooperation between workers and managers in fact vary across capitalist countries, Germany experiencing higher levels of cooperation than conflict compared to Canada or the United States (Baethge and Wolf 1995).

Furthermore, Braverman's perspective does not systematically incorporate the influences of the larger society, including institutional, historical, market, and political influences. Specific changes in the workplace, and consequently changes in the skill levels, are influenced by historical traditions within an industry or a society, the relation between an organization (firm or agency) and surrounding institutions such as education, governmental regulatory agencies, and organized labor. Conversely, the latter are influenced by changes in the social and technical organization of work.

THEORETICAL EXTENSIONS

For present purposes, I seek to elaborate the arenas of control in which the elements of labor processes are organized in an attempt to regulate various amounts of human effort. The fact that labor processes are controlled is not an issue; instead how and by whom they are controlled, and how the outcomes (such as incomes) are distributed are the pivotal questions. For practical purposes, the following discussion will be limited to labor processes within capitalist employment relationships and, therefore, they should have some common elements, despite institutional variations across national boundaries (Lane 1987; Smith and Meiksins 1995). At the same time, labor processes are expected to vary, as are the patterns of control and resistance embedded within them. In doing so, employment relations are seen as social relations, containing race and gender dimensions, as well as a class dimension, and each dimension contributes to an overall understanding of labor processes.

Labor processes, regardless what the output happens to be, are structured within arenas of control specific to particular work settings. Objective and subjective experiences within a labor process can be contextualized in terms of the activities within and the combination of those arenas, among which are: (1) management; (2) social and technical relations in the workplace; (3) human resources practices; and (4) industrial relations.[2] None of these arenas can be assumed to be either a harmonious whole or the primary source of control over labor processes. Rather, each must be seen as a social arena in which efforts are made to control the flow and outcomes of a production process. To that extent, each arena also must be seen as a social setting in which various actors express different, if not conflicting, interests. As they do, each arena contributes a certain amount of control in the actual production process. Furthermore, the first two arenas largely reflect the sites of most labor process research to date mainly because they were obvious foci in Braverman's analysis, whereas the latter two arenas were ignored for the most part by Braverman.

Adding the other two rounds out analyses of labor processes by incorporating critical arenas that bear directly on the organization of activities, experiences, and identities of the various actors, as well as outcomes of their efforts.

The management arena refers to the strategies and basic regulatory practices for maintaining and developing current operations, which include views on the role and value of workers, shape and size of the organizational structure, pattern of employee accountability, assessment of market conditions, and planned transformations in basic products and processes. Examples range from Taylorism to Total Quality Management and lean-and-mean production. The management arena, though, too often is seen as a rational monolith driven by principles of efficiency and the bottom line, when in fact it is fractured by political and ideological differences, some of which are based on gender and race (cf. Cockburn 1991; Collins 1997). Thomas (1994), for instance, observed that the management arena can be fraught with conflicting agendas and initiatives, making the road to launching an initiative very difficult. Furthermore, any plan launched by management faces modification, limitation, and opposition by actors and practices in the other arenas (P. K. Edwards 1986; A. Friedman 1990).

The social and technical relations in the workplace involve job design, including the sequencing and regulating of tasks, types, and use of technology, as well as deployment of workers, such as teams, job rotation, and shift work. They also include informal relations and workplace cultures workers establish with each other. This arena is the closest to the actual physical labor process, and for this reason, largely represents the site of a vast number of case studies (cf. Burawoy 1979; Zimbalist 1979). It also represents the focus for much of the skill debate and much of the research regarding workers' resistance.

The human resource arena includes job and skills training programs for workers, advancement opportunities, compensation and benefit packages, and safeguards for employee rights. Piece rates, pay for performance, safety training, childcare, health and pension plans, mentoring programs for women and people of color, comparable worth, and affirmative action programs are examples of different human resource practices. The human resources arena focuses less on shopfloor activity per se and more on the overall behavior and commitment of workers, with the intent of influencing their performance.

The industrial relations arena refers to the formal relations between management and workers, including the various ways employers and workers are represented. Employer associations, unions, work councils, and the various laws and governmental administrations that mediate labor–management relations are included here. This arena has been called a labor relations regime by P. K. Edwards (1994), and historically, the arena has regulated access to jobs internal to a firm and across an industry, while regulating wages and the overt expression of conflict between labor and management. When seen as a labor relations regime, this arena of control also includes cultural and institutional traditions within and between labor and management.

By no means are the arenas necessarily integrated by coherent strategies, nor are they necessarily mutually supportive domains or equal contributors in controlling labor processes. Many companies establishing greenfield sites in foreign countries adopt the management strategies found in the other country (cf. Milkman 1991), while attempting to impose a labor relation regime from one country onto the labor processes of another country can be extremely problematic, even after the two countries have united (Lane 1987; Hyman 1996). Additionally, at various historical moments, one arena might be more influential than the others. From the late 1930s through the 1970s in the United States, most mass production work environments were influenced heavily by an industrial relations regime, in tandem with a bureaucratically controlled workplace (R. Edwards 1979). Throughout the 1980s and 1990s, an increased emphasis was placed on the human resource arena, along with flexible technologies and job redesigns, following the path carved by companies such as IBM, Cummins Engine, and Hewlett Packard in the 1960s (Doeringer 1991). Control in these situations is embedded within an employment culture stressing flexibility and commitment, while often tending to avoid or break from the forms of control associated with rigid work rules and seniority found in the traditional industrial relations regime. Numerous observers have seen this development as challenging, if not threatening, the conventions found in the industrial relations regime in the United States (Kochan, Katz, and McKersie 1986; Parker and Slaughter 1988).

For example, contrast self-managed teams, comprised of workers with multiple skills who have been cross-trained to do each other's jobs, with rigid job classifications in a highly centralized authority structure (cf. Bluestone and Bluestone 1992). Osterman (1992) observed that self-managed teams can create fundamentally different internal labor markets from those with strict job classifications and a bureaucratically regulated evaluation process, thereby undermining job stability. As workers increase their commitment to an employer, they might become more vulnerable to management, especially if not represented by a labor organization, because of the reduced job classifications and the expanded skill requirements. Parker and Slaughter (1988) saw this as a formula for management-by-stress.

Women, in particular, might be the most vulnerable in this arrangement. V. Smith's (1993) review of literature revealed the possibility that self-managed teams in manufacturing favor men over women because the latter lack the training and the skills needed to work in a team-oriented production process. Moreover, middle management positions are the ones that only recently were opened to women, but are among the positions most endangered in a transformation to self-managed, high-performance work teams (V. Smith 1993:208).

According to others, however, training, skills, and teams do not necessarily conflict with union representation. Osterman (1995) reported skill training in high-performance workplaces is greater with the presence of a union. Turner, Bertelli, and Kaminiski (1996) reported that transformation to a flexible, high-performance workplace can be accomplished without undermining the union's position or shareholder value, but the transition requires greater communication between union leadership and management. Unions might well have to learn to play a new role in team-oriented workplaces, as Shaiken, Lopez, and Mankita (1997) observed at Saturn and Chrysler, resulting in promising outcomes for workers and management. From management's perspective, teams can reduce the job classifications and management hierarchy, thereby reducing variance in wage scales of workers while reducing the ranks of middle management, another cost savings (Ichniowski 1992; Berg et al. 1996). From the workers' perspective, self-managed teams can enlarge the responsibility of individual workers. According to Batt and Applebaum (1995), firms benefit from improved worker performance and commitment, while workers gain satisfaction for their jobs and experience more positive relations with co-workers.

In sum, the composition of all four control arenas bears directly on the effort workers put forth and the character of their relations with each other, their supervisors, and management.[3] Labor processes will vary, depending on how the four arenas are composed and related to each other, along with the racial and gendered characteristics of the workplace and actors within it. From a labor process perspective, then, identical tasks, whether sewing blue jeans, providing health care in intensive care units, assembling auto parts, or offering customer services can be constituted and experienced differently. Indeed, work processes that outwardly look very similar might well be constituted by quite different control patterns (Bélanger 1994), indicating quite different labor processes.

Temporary work nicely illustrates this point. Temporary workers perform the same or similar tasks as permanent workers, at nearly all levels of the occupational hierarchy. However, instead of being employed by the organization where they work, temporary workers are employed by a temporary help supply firm who contracts with a client firm or an organization for specific types and amounts of labor. This might seem like a subtle difference, but the control structure governing temporary workers is quite different from the one governing permanent workers. In terms of the management arena, temporary employees are often strategically sought because, as a rule, they are cheaper (Segal and Sullivan 1995:7). Temporary workers typically are paid less per hour than permanent employees, but more important, the client firm does not have to pay for benefits. Also, temporary workers enable a firm to create a dual labor market consisting of a core of permanent workers, who might receive above-market wages, and a periphery of temporary workers who can be purchased on an as-needed basis. Managers in client firms often see temporary workers as a means by which to screen potentially permanent employees (Segal and Sullivan 1995:8). Even though temporary workers might create the same amount of value-added as permanent workers performing the same tasks, the temporary workers effectively are devalued by management and are dependent on the client firm as well as the temporary services firm. They essentially have two employers to satisfy instead of only the one permanent workers must satisfy.

In terms of social and technical relations in the workplace, temporary workers, by definition, are not lifetime employees working in the same social and technical work setting. Temporary workers, as a rule, face different technologies, job designs, and supervisory methods in the course of their employment patterns. Even if they return to a particular work site, the permanent workers most likely do not interact with temporary workers in the same way they interact with each other, connoting temporary workers are not their equals. In some instances client firms deliberately limit the interaction between temporary and permanent workers (Gottfried 1992). Permanent workers, too, might well feel their job stability threatened by the presence of a cadre of temporary employees, which could exacerbate their negative view and treatment of temporaries. For temporary women workers in particular, this social context might make them more vulnerable to sexual harassment than would be the case for permanent women workers (Rogers and Henson 1997).

Similarly, the human resource practices affecting temporary workers are those largely supplied by the temporary services company. Some temporary service companies provide training, though nothing like the on-site training provided to permanent workers. Temporary workers do not benefit from mentoring or childcare programs unless provided by the temporary services employer, and they do not have immediate access to the internal labor market of any client firm. Segal and Sullivan (1995:7) observed that about one-fourth of temporary workers have hospitalization, surgical, and medical insurance compared to four-fifths of permanent workers. Temporary employees, especially if single or single parents, definitely experience a different connection between taking care of their job and taking care of their health, educational needs, and those of their family, than permanent workers.

The industrial relations arena in certain respects is largely inconsequential for temporary workers since they typically do not work in settings governed by a formal labor–management relationship. In effect, the industrial relations regime has little influence over the behaviors of temporary workers, their employer's, or the client firm's. On the other hand, the industrial relations arena does have some control over the process by which temporary workers could be collectively represented. If temporary workers want to join a union at the client firm, they must demonstrate first that the client firm and the temporary service firm are joint employers and second that the temporary workers have a community of interest similar to the permanent workers in the client firm's union (Carre, duRivage, and Tilly 1994). Other aspects of the industrial relations regime designed to protect workers in general frequently do not apply to temporary workers. In the case of unemployment compensation, temporary workers are much less likely than permanent workers to log the requisite minimum number of hours in the course of a given time period to be eligible. Thus, the traditional industrial relations regime has little direct influence over the labor process of temporary workers, but it does disadvantage them relative to permanent workers in being able to influence the conditions of their employment and work through collective representation.

The labor process of temporary employees clearly deviates from that of permanent employees, even though the two types of workers could be working side by side performing the same tasks. As Gottfried (1992) noted, temporary employees might well put in more "real" time working than permanent workers because of the insecurity of their employment status and the different controls regulating their labor processes. In this instance, temporary workers would be adding more value to the production of goods and services relative to permanent workers, but would be paid less, would have fewer benefits and advancement opportunities, and would not have the clear right to union representation. Obviously, simple physical activity does not define a labor process as much as the social and political-economic relations that control the activities of those involved. Significantly too, labor processes of temporary workers reveal the importance of the various arenas of control in producing and reproducing social inequities within capitalist societies.

CONCLUSION

The labor process perspective has wide-ranging applicability, and while Braverman popularized it, clearly his words were not the last. As we enter the twenty-first century, employers' pursuit of profits are no less salient than decades ago, and their need to employ labor is not any less. In a global market context, how much labor, where that labor is located, and how it is utilized and compensated will remain the significant issues for employers, managers, and employees.

If the trend toward greater uses of contingent employment, such as temporary workers, continues, concern about skill levels will become overshadowed by questions regarding the value of labor, how work-related issues influence family stability, and how the labor processes of contingent workers differentially disadvantage them in providing for their families relative to other workers.[4] If employers increasingly attempt to escape the responsibility of health and pension coverage, that burden will become more the responsibility of the individual worker, and how other arenas are configured will be critical in the ability of workers to maintain their health and that of their families', as well as provide for their own retirement. How workers approach their jobs, the way they view themselves and their co-workers, the amount of effort they willingly give, and the outcomes they and others derive from their total effort, certainly will be influenced by the degree to which they must be preoccupied about health, retirement, and family concerns.

The ongoing changes in employment and work raise multifaceted issues, requiring equally multifaceted approaches to understand their complexity. Braverman provided some insight that remains useful, but we can expand upon his foundation. A labor process approach encompasses a broad integrative view that draws liberally from a variety of disciplinary backgrounds. Therein lies its utility as a means by which to critically understand the changes and issues that will arise and how these differentially impact women and men, permanent and contingent workers, people of color and whites, plus professional, technical, and supervisory employees.

NOTES

Special thanks go to Peter Meiksins and Tom Steiger for their very thoughtful reading and commenting on earlier drafts. I benefited greatly from discussions with students in my graduate seminars and with my colleague, Jackie Rogers.

1. While the conceptions of work and labor processes found in this chapter could be used to analyze both paid and nonpaid labor, the chapter will focus on paid labor work arenas.

2. These domains will not be new to many readers. Rather, they represent common areas of scholarship that most often are treated independently of each other. The analytical power of a labor process perspective evolves from the theoretical breadth gained by integrating these domains.

3. The content and alignment of the four domains also bear directly on the relations workers have with their dependents, including family members.

4. Evidence exists that balancing work and family issues in some cases has a greater influence on overall job satisfaction than matters such as skills training and employment security (Berg 1997).

2

To Control and Inspire

U.S. Management in the Age of Computer Information Systems and Global Production

PHILIP KRAFT

I wonder if TQM is a strategy which is restricted to the internal functioning of a single company, or if it sees single companies as simply part of an economy which could be managed with total quality as its goal? I read about the futility of the us. vs. them mentality within the functioning of a single company . . . would this also apply to the functioning of an economy?
==================
TQM applied to a firm is capitalism.
TQM applied to an industry is communism.
See the difference?
(Exchange on an Internet discussion group on TQM in Manufacturing and Services Industries)[1]

The worst thing an organization can do when it empowers people is to tell them to go out and make decisions.
(Lynda Applegate, Harvard Business School, from a lecture on "Managing in an Information Age" at the Transforming Organizations with Information Technology conference, University of Michigan, Ann Arbor, Michigan, 12 August 1994.)

Early in 1993 the *Harvard Business Review* carried a celebratory article about time-and-motion management methods in a U.S. auto factory (Adler 1993). The article is less important as an official rehabilitation of Frederick Winslow Taylor than for its singular standing: the *Harvard Business Review* had not published a full-length article about traditional production work in years—and it has not published one since. Other trend-setting management journals, including the *Sloan Management Review*, *Administrative Science Quarterly*, and the *California Management Review*, have shown a similar lack of interest in what managers call "direct" work and workers.

Production work and production workers have been displaced from the pages of America's premier business press by the most important economic transformation since the end of World War II: the emergence of global markets. The advantages of global production have been quick in coming for U.S. firms: lower wage bills, fewer union members, higher profits, and, as a kind of bonus, rapid privatization of public services. There have been costs as well: unprecedented levels of competition and the need to produce for constantly changing niche markets. U.S. industry has had to learn how to make a profit by quickly turning out relatively small quantities of high-quality products rather than large runs of standard products for protected domestic markets.

If the global market confronts U.S. managers with new competitive problems, computer-based technologies promise to provide them with some of the solutions. New technologies, especially computer-based information technologies (ITs), offer unprecedented opportunities to speed up data collection, analysis, and distribution. They facilitate process integration and smooth workflows, and use unobtrusive, embedded command-and-control systems. They therefore offer unprecedented opportunities to redefine work relations. Specifically, U.S. managers have seized upon the control possibilities of IT as a way of satisfying their need to more systematically exploit labor (cf. Stalk and Hout, 1990; Porter 1985, 1990; Simons 1995).

When combined with telecommunications networks, computer-based information technologies offer the prospect of nearly instantaneous communication and therefore the possibility of continuous surveillance and direct control over work almost anywhere in the world. IT, furthermore, makes it easier to monitor all kinds of workers, not just traditional direct workers. Continuous feedback loops in manufacturing, monitoring phone conversations between service representatives and customers, automated testing of computer software and hardware, and automated validating of banking transactions can all be done cheaply and discretely—and often invisibly—twenty-four hours a day. In design work, powerful computer-based systems offer managers positively irresistible opportunities. Designers and engineers can model entire finished products and production systems before a single physical prototype is built. Engineers, architects, systems designers, marketing specialists, and accountants can exchange, test, and modify ideas, plans, and images over a telecommunications network without ever meeting each other.

So powerful are the new technologies that they have inspired management theorists and futurists to vision postmodern "virtual" organizations. Enterprises will be held together by telecommunications systems while they adroitly enter, exploit, and then abandon markets over the globe. At the same time they can dispense with the impediments of conventional organizations, including buildings, permanent employees, unions, and even middle managers. In short, the new computer-based technologies make the global market possible—and immensely profitable.[2]

GLOBALIZING COMMAND AND CONTROL

Global markets mean not just more competition between firms, but competition of a different kind. In a world of "agile enterprises," every agile enterprise is compelled to pursue shorter product development times, lower costs, and fewer defects. For U.S. managers, globalization and computer-based production and communications technologies intensify an old problem: they accelerate the need to rapidly as well as efficiently appropriate the labor of "value-adding" workers.[3] Value-adding workers directly contribute to the process of transforming partially completed products into deliverable commodities (Stalk and Hout 1990). Those who do not add value, in contrast, only bookkeep or police goods-in-process. In contrast to such transformational labor, James O'Connor (1973) has called this work "guard labor."[4]

It is easy to understand why U.S. management researchers so heavily stress the changing roles of a particular kind of transformational worker: designers and supervisors. The most pressing management problem left is how to make "creative" workers—Robert Reich's (1991) "symbolic analysts"—think faster.[5] The centrality of "creative" labor is underscored by the pivotal role played by design workers in planning and implementing the computer-based information technologies themselves. Systems designers, programmers, computer hardware engineers, systems engineers, and telecommunications specialists are crucial to making production global. Their work is unique: it produces some of the most valuable commodities of the global economy—computer programs and hardware, automatic switching equipment, marketing strategies—which at the same time provide the means to regulate and control the market itself. The intimate connection among design, production, and control is rapidly forcing a fundamental change in the way managers conceive the production process and the nature of transformational labor itself.

For U.S. managers there are two important kinds of transformational workers. The first is traditional production workers broadly defined: extractive workers, fabricators, assemblers, data-entry clerks, fast food preparers, and other "direct" workers. In some U.S. high-tech manufacturing firms direct labor can represent as little as 2 or 3 percent of total product costs. Traditional production workers, therefore, present less of a control problem than they did even twenty years ago. There are fewer of them and those who remain are effectively disciplined by the global market itself, that is, standardized and easily replicable tasks, as well as worldwide sourcing in a global labor pool, falling wages, and the insecurities of uncertain employment. With an essentially "union free" workplace and a large supply of legal "replacement" workers, U.S. managers see the battle to control direct labor as essentially over.[6]

The second kind of transformational worker is Reich's (1991) "symbolic analysts." These are technical and administrative specialists who manipulate ideas or data rather than things.[7] For Reich and many management theorists, the "creative" and "data-driven" labor of design, engineering, marketing, coordination, communications, and customer service are no longer simply adjuncts to the global value-adding production process: increasingly they *are* the production process. Coordination delays and conceptual bottlenecks in the work of these symbolic analysts—the modern equivalent of Taylor's planning department—are the principal remaining obstacles to the timely production of competitive goods in an increasingly competitive global market. Eliminating such bottlenecks is the key to maximizing both "flexibility" and profits.[8]

THE LIMITS OF TAYLORISM: FROM COMMAND AND CONTROL TO CONTROL AND INSPIRE

For nearly a century U.S. management theory has honored a fundamental Taylorist assumption: capitalist commodity production compels managers to spin out the processes of routinization and fragmentation as far as possible. Only those workers whose jobs ultimately resist routinization—managers, designers, engineers, and other "conceptual" workers—are permitted inside Taylor's "planning department." The rest check their brains in at the door. Even when studies of unskilled workers show them routinely using their imaginations and tacit skills (and when other studies show conceptual labor routinely subjected to rationalization),[9] such findings are declared exceptional.

In practice the "American System" of production has always relied on pragmatic and constantly shifting combinations of direct and indirect control, of rationalized work and "responsible autonomy." The latter is reserved chiefly but not exclusively for design and administrative workers (A. Friedman 1977). The relatively benign attitude toward design workers was possible because, more than most other U.S. employees, engineers, designers, and managers could be expected to display admirable loyalty to the enterprise. When necessary, they could also be induced to heroically self-exploit.[10] The most compelling reason to treat such workers gently, however, was neither technical nor ideological, but economic. Apart from some engineering-intensive industries, design and administrative work has been until recently a relatively minor cost of production. Labor-intensive industries producing for protected mass markets—a description that applied to most U.S. economic sectors between 1918 and 1977—generally could afford to absorb the costs of intellectual slack time.

Employers now see a radically different marketplace. Efficient and rapid product development, intricate coordination, reliable communications systems, and quickly dealing with "exceptions" are the basis for getting competitive products to global markets in a timely way. Managers also see a dilemma: if design, coordination, and dealing with "exceptions", that is, unanticipated disruptions in the process, are the most important value-adding work in the global production system, how can managers regularize and make predictable the work of employees whose work deals with nonroutine problems?[11]

Even under the most stable and predictable conditions, Taylorist command-and-control systems alone have never been adequate to manage these "creative" workers. The core of Taylorism is functional decomposition of tasks and direct supervision. Taylorism "scientifically" fragments work processes and relentlessly removes "waste": wasted motions, wasted materials, wasted time, wasted people. It does so in order to maximize output and minimize costs, chiefly wages and materials. It is able to do this by invoking the formal right of the employer to control the physical behavior of the worker while on company time. Behavior is controlled by direct monitoring and by the swift and predictable application of carrots and sticks, for example, variable piece rates, bonuses, and threats of discharge. It is the classic expression of what Gouldner (1954) called "punishment-centered" control systems.

Taylorism's chief shortcoming is that it can be applied to some aspects of design and administrative work but not to others. When employers try to extend Taylorist control techniques to design workers and managers, the results are at best ambiguous.[12] The problem is fundamental: managers seeking to extract the greatest value from "creative" workers need to manipulate not only behavior but imagination. They must inspire as well as control.[13] But the techniques most favored by American employers to inspire imagination—cheerleading and appeals to an uncertain professionalism—have also been the least reliable. The results, even when useful, are short-lived. Cheerleading—motivational seminars and tent revival inspirational meetings—takes time. If invoked too often it might generate cynicism. Similarly, appeals to professional loyalty may backfire.[14] Praising and rewarding engineers for their technical competence or managers for listening to the "voice of the customer" run the risk of divided loyalties. What to do?

Management's earliest attempts to regularize imagination were thoroughly Taylorist in spirit, if not in the literal application of the "one right way." Managers attempted to graft work decomposition techniques onto operations research methods (OR) and management by objectives (MBO) systems. Neither combination was particularly satisfactory. OR is a modeling system for laying out and scheduling the individual tasks broken down by workflow designers. Operations research itself is therefore only an extension of the rationalist assumptions of Taylorist fragmentation: it "scientifically" recombines the labor of individual workers whose work had been decomposed earlier by "scientific" work rationalization. It offers little in the way of facilitating design work itself. Similarly, MBO attempted to rationalize the decision-making process for managers and other administrative workers. To facilitate the ability of managers to think innovatively, MBO encouraged them to start with the desired long-term and intermediate outcomes rather than a standard set of administrative procedures and control techniques. MBO would help managers develop creative "problem-solving" tools to achieve goals that were constantly changing. Organizationally, MBO was the first widely used management system to lay out procedures and guidelines for making choices in ambiguous situations. Analytically, it was thus the opposite of Taylorism, which was constrained by the one-size-fits-all practices mandated by Taylor's "one right way." If MBO in practice was a variant of Taylorism, it was a reverse-engineered Taylorism.[15]

Although OR and MBO did not succeed in systematizing creative decision making, they did prepare the way for a major departure in the management of design and administrative workers. They were among the first attempts to systematize indirect command-and-control systems aimed at "creative" workers.[16] MBO in particular showed managers they did not have to choose between either "hard" (measurement-based) control systems designed by industrial engineers or the uncertain effects of "responsible autonomy" and tent revivalism. Engineering-based measurement of behavior could be combined with carefully constructed "soft" systems of the kind March and Simon (1958) call "bounded rationality." The trick would be to find the right balance.

FROM RATIONALIZATION TO OBLITERATION

The past two decades have produced a flood of command-and-control systems claiming to provide just that right balance. Among the most well known are continuous quality improvement, or just Continuous Improvement (CI), Total Quality Management—the now ubiquitous TQM, commonly associated with Deming, Juran, Crosby, and Ishikawa—and Business Process Reengineering (BPR), whose most famous theorist is Hammer. In the spirit of MBO, the goal of these "quality" and "process" movements is to provide managers with reliable ways to predict and control "outcomes" rather than measure and monitor behavior. Their common formal purpose is to reduce value-adding time, product and process defects, and costs. In this respect, they all owe large and obvious debts to Taylorism. TQM and BPR have been enthusiastically adopted by U.S. managers in part precisely because they legitimate and rejuvenate the traditional Taylorist obsession with unnecessary motions and unnecessary people. Taylor's cry of "eliminate waste!" finds an echo in Deming's cry of "shrink, shrink, shrink variation!" and Hammer's command to "obliterate" duplicative and non-value-adding work processes.

Like Taylorism, the process-centered command-and-control systems assume that all workplaces are systems that can be rationally designed, modified, and made routine, predictable, and efficient. Taylor's "eliminate unnecessary motions" is transformed into "continuous improvement." "Soldiering" is rooted out through kanban and lean production or some other form of "management by stress" (Parker and Slaughter 1988; see also Wood 1993). Their practice, if not their rhetoric, is top-down. Like Taylorism, all are concerned chiefly with getting fewer workers to produce more in less time and ultimately at lower costs. All rely heavily on techniques that operationalize workflows in order to measure outcomes ranging from time-to-market cycles to deviations from specifications to customer satisfaction. Increasingly, they rely on a variety of sophisticated computer-based real-time, that is, continuous, measurement systems—a sci-fi version of the time clock. Time-and-motion studies are supplemented with Statistical Process Control measurements monitored by cheap desktop computers and Local Area Networks.

For U.S. workers—whether engaged in "creative" or "routine" work—the consequences of the new work redesign systems are usually the same as those produced by Taylorism: intensified labor, more job competition and job insecurity, and downward pressure on wages (cf. Parker and Slaughter 1988, 1994; and Robertson et al. 1993).[17] For example, the following was part of a posting on an Internet TQM discussion list for managers:

> I am not a consultant or a quality guru. I am just a blue-collar worker. I am not stupid. . . . My company has been in the process of switching to TQM for over two years. My wife went to work in a new factory about a year ago that opened up under the TQM concept. . . . The workers get half the pay and twice the work that they would get if they were employed by the same company in one of their other non-TQM plants. They work long hours under brutal conditions and have absolutely no input in plant decisions although that is what was preached to them during indoctrination. They have no bosses only "resources" who have more authority and are less responsive to the employees than any boss [they] ever had. After all since this is a "team concept" if work doesn't get accomplished it obviously can't be the fault of the "resource" so it must be the fault

of the team members. . . . I don't have reams of research to offer you. I can only say that TQM sucks. It is a return to the stone age for the working person. It is nothing but stretch out and company unions wiping out worker gains and worker rights for the benefit of management. It is just another tool for manipulation. Nothing new about that. (QUALITY List)

The list was deluged by dozens of responses from sympathetic "quality" researchers and practitioners. Their unanimous response was that either the writer's employer had not applied TQM "right"—or the post was some sort of hoax.

The new command-and-control systems differ from each other in some important ways. Continuous Improvement and Total Quality Management on the one hand and Business Process Reegineering on the other are the extremes of the new management systems. If not exactly the yin and yang of command-and-control, they are its Laurel and Hardy. CI and TQM are the more incremental approaches. They seek steady decreases in product and process variations, that is, defects, and the constant evolution of "robust" design and production processes. BPR, at the other extreme, demands more fundamental results: a massive restructuring of process and work flows. BPR's goal is to reduce not just defects and variations, but to do so through radical simplification and "downsizing." A reengineered workplace has fewer, not just better, designed tasks, fewer, not just better, robust processes, and "multifunctional"—as well as fewer—workers. TQM and CI maintain an uneasy silence on speedup and job loss. BPR openly advocates stripping organizations down to their "core competencies" and "core processes" while aggressively outsourcing the rest. BPR is the proud godfather of lean and mean.

THE COLLECTIVE VERSUS INDIVIDUAL WORKER

If CI, TQM, and BPR share with Taylorism a preference for "hard" command-and-control systems, they are not simply modern variations of work measurement and direct control. Deming, Juran, Crosby, Ishikawa, and Hammer share with Taylor the engineer's credo: *measure everything*. But CI, TQM, BPR, and their variations go considerably beyond simple measurement, task decomposition, and speedup. TQM and BPR are preoccupied with the design of the production system itself. With Taylorism, they seek to maximize output and product quality at the lowest possible unit costs. Unlike Taylorism, TQM and other process-centered strategies also seek to eliminate defects in the *organization of the production process as a whole*. In a radical departure from Taylorism, these process-centered systems reject rigid distinctions between design and production and therefore rigid distinctions between design and production workers. On the contrary, CI, TQM, and BPR value—even covet—the ideas and tacit knowledge of all workers, including traditional direct workers. If Taylorism is about separating mental and manual work and then constructing a rigid hierarchy to administer and police that separation, process-centered management systems are about systematically appropriating ideas and knowledge from all workers through a system Harvey (1990) calls "flexible accumulation." It may just as accurately be called flexible appropriation and flexible control.

This is a fundamental difference between the old and new control systems and it warrants further explanation. Taylorist rationalization is linear, serial, and segmented. Taylorist control systems are concerned with three organizationally intertwined, but conceptually separate and distinct, problems. First, what is the best way of decomposing a product? Second, what is the most efficient (that is, fewest, cheapest, and fastest) set of actions required to produce each fragment? Third, what is the best way of combining the fragments into a finished product? Furthermore, from the perspective of Taylorist designers, product definition and development (the work of specifying, designing, prototyping, and testing a product) and the design of the technology, tools, and processes used to make the product are all separate and largely irrelevant activities. Both the finished product and the processes used to design it are givens. More to the point, product design and the design of the production process are the responsibilities of other managers, engineers, or designers. Each fragmented part of the total process, in other words, is carried out with little regard to what comes before or after it. Management critics of traditional serial organization call this system "over-the-wall" production.

In contrast, work systems organized along the principles of continuous improvement, TQM, and BPR stress the *identity between the design of the product and the design of the process required to make it.* Whether steadily reducing defects or radically reengineering entire processes, managers and engineers must therefore have a tighter and more immediate control over process as well as product variations. Process-centered command-and-control techniques offer managers a way to do this. Over-the-wall design, production, inspection, testing, and service are replaced by "design for manufacturability" and "concurrent engineering." In the language of TQM, it is the difference between quality control on the one hand and "building quality in" on the other, that is, inspecting finished products for defects rather than reducing variation and defects in the process itself.

The shift in focus reflects the worldwide raising of production standards and the need to minimize product design, development, and production cycle times. The obsession with reducing process as well as product variation means that CI, TQM, and BPR must go considerably beyond wringing out "slack time" in direct production or getting design and administrative workers to think more quickly and more effectively. Traditional Taylorism assumes that a finished product is the sum of individual tasks and individual "value-adding" transformations. An individual's work is decomposed, recombined, and then inserted in a linear process populated by similar individual workers whose behavior is similarly fragmented and closely coordinated by supervisors. Taylorism, in other words, focuses on the labor process of the *individual worker* rather than the production process as a whole. The "worker" is an individual from an engineering as well as a social point of view. Hence Taylorism's emphasis on piece rates and on direct surveillance and control, even for design workers and managers. Control the behavior of the individual worker and you control the "efficiency" of the total process and the cost and quality of the product.

Critics of Taylorism (and of Braverman's analysis of Taylorism) have always pointed out that in practice U.S. managers routinely ignore the presumptions of radical individualism and hyperrationality. Experienced managers know that Taylorism often backfires, particularly when crucial parts of the labor process rely on tacit knowledge and illicit coordination among workers. Moreover, the focus on the individual labor process becomes positively self-defeating when global competition increases the demand for "flexibility," "quality," and speed. Global production requires the coordination and administration of diffuse, constantly changing, and even "virtual" organizations. Under these conditions Taylorist hyperrationality can only *increase inefficiencies* in design, development, production, and distribution.[18] What was the essence of rationality becomes the source of irrationality and, worse, loss of control.

Global production therefore compels managers to conceive of *production as a system rather than a collection of individual tasks.* The new computer-based information technologies make it possible—necessary—to act on that assumption. This is precisely the strength of the new process-centered command-and-control systems. Juran, Deming, Ishikawa, Hammer, and Davenport[19]— each in some way Taylor's pupil—have seized upon a truth familiar to both Roethlisberger and Dickson (1946) and Braverman, if not Taylor: *labor may be individual, but production is collective.* This new understanding has forced managers to make still another fundamental break with traditional Taylorism. Taylorism is about individual workers and decomposed tasks. CI, TQM, and BPR are about collective workers and workflows. Controlling the collective worker requires managers to reject more than the traditional divisions between design and production and between product and process. It compels them, however reluctantly, to reject rigid distinctions between conceptual and manual labor. Wringing "unproductive" labor out of the new "agile" production processes means rejecting traditional assumptions about what constitutes transformational labor. For managers, this means acknowledging that work and production are *social activities*.

FROM OBLITERATION TO INCORPORATION TO EMPOWERMENT

U.S. management's reconceptualization of work as a collective activity has pushed them, however reluctantly, to define new truths and to discard older ones that no longer work in the global market. Computer-based process-centered control systems permit managers to concentrate on concurrent (direct and indirect) control systems, process integration, and recomposition rather than merely on task decomposition. In doing so, however, they are forced to rely on normative control mechanisms, for example, group/peer pressure and identification with the firm. And they must look for new ways of determining the value added by formerly invisible but crucial "indirect" workers, such as systems designers and technical support staff. Product development and data processing are redefined from overhead activities to products with "internal customers," that is, other transformational workers in the overall workflow of the "value chain." Hence, work that was considered merely overhead, such as communications and warehousing, or peripheral, such as process design and customer service, is now reconceptualized as integral to the larger production process and the overall "value chain."

If formerly peripheral work is now part of the "value chain," managers need new ways to measure, monitor, and maximize "value." In the end, this is accomplished by requiring *all* workers—old-fashioned direct workers and guard labor as well as "creative workers" such as engineers and managers—to become "design workers." Managers can control value-adding workers by *making everyone standardize, speed up, measure, monitor, and control his or her own work*. CI, TQM, and BPR are, in other words, attempts to dissolve the distinction among production, design, process flow, and control. If true, this is the reverse of Taylorism: process-centered production control collapses (or claims to collapse) the distinction between conception and execution and between productive and unproductive labor.[20] How, then, do managers do it? Controlling and inspiring the collective worker means reinventing an old management tool, the team.

REINVENTING THE TEAM

Management-defined and -controlled teams are nothing new. They have been a part of formal management theory since at least the days of Edward

Filene and welfare capitalism. Conventional teams were specialized and prone to the same shortcomings of serial, over-the-wall functional divisions of labor. Management critics call them "silos." In contrast, CI, TQM, and BPR teams are simultaneously normative and organizational systems.[21] They are normative systems because they formally acknowledge, even reward, the ability of workers—all workers—to decompose, recombine, chart, and monitor their own work. If TQM and BPR, with their obsession for facts and data and controlling variation, are "hard" control strategies, at the same time they also use "multifunctional teams" to shift some decision making from managers to "the people who actually do the work." In other words, the process-centered command-and-control systems are prepared to permit some workers some flexibility in fragmenting and recombining some of their work processes under some circumstances. Instead of relentlessly stamping out tacit knowledge—a cardinal principle of Taylorism, with its horror of "rule of thumb"—TQM and BPR encourage employees to "surface" tacit knowledge in order to systematically incorporate it into "rational" processes. Managers call this transformation of worker knowledge into "fact-based management" *empowerment.*

The practice of "empowerment" depends in turn on two major "soft" innovations. Both are rejections of traditional systems of fragmentation. The first is an emphasis on *flexible organizational structures.* BPR and TQM in particular provide managers with tools for inventing new "hard" metrics of work effort and "value-adding" activity. At the same time TQM and BPR are also strategies to restructure social relations in the workplace. Operationally, the goal is to shorten communications times and reduce communications "distortions," that is, to reduce the production of "bad data" or "inaccurate information." This is done frequently through the creation of teams equipped with appropriate computer-based technologies, for example, computer-numerically controlled machines, e-mail, teleconferencing, computer-aided systems engineering and design tools, and so on. In practice, teams are ways to push traditional policing, coordination, and reporting functions down the production and process chains of command. The decision-making authority offered to "self-directed work teams" is a perfect expression of March and Simon's (1958) bounded rationality. The decision-making authority is the right to choose among a limited range of options that have been designed into the system at a higher level of design or coordination (cf. Perrow 1986).[22] Computer-based technologies, which can be used to monitor in "real time," provide built-in surveillance and control. In some workplaces, technology and bounded rationality combine to produce flexible organizations that are nothing less than surreal: Oticon, the Danish maker of hearing aids, has abolished fixed workspaces for nearly all its workers. Instead, designers, clerks, secretaries, and technicians pull mobile filing carts and work benches from terminal to terminal as production workflows shift. Continuity, communications, and control are provided by local area computing networks and wireless telecommunications devices. Only the CEO has a permanent desk and a private office (cf. Bjørn-Andersen and Turner 1994).

The second "soft" innovation is a systematic emphasis on *ideology* or *"culture" as a control mechanism*. BPR, TQM, and their variations are comprehensive "philosophies" of workplace relations. There is nothing new, of course, about managers trying to influence the way workers think and feel about their condition and their relationship to their employers. Even Taylorism itself is about a deal employers offer to workers: check your brains in at the door, do what we tell you, and in return we will share (some) of the increased productivity in the form of higher wages.

The normative offensive that accompanies TQM and other process-centered work reorganization is of a different sort. To the extent that the work of imagination cannot be standardized, TQM and BPR are obliged to deploy a cultural strategy, that is, rearrange attitudes, mostly about relations of power and control. Normative control mechanisms are intended to alter the beliefs and behavior (the "corporate culture"), chiefly with regard to the definition of "customer" and the functions of middle management. Power and control are usually given labels like flexibility and cooperation. The notion of customer is broadened to include all transformational workers in the value chain. Middle managers are transformed from police and supervisors to "coaches," "leaders," "facilitators," and "resources" who inspire rather than flog. At the other end of the transformational chain, direct workers, newly empowered on self-directed multifunctional work teams, are informed they are engaged in a "win-win" quest with their employers. Cooperation and jointness replace us versus them adversarial relations, except, perhaps, when joining forces against a common enemy, for example, foreign competitors. Obviously, employers can quickly turn such arguments into a case against unions.

Finally, TQM and CI in particular are, in a commonly employed phrase, a "belief system" as well as a philosophy. Invoking a belief system allows managers to "surface" hidden agendas as well as tacit knowledge. The unrelenting pressure of "satisfying the customer"—that is, to work faster and produce more—combined with the social pressures of team membership can get team members to reveal their attitudes and opinions, to confess their individual sins and seek forgiveness from the group. In other words, teams make it easier for managers to apply group pressure to slackers.[23]

The ideology of "empowerment" reflects the new management conviction that "delayered" or flattened organizations—in other words, organizations in which teams monitor and intensify their own labor—can extract value more efficiently and more quickly than traditional systems of fragment and flog. This is the most explicitly ideological component of TQM theory, in the sense that theorists of process-centered command-and-control systems are quite open about the need to achieve a "world-class paradigm shift."[24]

Table 2.1 suggests where the new process-centered control strategies differ from their more conventional predecessors. The real power of CI, TQM, BPR, and similar process-centered systems is clearest when they are combined in a multitiered control strategy. Together, they continually refine engineering-based control systems for routine processes, radically reorganize whole production systems and workflows, and review the "core competencies" of the enterprise on an ongoing basis.

The tiers look something like this:

1. *Continuous Improvement for routine processes characterized by simple, repeatable events.*

   Repeatable events range from conventional mass production processes in manufacturing and data entry work to customer service, sales, or other activities relying on scripts or similar limited "decision trees," to combining "off-the-shelf" modules to write computer software. The goal is to wring out both variations in the product and "slack," mostly slack labor. This is the stuff of traditional Taylorism and it increasingly makes use of IT-based fragmentation and decomposition. The focus is still largely on the individual and individual tasks.

2. *Total Quality Management for "problem surfacing" and dealing with less routine and more "creative" work.*

   This is where responsible autonomy meets kanban to produce "self-directed, autonomous, high-performance work groups." It is also where "hard" (engineering) and "soft" (human resource) managers struggle over the exact balance of measurement and inspiration. The focus is more squarely on systems—and embedded control structures—than on tasks, and the goal is to devise ways to eliminate defects in the production system itself (the "process"). Here "defects" means employing more people than necessary, not just deviations from product specifications. Successful TQM makes "exceptional" work routine. It can then be pushed down the command-and-control chain and managed by continuous improvement techniques.

3. *Business Process Reengineering for effecting radical change and solving complex or crisis-level problems.*

   Usually BPR is done under the direction of senior managers and consultants who have a warrant to "downsize" or otherwise sharply reduce costs and cycle times in a hurry. Once an enterprise is radically engineered, its "systems" can be managed by TQM and CI teams and processes.

Table 2.1. Conventional Versus Process-Centered Control Strategies

Traditional Taylorism	*Control and Inspire*
FORMAL GOALS	
Management/worker "hearty cooperation"	"Win-win"
Reduce worker fatigue/injuries	Empower employees
Increase output/wages	Become more competitive ("save jobs")
WORK/WORKER FOCUS	
Individual workers	Collective workers/teams
Production/clerical workers	Designers, engineers, managers
"Routine" work	All "value-adding" work
Working hard	"Working smart"
PRODUCTION GOALS	
Increase productivity	Add value/reduce cycle time/"quality"
Quality control (inspect for defects)	Statistical process control ("build quality in")
ORGANIZATIONAL STRUCTURES	
Top-down	Top-down
Integrated organization	"Virtual organization," i.e., outsourcing
Decomposed labor processes	Controlled recomposition of labor process
Tightly drawn hierarchy	Controlled "delayering"
Permanent workers	Contingent workers
MANAGEMENT FOCUS	
Speedup	"Continuous improvement"
Root out soldiering	Lean and mean
Conflict	Problem management
WORKER ORGANIZATION	
Hierarchical unions	"Union-free" independent contractors
Individual piece rates	"Collective" (team) time-based production
Adversarial bargaining	Jointness and cooperation
SCALE	
Local/regional competition	Global competition wage
Local wage scales	Global wage scales
PROBLEMS	
Never applied "right"	Never applied "right"
Employers "cheat"	Inadequate support from top management
Employees "cheat"	Employees inadequately motivated

To take Hammer and Champy at face value, BPR provokes fundamental questions about the very purpose of the enterprise. Continuous improvement and TQM focus on the middle and bottom of the process hierarchy. The goal of each separately and in combination is to minimize exceptions—variations, defects, waste, scrap, anything that does not "add value"—and to codify and regularize as many "erratic" processes as quickly as possible.

Together, these are considerably more than a repackaging of older direct and indirect control mechanisms. The process-centered control systems are no longer interested in the distinction between conception and execution. They are concerned instead with the distinction between routine and replicable labor on the one hand and nonroutine and exceptional labor on the other. If the goal is to maximize all value-adding activity, inspiration labor has to be made predictable in the same way routine processes have to be made organizationally flexible. If managers can do this, their dilemma is solved.

CONCLUSION

Every opportunity is also a problem. The global competition that has accompanied global markets has forced U.S. managers to reexamine and change long-established production relations. Continuous Improvement, Total Quality Management, Business Process Reengineering, and similar command-and-control systems are as much a departure from Taylorist command-and-control systems as Taylorism was a departure from craft-based control of production. This has not happened because some forms of crucial "creative" work resist routinization. It has happened because employers have run out of ways of appropriating the "added value" of all workers as quickly as the new global market demands.

The original Taylorist deal—when it was honored by managers at all—was "Check your brains in at the door and in return we will share some of the increase in productivity with you in the form of higher wages." TQM, CI, BPR, and especially "empowered" teams are formal acknowledgments by managers that a century of relentless rationalization has reached its limits. They are also a recognition that all work is, contra Taylor, conceptual and creative. *It is therefore a recognition that all labor sooner or later, formally or illicitly, deals with exceptional rather than routine demands. Even work that is predictable is not necessarily replicable and work that is replicable is not necessarily predictable.* It is, finally, a recognition that a more efficient expropriation of the "value-adding" potential of all workers depends on defining and exploiting a broader range of their conceptual labor.

It is the major breakthrough of Deming, Hammer, and others to attempt the intensification of all labor by collapsing social distinctions among design, production, and even service work on the one hand and management, coordination, and communications on the other. In doing so, they have presented managers with tools to systematically combine "soft" normative and "hard" engineering control systems in remarkably flexible ways. These "hard" and "soft" combinations have little in common with the heavy-handed combinations of human relations inspiration and Taylorist task decomposition. CI, TQM, and BPR acknowledge the truth of Braverman's insistence that human labor is simultaneously routine and creative, unique and replicable, instinctive and conscious. That managers have done so in order to extend still further the "ambit of capitalist production" should not prevent us from either appreciating the vindication of Braverman's analysis or the ongoing need to revise it to reflect changing realities.

NOTES

1. Here and in other "off the net" extracts I have standardized spelling and grammar.

2. Emergent, virtual, and agile organizations have received a lot of attention from theorists of postmodernity. How much of this is real and how much is wishful thinking is still to be determined. My favorite combination of description and fantasy, simultaneously tacky and insightful, is the collected work of Newt Gingrich's inspirations, Heidi and Alvin Toffler. The most trenchant scholarly analysis of modern and postmodern organizational theories is Harvey (1990). See in particular his deconstruction of control systems in Chapter 10, "Theorizing the Transition." Harvey, alas, wrote *The Condition of Postmodernity* before the current waves of TQM and BPR. See Roseneau (1992); Boje and Winsor (1993). A much more modest example is Kraft and Truex (1994). See also Lyotard (1987).

3. Parker and Slaughter(1994) among others have properly attacked "phony competition" as a weapon to whipsaw workers. Here I address a different issue: the mechanisms that permit (and, from the perspective of managers, require) extraordinary and concurrent control strategies.

4. The management concept of value-added was popularized by Porter (1985; 1990) in his "value chain" analysis. Some of the most interesting theoretical critiques of "value-adding" come from the so-called radical accountancy school (cf. Yuthas and Tinker, 1994).

5. Cf. Simons (1995); see also Gouldner (1954); Perrow (1986); Kusterer (1978); Klein and Kraft (1994a; 1994b).

6. The relative lack of interest does not mean, of course, that routine work and mass production no longer exist. It means only that the displacement of much formerly U.S.-based mass production work to low-wage (and

often politically repressive) regions makes control of mass production workers less urgent for U.S. employers. Justified or not, employers have shifted their focus. An unusually clear management statement of this is Simons (1995). See Boje and Winsor (1993). Ironically, while union density in the U.S. private sector has declined to its lowest rate since World War II—about 10 percent— the U.S. telecommunications workers union, the CWA, has actually seen a substantial increase in its membership of workers in the crucial IT sector.

7. Reich's distinction comes from the "people, data, things" classification scheme long used by the U.S. Bureau of Labor Statistics.

8. Stalk and Hout (1990) call this "time-based competition"; see also Hammer (1990); Hammer and Champy (1992); Davenport and Short (1990); Deming (1984); Porter (1985; 1990); Clark and Fujimoto (1991); Ishikawa (1985); Goldratt (1986).

9. Two very different examples are Kusterer (1978) and Berggren (1992).

10. Cf., Kunda (1992); also Kraft (1977); Friedman (1977); Meiksins (1988); Jackall (1988); Kidder (1981).

11. Kusterer (1978), in his early critique of *Labor and Monopoly Capital*, pointed out that "routine" work routinely calls for imaginative and often illicit solutions from "unskilled" workers. The problem of routinizing imagination, it seems, is important for managers only when imagination is both the process and the product.

12. Kraft (1977); Kraft and Dubnoff (1986); A. Friedman (1977).

13. Cf. Stalk and Hout (1990); Pine (1993); and Simons (1995). This is sometimes called the "effort extraction problem" by labor economists.

14. Cf. Kunda (1992) and Barley and Kunda (1992). See also Meiksins (1988).

15. One of the earliest, and still clearest, statements of MBO is Drucker (1954; 1964). See also Odiorne (1965).

16. This in distinction to older human relations efforts to systematize the "psychic reward system" U.S. managers have used to affect worker behavior and attitudes. See note 18.

17. The Canadian Autoworkers Union (CAW) has produced a remarkable film, *Working Lean*, which documents the similarities of the new "working smart" to the old Taylorist speedups.

18. This raises a rich set of issues. Taylor assumed regional, or at most national, markets, including labor markets. The first modern systematic work rationalization schemes—those of Taylor, Fayol, the Gilbreths, Gantt, Mogenson, Shewhart—examined the tasks of individual workers or, at most, a single department at a single site. Fragmented work was redistributed and eventually recombined within the same workplace. "Postmodern" managers literally face a different world. Work, including creative work, can now be moved around the globe to suit employers' requirements for low labor costs,

predictability and timeliness (cf. Shaiken, 1984; Aronowitz and DiFazio, 1994). Skills have been transformed into "knowledge," knowledge is operationalized as "data analysis" and "just-in-time knowledge transfer" and finally retailed as "expert systems."

The local perspective also meant dealing with local labor supplies and roughly predictable market cycles. The new systems of work rationalization, although always applied in specific times and places, are conceived globally. The shift has fundamentally changed the way managers conceive the labor process, the workplace, labor markets, and even the definition of work itself (cf. Chandler 1977). Finally, ever since the Western Electric studies, management theorists have understood perfectly well that production is a social activity. As Braverman (1974) points out, management's initial response was to try to capture the subjective bases of worker "resistance" and turn it to their own advantage. The result was human relations theories of various kinds, which "scientific" managers generally rejected as too soft and squishy. The process-centered control systems described in this essay go far beyond these crude "contented cows give more milk" manipulations.

19. "Total Quality," in the form of "total quality control," was probably first used by Feigenbaum (1951). The person popularly associated with TQM, Feigenbaum's junior colleague, W. Edwards Deming, refused to use the term; he preferred instead to talk about "quality" and continuous improvement. Deming's own acolytes and commercial competitors have been less reluctant to use what has by now become a generic label (Berry 1991).

20. Feminist critics of Braverman have pointed out that his use of waged craftwork as the model of skilled labor effectively renders women's work invisible as well as unskilled. Management's recognition of the collective nature of work raises still more questions about gender, work, and skill (cf. "What Gender Is the Collective Worker?"—Kraft, in preparation).

21. The following discussion is drawn in part from Klein and Kraft (1994a).

22. For a more detailed discussion, see Klein and Kraft (1994b).

23. The best single analysis of collective pressure on the team-member/collective worker is Parker and Slaughter (1988). See also Robertson et al. (1993) and the CAW film, *Working Lean*.

24. Note the following explicit melding of engineering measurement and normative control (and the implicit criticism of Taylorism) in this suggestion for dealing with affirmative action reporting requirements:

> Appreciating the need for diverse opinions, ideas, etc. is at the very heart of problem solving. A part of affirmative action also applies in a similar manner as the legislation banning discrimination due to disabilities. Both to maintain effective work and to comply, compa-

nies have to be able to (or should be able to) document each job/
position by the tasks that when bundled together make up that task.
At present most companies don't have a clue why certain tasks are
attached to particular jobs. They grow and are or have been passed
down through the firm's history. Step number one in most quality
and participation processes should be to document and flow chart all
the tasks actually done within the workplace. Step two is to determine the value added or not by the task as a whole of the individual
steps with the task. If companies/agencies would do this, they would
not only be prepared to better deal with becoming more effective
and more efficient, they would be able to fully comply with affirmative action policies regarding race, gender or ethnicity, but to dis-
abilities as well. Once the tasks are documented, you can see how
they can be rebundled differently to suit the talents in the company
and applicants who have been discriminated against in the past.
(QUALITY discussion list)

3

Braverman, Taylorism, and Technocracy

BEVERLY H. BURRIS

Harry Braverman, who took on the ambitious task of updating Marx, must now himself be updated. In the years since *Labor and Monopoly Capital* was published, the social and historical context has changed dramatically, for capitalist and state socialist countries alike. If the Neo-Marxist tradition that Braverman pioneered is to remain a viable theoretical perspective, it must continue to develop so as to promote understanding of contemporary realities. Contemporary Neo-Marxist theorists must continue to promote ongoing reconsideration of both Marx and Neo-Marxist theorists such as Braverman.

Certainly the labor process continues to be of central importance. During the past twenty years, a fundamental restructuring of work organizations and labor markets has occurred, as the internationalization of the division of labor and the implementation of computerized technology and advanced information systems have transformed production. As I have argued elsewhere (Burris 1989a; 1989b; 1993), these changes have been sufficiently substantial to imply a fundamentally different organizational control structure, which I call *technocracy*.

Given technocratic restructuring, which I describe in more detail below, Braverman's key insights into the capitalist labor process must be revised. Braverman strongly emphasized the salience of Taylorism for capitalist work organization. Although some features of Taylorism are of ongoing importance, for instance, the ideology of the "one best way," the one best technical solution to any problem, in general Taylorist control has been superseded by technocratic control, which is a more sophisticated and heavily legitimated control structure. In recent decades, capitalist administration has been rationalized and has more effectively utilized scientific expertise and advanced technology to further its goals.

A specific feature of Taylorism that has been modified is the relationship between conception and execution. Braverman analyzed the way in which Taylorism dissolves the unity of conception and execution. Conception and execution remain separate, but the dissolution has now been amplified and extended. Rather than a small group of managers and technical workers presiding over a much larger sector of deskilled workers, we find a much larger technical/expert stratum and a polarized workplace. Moreover, conceptual and executing sectors are often widely separated by geographical distance, and experience widely disparate working conditions (Burris 1993).

A final way in which Braverman must be updated concerns the new configurations of class, race, gender, and expertise that are emerging in contemporary workplaces. Although Braverman, like most Marxist theorists, emphasized class relationships, contemporary socioeconomic realities demand an analysis of the ways in which class relationships are influenced by gender, race, and other variables. Contemporary workplaces manifest a complex constellation of inequality that must be analyzed and deconstructed if progressive change is to occur.

The essay that follows is divided into three sections and a conclusion. First, I discuss the main features of the technocratic reorganization of production. Next, I analyze the relation between Taylorism and technocracy. Then I discuss the interaction among class, race, gender, and other variables in contemporary workplaces. Finally, I conclude with a discussion of the implications of these recent socioeconomic changes for Braverman's analysis and for Neo-Marxist theory of the labor process more generally.

TECHNOCRATIC REORGANIZATION OF PRODUCTION

Organizational control structures include structural characteristics and corresponding ideologies that work together to ensure managerial control of the labor process, subordination of the labor force, and legitimation of this subordination.[1] Different forms of organizational control have evolved in the course of historical rationalization: precapitalist craft/guild control, simple control, structural forms of control (technical, bureaucratic, professional), and finally, in recent decades, technocratic control.[2] Although technocracy currently coexists with earlier forms of organizational control, it has become sufficiently prevalent to demand analysis.

Technocratic organization is currently most apparent in workplaces centered around computerized technology: highly automated production workplaces, "high-tech" research and development corporations, and service corporations heavily reliant upon computerized systems. Technocracy emerges as certain factories, bureaucracies, and professional organizations are restructured around computerized technology and technical experts. The central features of technocratic organization include a polarization into expert and nonexpert sectors and a corresponding flattening of bureaucratic hierarchies, flexible configurations of centralization/decentralization, skill restructuring, and increased salience of expertise as a central source of legitimate authority. I discuss each of these briefly below.

Polarization

Polarization into expert and nonexpert sectors is a fundamental aspect of technocracy. As organizations are systematically reorganized around computerized technologies, which substitutes technological complexity for the organizational complexity characteristic of bureaucracy, the hierarchical division of labor is broken down, middle-level positions are eliminated, and distinct expert and nonexpert sectors emerge (Burris 1993; Colclough and Tolbert 1992; Hodson 1988; Noyelle 1987). The expert sector, composed of managers, technical experts, and professionals, is clearly differentiated from the nonexpert sector, which is composed of clerical or production workers (or both). This polarization is paralleling and reinforcing race and sex segregation, with white males predominating in the expert sector, and women and racial minorities disproportionately found in the nonexpert sector (Cockburn 1985; Colclough and Tolbert 1992; Feldberg and Glenn 1980; Glenn and Tolbert 1987; Murphree 1984). The nature of the labor process varies dramatically according to sector. Expert and nonexpert jobs differ not only in their level of skill, but also in remuneration, fringe benefits, and working conditions. At expert levels, much of the rigidity characteristic of bureaucratic rules and task specifications is replaced by more flexible and collegial types of work. Tasks tend to be organized around ad hoc projects, with formal communication channels and chains of command routinely bypassed, leading to decentralized authority among the experts, an emphasis on horizontal communication, and a sense of "adhocracy."[3]

Expert sector workers and elite professionals are therefore in a position to benefit from computerized production and information systems, which enhance their work by providing them with expanded access to relevant data, enlarge collegial networks (both intra- and interfirm), and provide technological support for conceptualization and decision making.[4] Indeed, telecommunications systems now link experts around the world, making it possible for experts such as engineers to work together on the same project (Shaiken 1984). Internet communication facilitates collegiality and resource acquisition in ways reminiscent of science-fiction utopias.

Conversely, at nonexpert levels, the tendency has been for tasks to become more routinized and stringently monitored via the computerized technology. However, the nature of nonexpert sector working conditions depends upon social and political choices, constrained but not determined by technology. Advanced technology can also be implemented so as to enhance nonexpert sector work: to "increase employees' feedback, learning, and self management rather than to deskill and routinize their jobs or remotely supervise them" (Zuboff 1982:151). In some firms, nonexpert workers have been organized into multiskilled teams, with opportunities to acquire more comprehensive understanding of their jobs (Hirschhorn 1984; Kanter 1983; Zuboff 1988). However, empirical evidence indicates that this type of organization of nonexpert sector work is currently the exception rather than the rule; more commonly, superficial types of worker participation mask managerial control and expert privilege (Gregory 1983; Gutek 1983; Machung 1984; National Research Council 1986; Shaiken 1984).

Centralization/Decentralization

In technocratic organizations, centralization is combined with decentralization in varying configurations. Traditionally, organizational control has been kept highly centralized, but while centralization of control is the norm, it is not inevitable. In blue-collar and white-collar production workplaces alike, microcomputers have opened up new opportunities for decentralization.

Centralized numerical control (CNC), for instance, can be used to facilitate worker programming and editing, and microcomputers can serve to provide information and communication links to relatively autonomous satellite stations or work teams (Murphree 1984; Shaiken 1984). However, the same technology can also be used to enhance centralized managerial control, surveillance, and monitoring of worker performance. The technocratic system often assumes the form of *visible* decentralization (e.g., a computer terminal in every office or throughout the shopfloor), but with an underlying centralization of control that is programmed into the design of the computer system (see Burris 1993). The technology can therefore be used to both promote and obscure the polarization of power. In practice, control tends to be kept quite centralized, although at expert levels access to power and information is more widely distributed (Burris 1993).

Skill Restructuring

Another corollary of technocratic restructuring is "skill restructuring" (Cockburn 1983), "skill disruption" (Hodson 1988), and new types of alienation, stress, and occupational hazards (see Hirschhorn 1984). Both deskilling and reskilling occur, and the balance between the two depends upon both the design of the technology and the way in which it is implemented. Social and political factors interact with technical ones, yielding complex outcomes.

Expert and professional work tends to be enhanced by recent sociotechnical changes. Technological support systems expand the amount of data available and facilitate professional decision making, collegial networks are extended by telecommunication systems, and often the more routine parts of the job are computerized. For expert sector workers, conceptualization, creativity, and innovation are emphasized.

Conversely, nonexpert work is often deskilled in the process of technocratic reorganization, although there is considerable ambiguity and variation present. For instance, numerical control of machines using microcomputer terminals can be implemented so as to deskill/monitor or enhance the work of the machinists. The central question concerns who programs the technology: professional programmers or the machinists themselves (Shaiken 1984).

Whether a job is deskilled or upskilled also depends upon the skill level of one's *previous* job. For instance, in the insurance industry, skilled clerical workers now use computerized programs to perform underwriting tasks; whether the job is perceived as deskilled or upskilled depends upon whether one is looking from the perspective of a former underwriter, or a former clerical worker entering the occupation for the first time. Similarly, newspaper photocomposition appears deskilled from the point of view of traditional craft compositors, but upskilled from the point of view of a clerical worker (Cockburn 1983). As Cockburn discovered, perceptions of skill are also influenced by gender. The male compositors perceived photocomposition as deskilled because "girls could do it" (Cockburn 1983). As technological innovation turns formerly blue-collar workplaces into more white-collar settings, both class and gender confusion accompany skill restructuring.

Another dimension of the restructuring of skill is the fact that work that involves computerized systems, whether computerized production systems or advanced information systems, involves new types of analytical skill. As Zuboff (1982:145) put it:

> The distinction in feedback is what separates the Linotype operator from the clerical worker who inputs cold type, the engineer who works with computer-aided design from one who directly handles materials, the continuous process operator who reads information from a visual display unit from one who actually checks vat levels, and even the bill collector who works with an on-line . . . system from a predecessor who handled accounts cards. Computer-mediated work is the electronic manipulation of symbols. Instead of a sensual activity, it is an abstract one. (See also Zuboff 1988)

New types of abstraction and diagnostic skills are needed, particularly when systems malfunction. The increased emphasis on abstraction does not necessarily imply that computer-mediated jobs are challenging or rewarding, however; tasks can be routinized and boring while nonetheless requiring focused, abstract attention. Sociotechnical theorists contend that workers who work with advanced computer systems must be given opportunities to acquire comprehensive knowledge of the system and to forge cooperative working relations with other workers if they are to be able to adequately contend with the new tensions resulting from "the counterpoint of watchfulness and boredom" (Hirschhorn 1984:70).

Expertise as Authority

A final characteristic of technocracy concerns the fact that demonstrated expertise and credential certification tend to become more important than rank position as the basic source of legitimate authority. In contrast to the more personalized managerial authority characteristic of bureaucracy, technocratic authority rests on allegedly neutral decision making derived from expertise. Although managers and technical experts continue to make political decisions, they increasingly do so behind a veil of technocratic ideology that purports to reduce politics to technical decision making. In actuality, power interacts with technical expertise in complex ways (Feldman and Milch 1982; Straussman 1978).

In organizations where rank authority is not yet based on technical expertise, and where managers may have less technical knowledge than their subordinates, conflict has been a frequent occurrence (Kraft 1979; Hodson 1988). Rank authority alone does not provide sufficient legitimacy in technocratic workplaces. Managers increasingly need technical expertise, external credentials, as well as managerial expertise in order to maintain legitimate authority. Moreover, technical expertise is becoming an important precondition for traditional managerial functions: supervision, planning, marketing, and the like.

Given the increased emphasis on expertise as the basis of authority, new types of politicking centered around "conspicuous expertise" (Burris 1983; 1993) become apparent in technocratic organizations. Formerly, successful bureaucratic careers depended on who you knew more than on what you knew; technocratic careers may depend not only on who and what you know, but also upon how well you can *appear* knowledgeable. "Knowledge has become a critical resource in the politics of class struggle, both inside and outside the workplace" (Fischer 1984:188).

FROM TAYLORISM TO TECHNOCRACY

Frederick Taylor, writing at the turn of the twentieth century, brought positivist philosophy from the Continent to the United States, giving practical and concrete expression to the concern with societal restructuring along more scientific lines. For Taylor, the labor process itself created the greatest inefficiency and waste, and he advocated scientific management in order to find the "one best way" to solve any industrial problem:

> . . . Among the various methods and implements used in each element of each trade there is always one method and one implement which is quicker and better than any of the rest. And this one best method and best implement can only be discovered or developed through a scientific study and analysis of all the methods and implements in use, together with accurate, minute, motion and time study. This involves the gradual substitution of science for rule of thumb throughout the mechanic arts. (Taylor 1913:25)

For Taylor, the one best scientific method is too complex for ordinary workers to understand; therefore, expert management based on scientific principles is necessary. The rather rudimentary scientific principles he advocated included time study, standardization of tools and movements, establishment of a separate planning room, use of time-saving implements (such as slide rules), and use of differentiated piece rates (see Taylor 1913:129 and passim).

Taylor presented his project not as a tool of the capitalist, but rather as scientific and politically neutral. According to Taylor, the scientific management of industry (and ultimately of society as a whole) would reduce production costs and increase efficiency and productivity; it would also lower prices and increase wages (see Taylor 1913:10ff.). Obviously, in such a scenario, capitalists, engineers, workers, and consumers stood to benefit. For Taylor and his followers, scientific management became a moral mission, one that was guaranteed to reward the hardworking, punish the lazy, eliminate politics, and restore societal harmony. In the private sector, there was considerable interest in Taylorism, combined with resistance from both managers and workers. In the public sector, Taylorism was embraced by the Progressive reform movement, which sought to "engineer the transition to a new and 'more rational' form of governance . . . to replace . . . political irrationality with scientifically designed decision processes" (Fischer 1990:81). However, as Braverman pointed out, Taylorist methods are noteworthy not for their scientific qualities but rather as an expression of capitalist management ideology: "[Scientific management] enters the workplace not as the representative of science, but as the representative of management masquerading in the trappings of science . . .

behind these commonplaces there lies a theory which is nothing less than the explicit verbalization of the capitalist mode of production" (Braverman 1974:86).

The long-term significance of Taylorism was that a new class of scientific experts began to coalesce, legitimated on the grounds that it would be above politics and class conflict. As David Stark (1980:119) put it:

> The period of the transformation of the labor process during the early decades of this century was also an important period of class formation with significant consequences for the contemporary constellation of class relations. . . . What the reorganization of work did accomplish was to provide the basic conditions for the ideologically sharp division between 'mental' and 'manual' labor. . . . The creed of specialized knowledge and expertise became the formative basis of a new and more complex ideology around which a class could cohere.

Taylorism thus represented the beginning of the process of technocratic rationalization of the labor process, and Braverman was correct to assert that this restructuring bore the imprint of capitalist power relations. Knowledge and skill were increasingly dissociated from workers and consolidated and codified in the hands of management and technical experts (see Braverman 1974:112ff.). The twin goals of increasing productivity and enhancing capitalist control of the workforce shaped the restructuring.

In Braverman's analysis of Taylorism, the dissolution of the unity of conception and execution figures prominently. Under capitalism, work is typically divided so that some workers conceptualize, and others execute. This division, which Marx discussed as the split between mental and manual labor, is extended and legitimated by Taylorism. Today, in the worldwide technocratic capitalist system, conception and execution remain separate, but computerization and related socioeconomic developments have altered both conception and execution.

One major change of the past twenty years has been the increased size of the conceptual sector. Braverman, for instance, estimated the size of the technical sector to be 3 percent in 1970 (1974:241). Currently in the United States, however, approximately one-third of all employed workers are managers, supervisors, professionals, or technical workers (U.S. Bureau of the Census 1991), and in high-tech workplaces the expert sector can be even larger. The technical sophistication of computerized systems, as well as the enhanced need for innovation in order that U.S. firms can compete effectively in international markets, have promoted the increased size of the conceptual sector.

As we have seen, this conceptual, expert sector generally enjoys advantageous working conditions: relatively high pay, considerable autonomy, collegial interaction with other experts. Moreover, computerization generally enhances expert sector work, eliminating the more routine tasks, expanding the information and data available, and providing technical support for decision making. Expert sector work is more purely conceptual than ever before, while expert collaboration is easier than ever before.

In general, the interaction between experts and nonexperts is minimal. Therefore, the breach between conception and execution has widened: instead of conceptualizing tasks that are closely related to nonexpert workers, the potential exists for conceptual workers to design products and services in greater isolation from those who will produce the products or perform the services. Indeed, the nonexpert workers are often widely separated by geographical distance, even national boundaries, from the expert conceptual sector. (See Greenbaum, this volume.) This wider separation of conceptual and nonconceptual workers serves to veil the class relationship, and gives conceptual workers the illusion of being "free-floating intellectuals," with only the imperatives of science and creativity as constraints.

Execution also is transformed by technocratic reorganization. In many types of computerized work, the computer performs much of the actual execution (Hirschhorn 1984; Shaiken 1984; Burris 1993). In some superautomated factories, a very small number of workers monitor an almost completely computerized system of production.[5] This trend is projected to intensify, as computer automation has the potential to eliminate most work in the execution sector (Rifkin 1995).

Under such conditions, the nature of nonexpert sector work is transformed. Workers must acquire new skills of monitoring, inference, and diagnosis (Hirschhorn 1984). Although these skills are not conceptual, they are more abstract (Zuboff 1982; 1988). The work is less concrete and physical, and workers must develop inferential reasoning from abstract cues. Under conditions of extensive computerization, workers must have some comprehensive understanding of the computerized system in order to be able to effectively monitor it and diagnose malfunctions (Hirschhorn 1984). In practice, however, workers are often not given this knowledge (Zuboff 1988).

In effect, technocratic restructuring has broadened the gap between conception and execution and has created a *bifurcation of control* in many workplaces. Conceptual and executing sectors typically experience dramatically different systems of control: expert sector workers are organized into work teams or task forces with considerable autonomy; nonexpert workers tend to be organized in more traditional ways, with stringent bureaucratic or technical control. Expert sector, conceptual workers are treated by capitalists and managers as "partners in power" (Baylis 1974) who will be more productive and creative if they work autonomously and collegially, whereas nonexpert sector workers are perceived to require closer supervision and control if they are to be productive. With this bifurcation of control, Taylorism has been modified, as a substantial sector of the population, the expert sector, has been, in effect, exempted from Taylorist control.

In recent decades, then, the process of workplace restructuring began by Taylor one hundred years ago has become far more sophisticated, and computerized technology has amplified and extended the process. As mentioned previously, as Taylorism evolved into technocracy, an expansion of the class of scientific and technical experts has been one result, further polarizing the capitalist workforce into expert and nonexpert sectors. Simultaneously, technocracy blurs capitalist power relations by emphasizing technical expertise as an alternative source of power in the workplace.

Where Taylorists attempted to legitimate their reforms as scientific, and did include some technical innovations as part of their restructuring,[6] in general they relied on religious fervor and crude and transparent control strategies: time and motion studies, speeding up assembly lines, and so on. Worker resistance, particularly from the craft unions and professionals, was considerable (Stark 1980; Clawson 1980). Conversely, technocratic control tends to be embedded in computerized systems, which are programmed and designed to restrict access to information, and which also have the potential to enforce a more veiled type of control than Taylorism. Managers and supervisors can surreptitiously monitor worker productivity, quality of performance, and rate of errors (Garson 1988; Gregory 1983; Gutek 1983; Machung 1984; Shaiken 1984). Some firms have even experimented with the use of subliminal messages that flash onto computer screens, such as "Work faster" or positive slogans about the employer (*In These Times* Editorial Board 1988:5).

Importantly, computerized systems that utilize microcomputer terminals may give the illusion of decentralization, but the system is typically programmed to maintain centralized control. Passwords, for instance, serve to preserve managerial and expert access to information and power networks. One manager candidly told Zuboff (1988:252): "Managers perceive workers who have information as a threat. They are afraid of not being the 'expert.'" A worker in the same firm demonstrated awareness of these managerial attitudes when he said: "It seems management is afraid to let us learn too much about how this system operates. The more we know, the more we could sabotage it" (Zuboff 1988:251). Restriction of access to information, then, is a central mechanism of technocratic control.

Moreover, technocratic control is often legitimated on the grounds of technological progress: "working with computers" is seen as important, and as necessarily involving close monitoring and discipline due to technical exigencies (Burris 1983). Another way in which technocratic control of the nonexpert sector is veiled is through an emphasis on the working conditions of the expert sector as generally characteristic of "working with computers." In both the scholarly literature and the journalistic media, working with computers is viewed typically as necessitating autonomy, promoting workplace democracy, and inherently interesting (see Burris 1993 for a fuller discussion).

Technocratic control is, then, a more sophisticated and rationalized alternative to Taylorism. With the development of computerized technology and advanced information systems, as well as related socioeconomic changes such as the international division of labor, the increased size of the state sector, and the perceived need to manage the economic system and perfect long-range planning, a new class of technocratic experts has emerged, grown, and reorganized production. The general societal esteem for experts has contributed to the legitimation of this new technocratic system, and has rendered it exempt from critical analysis.

CLASS, EXPERTISE, RACE, AND GENDER

That technocratic control purports to be more meritorious than earlier forms of control stems, in part, from its relation to rising educational levels and equal opportunity pressures (Noyelle 1987). In actuality, however, technocracy is fundamentally intertwined with various types of discrimination in the workplace. Expertise, class, race, gender, and other variables form a complex constellation of power relations. This complexity has served to blur power relations and further enhance legitimacy of the technocratic system.

Braverman's analysis focused on capitalist class relations, and attempted to update Marx's own class analysis by considering the class position of clerical workers, on the one hand, and scientific and technical workers, on the other. Braverman unequivocally placed the former in the proletariat,[7] whereas the latter he saw as embodying more contradictory characteristics.[8] More important, Braverman recognized that class categories are not static or fixed, but rather evolving and fluid, and that "difficulties" in class categorization will be inevitable:

> These difficulties arise, in the last analysis, from the fact that classes, the class structure, the social structure as a whole, are not fixed entities but rather ongoing processes, rich in change, transition, variation, and incapable of being encapsulated in formulas, no matter how analytically proper such formulas may be. (Braverman 1974:409)

The best tribute to Braverman is to analyze this ongoing process of the restructuring of class relationships. Today, class relationships cannot be considered in isolation from gender, race, and other variables. Unless class is understood as part of a more complex constellation of stratifying dimensions, it cannot be understood at all, for "the other social relations in which workers are enrolled will determine the manner in which they react inside the factory, and . . . the plurality of these relations cannot be magically erased to constitute a *single* working class" (Laclau and Mouffe 1985:167).

As we have seen, technocratic restructuring rests on a polarization into expert and nonexpert sectors. Technical expertise therefore becomes an important new currency of workplace stratification. The expert/nonexpert divide has tended to correlate with other dimensions of stratification, such as race and gender, with white males overrepresented among the expert sector, and minorities and women overrepresented among the nonexpert sector (Burris 1993; Feldberg and Glenn 1980; Glenn and Tolbert 1987; Machung 1984; Stroeber and Arnold 1987). The polarization of the technocratic workplace parallels and reinforces gender and race segregation so as to circumscribe mobility prospects for women and minorities (Noyelle 1987). Privilege, in other words, tends to be overdetermined, although technocracy is widely presented and perceived as meritocratic.

Some women and minorities have made incursions into managerial and professional ranks. For instance, during the 1970s women essentially doubled their numbers in managerial and professional sectors of the insurance industry (Baran 1987:50). Women and minorities are not universally disadvantaged by technocratic restructuring; rather, new types of structural and ideological barriers have differential effects on women, depending on their class and race, and differential effects on minorities, depending on their class and gender. Educational credential barriers, for instance, serve to disadvantage working-class and minority women, in particular (Hacker 1989; Noyelle 1987).

The culture of the high-tech professions is heavily gendered. Engineering, for instance, is one of the most male-dominated fields, and this disproportionality is both a cause and an effect of sexism within the profession. Sally Hacker argued that "engineering contains the smallest proportion of females of all major professions and projects a heavily masculine image that is hostile to women" (1990:113). The engineers she studied explicitly told her that engineering was a male activity: hard, clean, predictable, abstract, technical, mathematical, controlling (1990:passim). She found that in engineering classes, the professors used jokes to denigrate women and racial minorities as technically incompetent (1990:113ff.). Engineering was seen as closely allied with ideologies of control and dominance: control of women, racial minorities, the body, nature, and chaotic forces in general (Hacker 1989:35ff.).

Another feature of the expert sector of technocratic organizations is the reliance on task forces, team structure, and informality, and the corresponding relaxation of bureaucratic regulation. In such a context of "adhocracy" (Mintzberg 1979), the micropolitics of small group interaction becomes more salient.

Leadership of such groups has been found to be derived from such sources as "information, expertise, connections, energy, creativity, and charisma" (Hirschhorn 1984:146), and given the predominance of men in the expert sector, such micropolitics are likely to be gendered. Murphree, in a study of law firms, found that teams of lawyers exhibited patterns of gender discrimination, and that "the primary group nature [of these groups] may well encourage the same sexist and autocratic patrimony that characterized the former attorney-secretary dyads" (Murphree 1984:85–86). Natasha Josefowitz (1983) found that in small group discussions, men often failed to hear women's comments, or attributed them to a male participant.

One of the most salient types of politicking in technocratic organizations is the emphasis on expertise and the need to prove oneself and one's expertise: a constant fear of "not being the expert" and the common response of "doing a snow job" and projecting "conspicuous expertise" have been found to be characteristic of the micropolitics of the expert sector (Burris 1983; 1993; Zuboff 1988). Gender contributes to this insecurity over expertise in several ways. First, conspicuous expertise is more consistent with traditional male gender, giving men some advantages in the new types of politicking. There is also greater insecurity among men in the expert sector: fear of being unmasculine if one's expertise is found lacking or is questioned (Cockburn 1985:178ff.). It appears that this insecurity contributes to racism and sexism, since being perceived as less competent than a woman or racial minority appears as a double threat to masculinity and self-worth (Cockburn 1985).

Despite these indications of technocratic discrimination, some contend that technocratic restructuring, with its reliance on computer-mediated communication and abstract information and its deemphasis on face-to-face interaction, will undermine forms of discrimination based on ascribed, visible characteristics. Zuboff quoted one manager of a large pharmaceutical company as saying:

> DIALOG lets me talk to other people as peers. . . . All messages have an equal chance because they all look alike. The only thing that sets them apart is their content. If you are a hunchback, a paraplegic, a woman, a black, fat, old, have two hundred warts on your face, or never take a bath, you still have the same chance. It strips the halo effects from age, sex, or appearance. (Zuboff 1988:371)

However, the fact that this user of computer conferencing continues to associate women and racial minorities with social and physical handicaps undermines the veracity of his views. Whether computerized communication will become prevalent enough to undermine discrimination based on ascribed characteristics is unclear. What is clear, however, is that technical expertise can and does interact with traditional forms of discrimination in complex and insidious ways.

CONCLUSION

Harry Braverman made a major contribution to Neo-Marxist theory and the contemporary study of the labor process. He did so by extracting certain fundamental ideas from Marx's work, and showing their ongoing relevance to the capitalist labor process: the separation of conception from execution, the exploitation of the working class, and so on. If Neo-Marxism is to continue to evolve so as to remain a viable theoretical tradition, we must now go beyond Braverman's insights and formulate theory that illuminates the contemporary face of capitalism.

Technocratic capitalism differs from previous forms in certain crucial ways. Conception remains separate from execution, but the breach has widened, as advanced technology and the internationalization of production have transformed production. Moreover, the size of the conceptual or expert sector has increased. In contrast to the relatively small technical/managerial sector that Braverman discussed, we now have an expert sector that comprises approximately one-third of the workforce in advanced capitalist countries, and is projected to grow. The workforce is polarized into expert and nonexpert sectors, with widely disparate working conditions, a bifurcation of control, and frequent separation by considerable geographical distance and national boundaries.

Braverman strongly emphasized the salience of Taylorism in the development of capitalism in the United States, seeing it as capitalist ideology masquerading in scientific guise. Today, Taylorism has evolved into technocratic control and ideology, a more rationalized and heavily legitimated type of capitalist control. As science and technology have become more sophisticated and technically advanced, so has capitalist/expert control. Technocratic control is more heavily legitimated for several reasons: increased size of the conceptual sector and ideological exaggeration of expert sector working conditions; bifurcation of control; superficial decentralization masking underlying centralized control of the nonexpert sector; and general societal esteem for science, technical expertise, and credentialed workers.

Challenges to technocratic/capitalist control must become correspondingly sophisticated. If it is to be of ongoing relevance, Neo-Marxist theory must go beyond a narrow class analysis and develop a more multidimensional stratification theory, one that explores the complex interrelationships among class, race, gender, expertise, and other variables. Class is not the only salient dimension of stratification, nor is it necessarily the most important; rather, we have a shifting configuration of several variables, some achieving primacy in certain contexts, and others in other contexts.

In technocratic workplaces, expertise, race, and gender are often correlated, leading to overdetermined privilege, visible polarization, and a potentially volatile political situation. Neo-Marxism must go beyond a narrow class analysis, however, in order to theorize these new political realities. The overdetermined nature of privilege can only be confronted by a left that is willing and able to articulate the logic of a "radical and plural democracy" (Laclau and Mouffe 1985:passim).

This process will not be easy. Technocratic control and domination are more insidious and veiled than earlier forms of control, and the capitalist system is now worldwide in scope. In the context of technocratic restructuring, with its profoundly undemocratic privileging of technical experts, the struggle to retain, much less extend, democracy will be a long and difficult process.

NOTES

1. See Etzioni (1965); Heydebrand (1979; 1983); and Burris (1993) for fuller discussions of the concept of organizational control structure.

2. See R. Edwards (1979); Burris (1993) for fuller discussions.

3. See Mintzberg (1979); Kanter (1983); Burris (1993) for fuller discussions.

4. Some less elite professionals have experienced disadvantageous changes in their working conditions, leading some to speak of "deprofessionalization" (Haug 1977) or "proletarianization" (Derber 1982; Larson 1980) of the professions. Although some professionals working within technocratic workplaces do experience larger client loads and some reduction in autonomy, in general the deprofessionalization arguments are overstated, as elite professionals and technical experts generally continue to enjoy not only high status and prestige, but also advantageous working conditions (Derber, Schwartz, and Magrass 1990; see Burris 1993 for a fuller discussion).

5. Shaiken, for instance, described a Japanese machine tool factory: "The Yamazaki Machinery Corporation . . . cites some impressive figures. . . . The $18 million system has 18 machine tools, occupies 30,000 square feet of space, has a staff of 12, and can turn out 74 different products in 1200 variations. A comparable manual system . . . would need 68 machines, 215 employees, and 103,000 square feet to do the same job" (Shaiken 1984:146). See Burris (1993) for a fuller discussion.

6. For instance, the type of steel used for machining was improved. See Clawson (1980:243 and passim).

7. He said, for instance, "The apparent trend to a large nonproletarian 'middle class' has resolved itself into the creation of a large proletariat in a new form" (Braverman 1974:355).

8. He said, for instance, "there is a range of intermediate categories, sharing the characteristics of worker on the one side and manager on the other in varying degrees" (Braverman 1974:405).

4

Deskilled and Devalued

Changes in the Labor Process in Temporary Clerical Work

JACKIE KRASAS ROGERS

Over the past twenty years we have seen not only drastic increases in the numbers of temporary workers, but a change in the way companies are utilizing these workers. In the era of the "Kelly Girl," temporary clerical workers were used primarily for vacation, sick leave, and maternity leave replacement. Now, more and more companies are utilizing temporary workers as part of their staffing strategy (R. Parker 1994) to reduce benefit and other costs, to cover seasonal fluctuations in workload, and to avoid costs associated with layoffs (Fanning and Maniscalco 1993). Contrary to public portrayals, the boom in temporary employment is occurring primarily as a result of employer action rather than employees' desires for "flexible" work (Golden and Appelbaum 1992). And with over 90 percent of companies utilizing temporary help firms (National Association of Temporary Services 1992), temporary employment has indeed become institutionalized in the U.S. workplace.

But temporary employment is only a portion of the larger "contingent" employment sector that includes part-time, temporary, self-employed, casual labor, subcontracting arrangements, and job sharing—work arrangements that differ from the traditionally conceived year-round, full-time employment relationship. In fact, Belous (1989) estimated that between 25 percent and 35 percent of the U.S. workforce could be categorized as contingent workers. These numbers of contingent employment speak to the increasing insecurity of work for large portions of the population. Although many groups of workers historically have not had access to "core" jobs, the current trend toward contingent work will encompass more workers than ever before. While more white, male workers are being drawn into contingent work arrangements, women and people of color are still overrepresented in this sector. Nearly 50 percent of the workforce is female, but women comprise two-thirds of temporary workers. Likewise, while 10 percent of the workforce is African-American, African-Americans make up 20 percent of temporary workers. The overrepresentation of women and people of color in temporary employment indicates a need to investigate the gendered and "raced" nature of such changes in the employment relationship. The institutionalization of temporary employment has occurred most significantly in the female-dominated clerical sector, with approximately 63 percent of temporary jobs in clerical work (National Association of Temporary Services 1992). This is hardly surprising since women tend to be concentrated in occupations where nontraditional work arrangements, such as temporary work, proliferate (Negrey 1993).

Set against the background of societal racial and gender inequalities, increases in temporary work raise questions concerning the organization of technical as well as social labor processes in temporary employment. First, does temporary employment have an effect on the skill content of jobs? If so, are jobs upgraded or deskilled? Second, does temporary employment impact the social organization of work? If so, are employment relationships enhanced or downgraded? Finally, what are the consequences of these changes in jobs for the workers (disproportionately women and people of color) who perform them?

GENDER, LABOR PROCESS THEORY, AND SKILL

In the years since Braverman's (1974) landmark treatise on the deskilling thesis, social scientists have come to appreciate its continuing relevance as well as its limitations. Discussions of skill, deskilling, and upgrading are far from conclusive, yet it is becoming increasingly apparent that we are dealing with multiple and indeterminate labor processes rather than a singular, preordained, unidirectional labor process (V. Smith 1994). In her commemoration of *Labor and Monopoly Capital*, Vicki Smith (1994) outlined what she finds to be three fruitful areas of inquiry derived from Braverman's work (1974) that extend beyond simple questions of technical labor processes to include social aspects of the labor process: worker participation and resistance, gender and the labor process, and skill and worker control. Some of the staunchest criticism of Braverman (1974) and consequent labor process theorists (R. Edwards 1979; Burawoy 1979; P. Thompson 1989) has come in the form of feminist critiques (Acker 1990; West 1990; Westwood 1985; Cockburn 1983; 1985) that cite either the complete absence of gender from analysis, or the unquestioned acceptance of gender inequality as "natural" in discussions relating to both technical and social labor processes.

With regard to technical labor processes, some have noted that continued deskilling increases the number of deskilled workers at whose expense the skill of a smaller, more skilled segment of workers is maintained or increased (Braverman 1974; Thompson 1989). Yet Cynthia Cockburn (1983) reminded us that this process is not gender-neutral. There are material differences in the content of women's and men's work. With regard to technology, Cockburn (1985:12) added that "women may push the buttons, but they may not meddle with the works." Women tend to perform most of the truly monotonous and labor-intensive work in the world (Sassen-Koob 1984; West 1990), while an increasing division of labor aids men in maintaining their skill advantage over women.

While there is evidence that such material differences in men's and women's work do exist, other feminist writers remind us that "skill" is a slippery concept. What constitutes skill is at least in part, socially constructed (Phillips and Taylor 1980; Acker 1990; Milkman 1987), and the very notion of "skill" is gendered (Cockburn 1985; Acker 1990; Steinberg 1992)—men have skill, women do not. In her analysis of job evaluation systems, Joan Acker (1990) revealed how gender-neutral discourses help construct a "disembodied" and "universal" worker that obscures the embeddedness of gender in organizations. The scientific endeavor of job evaluation separates skills from workers as it "objectively" ranks jobs on the basis of skill rather than the workers who perform the jobs. This process reproduces gender hierarchies, as skills that women are more likely to possess are typically assigned less importance than the skills men are more likely to possess.

Taking this literature as a whole, it teaches us that women's work is both deskilled and seen as unskilled. Men are both better able to retain skilled jobs than women, and better able to define their jobs as skilled regardless of the actual content of the job. Both scenarios lead to a polarization of skill (either materially or ideologically) by gender. Yet as Joan Acker (1990; 1992) told us, organizational processes produce and reproduce gender ideologies implicated in the gender segregation of work.

Therefore, a discussion of potential changes in labor processes should include an understanding of how organizational processes, which bring change in either technical or social labor processes,[1] reproduce or mitigate gender and racial inequality. Both Joan Acker (1992) and Vicki Smith (1993) have commented that gender is embedded in the strategies organizations utilize to achieve flexibility. "Enabling" strategies of flexibility (those that upgrade the labor process and employment relationship) are most often pursued in male-dominated workplaces, while "restrictive" strategies (those that downgrade labor processes and the employment relationship) pervade in female-dominated workplaces (V. Smith 1993). With the overrepresentation of women and African-Americans in temporary employment (Belous 1989), we need to consider whether increases in temporary clerical employment represent a restrictive or an enabling strategy for workers.

METHOD

This research proceeds from the notion that workers' subjective experiences must be incorporated into labor process analyses (V. Smith 1994). I employed multiple-strategy field research (Layder 1993) to arrive at a midlevel analysis that works back and forth between structural and intersubjective understandings of temporary employment and labor processes.

I gathered data for this research through several sources: several months of participant observation as a temporary worker over a two-year period, twenty-eight in-depth interviews of temporary workers and five in-depth interviews of agency personnel, and documents collected from the field and other sources. Interviews were obtained through several sources: an ad placed in a local magazine advertising temporary jobs, a flyer placed at the temporary agency through which I worked, referrals from temporary agency contacts, and personal contacts made while on temporary assignments.

The interviews represent experiences with over twenty different temporary agencies in the greater Los Angeles area, and many interview subjects worked through several agencies. The range of temporary work experience is from five months to fifteen years, and interview subjects are drawn from diverse geographical locations all over Los Angeles County, including downtown, West Los Angeles, Santa Monica, San Fernando Valley, and South Los Angeles. Geographical diversity is important given the ethnic makeup of certain areas of Los Angeles County and local markets for temporary services. The ethnic makeup of my group of respondents is 51 percent white, 21 percent African-American, 9 percent Latino, 6 percent Asian-American, 6 percent Jewish-American, and 6 percent other (includes West African and Native American).

The organization of my interviews with the temporary workers followed three trajectories: relationship of the worker to the work, relationship of the worker to others in the workplace, and feelings of the worker about himself or herself. Questions for the interviews with temporary agency representatives were structured around the business of temporary employment, the client companies, and the temporary workers. Interviews were semistructured through the use of an interview guide, enabling the researcher to follow important lines of inquiry as they arose while maintaining consistency in the overall structure.

DESKILLED IN TECHNICAL LABOR PROCESSES

Deskilled

Clerical work encompasses a diverse array of job assignments from data entry and filing to receptionist and executive secretary, making it difficult to characterize clerical labor in singular terms with regard to skill content. Therefore, this research proceeds from the position that not all clerical work has been deskilled, or deskilled completely. Significant pockets of skill remain in clerical work, although they may be devalued.[2] This is not to say that an analysis illustrating the deskilling of clerical work in general would be incorrect. However, to understand skill in temporary clerical work we must first recognize the diversity of tasks within clerical work as well as the skilled content of some clerical work. Some skilled clerical work has been unrecognized as such because of historical changes in the gender composition of the clerical labor force (Game and Pringle 1983), while other clerical work can be said to be truly lacking in skill (Crompton and Jones 1984). Therefore, it is necessary when discussing skill in temporary clerical work that the content of those jobs be compared to clerical jobs that are not organized on a temporary basis. In other words, to what extent is the skill content of a job related to the fact that it is a temporary job?

Messages from the temporary industry about skill are complex and vary according to the potential audience. The industry uses notions of skill to their advantage in both marketing and eliciting consent from temporary workers. On some occasions, temporary workers are characterized as being highly skilled such as when the temporary industry claims to be filling a niche left by a dearth of skilled labor. In the following quote from a temporary agency's promotional kit aimed at generating clients, temporary workers are cast as possessing high-level, yet scarce skills.

> There is a chronic shortage of skilled clerical and technical help in this country. The Occupational Outlook Handbook, published annually by the Department of Labor, has outlined this fact since at least 1974. The forecasted growth in demand for skilled clerical and technical help is significantly faster than the growth for the workforce as a whole. At the same time, supply side factors, such as the *woman's movement* [emphasis mine], and aging workforce, the decline of the classic secretarial school, and increased labor force mobility and opportunity have created a supply imbalance/shortfall. This fact is reflected in the newspaper classified ad sections every week. . . . . Rapidly changing technology in both the clerical and technical fields have created new skill requirements to which the workforce in this country responds slowly. [temporary agency promotional kit]

Business and the temporary industry are cast as responding to a shortage and a rigidity in the U.S. workforce, for which the educational system and even the women's movement are to blame. The ideological sleight-of-hand acts to shift the impetus for temporary work from the temporary industry itself and employers to workers, when in fact Golden and Appelbaum (1992) have found it to be the opposite. The large increases in temporary work are employer- rather than employee-driven. By focusing on the "human capital" of workers, the temporary industry dodges questions regarding their role (and employers' roles) in creating a large contingent workforce.

However, the portrayal of temporary workers doing skilled work does not mesh with the consistent reports from temporary workers often feeling overqualified for assignments and performing unskilled work despite their "human capital" or capabilities. Specifically, the temporary clerical workers I interviewed consistently reported being given the worst work of the office, while only occasionally being called for the use of their "special skills." They referred to the work they most often received as "shit work," "dreg work," or "scut work."

> A lot of times you'll be called to do, you'll have to know this program and it's supposed to be a lot of word processing but it ends up being like opening the mail and answering phones all day. [Harold Koenig, twenty-nine-year-old white man]

> And at this assignment now I'm processing declination and reply letters for insurance. And it's basically all I do. And when it's done, I don't have anything to do. And when I was at the other assignment I was keeping a log of various telephone accounts because I was working in the telecommunications department. And keeping logs of the telephone bills and sending out the telephone bills to the customers. Very simple phones, nothing difficult. No real brains involved. Or at least the bare minimum. [Albert Baxter, thirty-one-year-old white man]

> I worked in a bank and stuffed envelopes for five days straight. It was terrible, it was sooo monotonous. He delegated me these huge boxes of stuff, so like I would only have to go to him two days later. I'd just go to him when I ran out of stuff to stuff. [Sarah Tilton, twenty-five-year-old white woman]

Despite the range of educational and work backgrounds among my interview subjects, they seemed to share a general feeling of overqualification for the work that they were performing. In this sense, temporary work can be said to be a form of underemployment (R. Parker 1994).

> They give you spelling tests, math tests, yeah, they do that too. The ten key test. And most of the time when you go to a job, you never

basically do those things. I mean it's like the ten key. Unless you're really doing an accounting job and you have to add up, I can see that. But the jobs I mostly got weren't like that. I was always over-qualified for the jobs. [Linda Mejia, thirty-one-year-old Latina woman]

Yes, there were some days when I thought, this is ludicrous. I am so miserable. I can't believe that I'm however many years old, thirty-six, thirty-seven, and I'm making nine thousand copies of this script or something. I have two master's degrees. [Ellen Lanford, thirty-eight-year-old white woman]

Again, to the degree that the temporary industry focuses on the human capital that temporaries bring to the job rather than the job itself, it misrepresents temporary workers' experiences by equating the skills of the worker with the skills required for the job. The worker and the job are treated as virtually the same. Any disjuncture of workers' skills and job tasks is not acknowledged.

If temporary clerical workers feel their work is lacking in skill utilization, then to what end is this occurring? Is it simply a by-product of the capitalist labor process that tends to result in job deskilling? Or are some workers maintaining or increasing the skill content of their jobs at the expense of temporary workers?

Either implicitly or explicitly, temporaries acknowledge that their performance of "dreg work" insulates permanent employees from having to perform those tasks they find unsavory.

Yeah, the temp is the one who gets the shit work. And the temp is the one who is last considered for anything. [Michael Glenn, twenty-five-year-old Asian man]

When you're a temp, you get all the shitty work. . . . You usually got stuck in the back to do the work that either someone put off or was on maternity leave or sick. Work that no one else wanted to do. [Doug Larson, thirty-nine-year-old white man]

These research findings also suggest that the deskilling process in temporary clerical work is not conducted by management alone. To the contrary, "permanent" workers participate in the assignment of tasks to temporary workers.

In fact, she was really gung ho about giving me all this grunt work to do and I spent the entire time typing in there while she was pigging out on Doritos and what not. So it seemed as though she had taken the opportunity to give me all her crap work. [Irene Pedersen, twenty-four-year-old white woman]

Temporary workers often report that the work assigned to them is work that has been sitting untouched because no one else in the office will do it. Furthermore, temporaries report that their entrance into an office is seen as a signal for other clerical workers to transfer to the temporary the work they do not want to do. Literature from the temporary industry demonstrates a similar understanding of the function of temporary work.

> Companies often call on temporary help companies for supplemental staffing during peak production periods, special projects, transitions, the introduction of new products or technology, and to relieve "core" employees of excess overtime and tedious work. [pamphlet from temporary help firm]

This is a notable contradiction to the scenario portrayed by temporary agencies in which temporary workers are hired as short-term experts. Thus it seems that the "expert" notion of the temporary worker does not apply, at least in the case of clerical work.

While temporary work does not necessarily change the overall technical labor process, it can result in two categories of jobs and differential experiences of work for permanent and temporary workers. Therefore, temporary employment can serve as a type of occupational segregation that "pushes up" the skill level in the core of workers while "pushing down" the skill level in the periphery of temporary workers. Permanent workers are relieved from monotonous work, and (happily for the employer) these higher-paid core workers do not spend their time doing routine tasks. Using temporary workers in this way provides a further realization of the Babbage principle, which cheapens labor through increasing divisions of labor (for a more complete discussion of the Babbage principle, see Braverman 1974). High-priced workers spend their time on high-priced tasks, while low-priced workers spend their time on low-priced tasks. So it seems that deskilling and upgrading of clerical jobs are occurring simultaneously with the introduction of temporary workers. Importantly, the core of skilled workers seems to be shrinking, for even in times of economic recovery the use of temporary help is rising (R. Parker 1994).

Devalued

The picture of temporary work as widening the division between higher-skilled jobs and lower-skilled jobs is accurate but incomplete. Another, seemingly contradictory, tendency in temporary work runs counter to notions of deskilling, namely, not all the work temporaries do lacks skill. Clerical temporaries often perform complex, skilled work either equivalent or superior to the work of "permanent" employees. In fact, the only distinguishing factors between permanent and temporary work often seems to be that temporary work is devalued and brief or uncertain in duration. On these occasions, the skilled work of temporaries is not recognized as such—it is ideologically deskilled. The result often is that temporary workers are provided lower compensation[3] than permanent workers for similarly skilled work. The following description is reflective of the type of skilled labor temporary workers perform.

> Nine dollars an hour. I am publication coordinator. I do all the billing for the magazine. I do all the billing for the advertisers, which means I'm sort of accounts receivable. Uh, I answer phones. I'm front office for phones. I do the filing of course for certain things. Um, I place the ads. I cut and paste and place all the ads. I proof the entire magazine before it goes to the printer. [Michael Glenn]

For those who come to the labor market highly skilled, their skills do not provide them with "market power" that translates into job security, high pay, and promotional opportunities. To the contrary, companies are getting highly skilled individuals at "bargain basement" rates by paying for a clerical temporary worker and utilizing the full range of the temporary worker's abilities.

> He was just used to having a girl who would answer his phone and take messages and type his letters. That's cool. But you don't get any more money for that, you don't get any more money for being smart. [Ludy Martinez, thirty-six-year-old Filipina woman]

> An applicant who if we tell her you're gonna be doing some word processing and the client asked if she can do some backup on the switchboard and [she] says, "I wouldn't do that. I'm above that. I may have a degree or I'm working on a degree, and I have good skills, why should I do that?" Well you know, in the meantime, you're out of work. We're paying you the same rate if you're gonna be answering phones or doing a proposal, so that would be someone we would consider a prima donna. [Manny Avila, temporary agency representative, twenty-eight-year-old Latino man]

Many temporary workers resented being brought into the workplace under the guise (and pay) of a clerical worker while being asked to perform complex tasks that often required extensive training or experience.

> And I went to some agencies right away, and they're like, well okay so do you speak Sanskrit, do you uh, do you ride a bicycle? It's like well no, I uh, I know this program fairly well and type and . . . Oh well, so does everyone so that's not good enough. You need to know Lotus and Windows and desktop publishing, and you need to have

had a masters' in finance. . . . Sometimes they get you in there and they want you to like be their junior CEO and still pay you nine bucks an hour. [Harold Koenig]

You know where certain businesses find it useful to hire overqualified temps if they can find them. Because they will get those extra skills out of them even though they're just paying an hourly wage. I mean it's like when certain businesses found out that I could at least spell and write and compose and that's how I ended up writing speeches and stuff like that. Um they're getting wise to the fact that not all the temps have the same skills and that they will try to bilk you. I mean it's like when people found out I could translate French and Spanish and they were like WHOA! [Ludy Martinez]

Furthermore, temporaries report that their education and work experience are seldom recognized by temporary agencies as having been instrumental in their development of work-related skills.

I have worked as a secretary in a law firm for twenty, over twenty years now. But that didn't matter to the agency, didn't seem to make a difference. They wanted specific programs and I hadn't used them. Sure I could learn them, I worked twenty years! Doesn't that count for something? [Ramona Geary, forty-eight-year-old white woman]

It was kind of depressing for me but I needed money. I remember being given like spelling tests and very simplified math tests to make sure I had a brain even through I had a resume that said I graduated [from college]. . . . I think they should say, "I recognize that this may be a bit condescending but it's just a way to screen. We know you're smart and you have a degree." Some sort of acknowledgment about that. [Carol Ketchum, twenty-nine-year-old white woman]

Thus, many temporary workers bring substantial skills and "human capital" with them to jobs that are defined and remunerated as unskilled. While employers find themselves in the fortunate position of paying for a receptionist who ends up doing accounting, computer-aided design, or translating documents from French and Spanish, the job remains defined as clerical, while temporary agencies and their clients benefit from temporary workers' education and work experience. Therefore, two additional scenarios regarding the technical labor process exist: there is either no change in the technical labor process, or there is an upgrading that goes unremunerated (by money or recognition). Agencies often fail to recognize (verbally or monetarily) the types of skills developed through education and work experience, while at the same time they are happy to market those skills to their clients.

The tendencies in temporary employment toward deskilling and devaluing, which originally appeared contradictory, can be understood if we recognize that one constitutes material deskilling while the other constitutes ideological deskilling. Analytically these are separate categories; however, experientially they are intertwined. Some temporary workers experienced mainly deskilled work while others experienced mainly devalued work. However, many temporary workers experienced a combination of or an oscillation between deskilled and devalued work. For example, Ludy, the woman who was translating French and Spanish as well as writing speeches, also had to spend hours typing up audiotapes of depositions. And Cheryl Hansen [twenty-five-year-old white woman] reported filing as well as running computer-aided design software while working as a temporary clerical worker in a bank. In my own experience as a temporary worker, I worked as a receptionist and at cleaning out old files, as well as rewriting personnel policies. In the first two types of jobs, I was hired as a clerk. In the situation where I rewrote personnel policies, I was also hired as a clerk. I received the same pay at each assignment.

Yet skill is but one consideration in the labor process. Labor process analyses can, and should, encompass the entire employment relationship which takes into consideration social, as well as technical, aspects of labor processes. There is strong precedence for doing this (Braverman 1974; R. Edwards 1979; Burawoy 1979; Westwood 1985), so the next stage of analysis will broaden to include the employment relationship, which will in turn buttress the arguments regarding skill.

CHANGES IN SOCIAL LABOR PROCESSES

Management by Uncertainty

While the overall physical and technical parts of the labor process have not changed (even though material and ideological skill seem to be reallocated between core and periphery workers), certain social aspects of the labor process have undergone significant changes with the use of temporary employment. When referring to the temporary employment relationship, I am specifically limiting my definition to the situation in which workers obtain work through a temporary agency. This situation differs from the one in which an individual finds temporary work on his or her own and from subcontracting relationships. In the first case, temporaries work directly for the hiring company, but only on a temporary basis. The temporary worker has but one employer, if only for a short duration. In the case of subcontracting, the worker is exclusively the employee of the subcontracting firm and has a "home base." Typically, the entire subcontracting firm (or a significant portion thereof) is hired by the client. The client does not become a co-employer.

Contrast this with temporary employment through an agency. The temporary agency acts as a mediary between the worker and the client. The agency and the client act as co-employers of the temporary worker. The temporary worker is not employed permanently either by the client or the temporary agency. The temporary agency has no obligation to employ a temporary worker for any duration of time. Termination from an assignment or the employment relationship altogether can occur with virtually no notice and no justification. For example, if an agency tells a temporary worker that an assignment will last for three days and it does not, the agency does not (and is not obligated to) pay the worker for that lost time. If the worker is fortunate, she or he may find something else to replace those hours. In fact, having assignments cut short is a common experience among the temporary workers I interviewed.

> One place I worked, there were massive layoffs coming down and permanent secretaries who were getting sacked were like pointing out people who were temps in other departments saying, "No, no, no, no, just transfer me there because she's a temp there." And in some ways they were within their rights, but I remember getting a temp gig cut short because of that. I was ordered for like six weeks and did only two. . . . I just remember that's when a six-week order suddenly became a two-week and nobody was apologizing about it. [Ludy Martinez]

> She had estimated that this job would take three days. Well it turns out my partner had her B.S. also. So we worked quickly together. The woman that hired us was surprised that a three-day job got finished in a day. And she goes, "That's fantastic, here's your reward, I'll cut your assignment short." Not, "I'll give you a bonus." So our assignment got cut down. I mean you're told it's going to be a five-day assignment and you arrange your schedule, but they get pulled from you. [Cheryl Hansen]

The obligations of the temporary agency to the worker appear even less compelling if we consider that the agency is paid by the client. The client relationship closely aligns the interests of the agency with the client rather than with the temporary worker. Consider the example wherein a client decides to cut short an assignment. Of course, this results in some immediate revenue losses to the agency in addition to the lost pay for the clerical worker. But, as I was told by the president of one agency:

We never call them on that, you know, it's not, it's just not good business. We'll make it up later. [Charles Morton, agency owner and president].

Therefore, in order to preserve the relationship with the client, the agency shifts the uncertainty (and the costs of uncertainty) to the temporary worker.

Furthermore, in matters of dispute between the temporary and the client company, it is in the interest of the agency to side with a client. In a climate where more temporary workers exist than needed on any given day, as well as many agencies clamoring for clients, it is easier to replace a temporary worker than a client. Temporary workers are keenly aware of who holds shared interests in temporary employment.

I think [the agencies] ought to stick by their employees. They don't know people so it's hard to. But then [clients] will just say then we'll get another temp agency. [Cindy Carson, thirty-eight-year-old white woman]

Who is looking out for the temps' interest? The agency isn't looking for the worker's interest. The [client] isn't looking out for the worker's interest. [Doug Larson]

Thus, the organization of temporary work creates a situation wherein client companies and temporary agencies can reap benefits through shifting the burden of uncertainty to temporary workers, who in turn have little recourse. Temporary workers are easily replaced relative to client companies, and that strengthens the agency's ability to control its workers. Thus, temporary work relies on management by uncertainty as a mechanism of control.

Divide and Conquer: Race, Gender, and Class

If temporary workers do not share interests in common with the temporary agency, they do not necessarily share interests with other temporary workers. Since clerical work is predominantly female, we must also recognize the divisions among women (and men) clerical and temporary clerical workers by race and class (V. Smith 1994). We must ask which women (or men) fall into the smaller "core" of employees who are able to have their skills upgraded at the expense of temporary workers, and which fall into the "periphery" of temporary workers, whose deskilled work supports upgrading of the core. Although these questions cannot be answered definitively here, they are crucial to a future understanding of temporary employment because these divisions between workers both rest on and reproduce gender and racial inequalities in the workplace.

It may be reasonable to suggest that the effect of temporary employment on the organization of technical and social labor processes in a predominantly female occupation such as clerical work may vary depending on the gender and race of the majority of individuals in an occupation. In the case of clerical work, thus far temporary employment appears to be a restrictive form of flexibility attainment because it downgrades skill as well as the employment relationship. Comparative studies are needed to ascertain whether temporary employment in other occupations represents restrictive or enabling strategies for flexibility attainment, and the extent to which differences in strategy reflect the predominant gender in an occupation. Still, preliminary work on lawyers who work through temporary agencies (Rogers 1994) suggests that at least in some professions, the position of temporary worker is feminized despite the male majority in the occupation.

However, what can be more fully addressed here are divisions among temporary workers. Temporary work is no exception to the cleavages in the workplace by gender, class, and race (Amott and Matthaei 1991). Since temporary work does not occur in isolation from larger social institutions, this is not surprising, and the increased uncertainty of temporary employment can exacerbate the extent to which these divisions are felt. Temporary workers talked a great deal about why they felt they were not given a particular assignment or opportunity.

Cindy Carson asked her "supervisor" at the agency for a raise and was told it would not be possible to pay that much money for an assignment like hers. She was being paid seven dollars an hour. Shortly afterward, she overheard two other agency representatives recommending another temporary at the same job location be given over eight dollars an hour. Cindy's explanation of the situation follows.

> I really thought it was sexual discrimination. I thought this is happening to me because I'm a woman. That's what I really thought. [Cindy Carson]

Men felt that the agencies favored women.

> At least in the entertainment field a lot of the execs are males and they want females in their office. And I think I wasn't even considered for jobs because of that. [Doug Larson]

Others felt that a premium was placed on appearance or wearing the right clothes (also see Henson 1996). Having a neat and "professional" appearance is stressed in most of the literature I collected from temporary agencies. Henson (1996) recounts the difficulty he had with his agency because he did not possess the proper corporate attire, while I was told that I was placed on certain "prize" assignments because I had "that corporate look" (which in part came from a wardrobe collected from several years of working in a conservative corporate atmosphere in a middle management position). The emphasis on "the look" operates on class distinctions among temporary workers. Had my experience prior to temping been in a lower-level service job or an entry-level clerical position, or had I been fresh out of high school or coming off a long stint of unemployment, I would not have had the clothes that helped me get higher-paying assignments such as executive secretary or administrative assistant. Furthermore, if I had been temping as my primary source of income, I doubt that I would have been able to then purchase the appropriate clothes with an unsteady income.

The following quote illustrates how "middle-class (and white) behaviors" are expected in temporary employment in order to obtain the better assignments.

> They didn't have a clue either of how to behave and read signals. . . . You know sometimes it was for economic social reasons, you know, not educated enough. Not really brought up to understand that they were working in the white corporate world and didn't really know how to blend in. You know, you don't speak Black English on the phone. You know, don't chew gum, you know, don't interrupt. [Ludy Martinez]

My discussions with temporary agency personnel illustrate that temporary workers are not imagining the emphasis placed on appearance, gender, race, and class. In fact, the notion of "proper appearance" is imbued with race, gender, and class divisions. Regina Mason, a temporary agency representative, described what he finds clients desire most in a high-profile temporary.

> Nine out of ten times it's a little blond girl with colored eyes. Or somebody with an English accent. Nobody overweight. And if it's a person of color, she's gotta be drop-dead gorgeous. Not just pretty, drop-dead gorgeous.

Another agency representative, Manny Avila, told me how an agency where he used to worked used code words to take orders from their clients based on ethnicity. For instance, "no Marias" meant no Latina women, while "no Kims" meant no Asians should be sent. Temporary agency personnel recognize that even when they do not wish to comply with discriminatory behaviors, they run the risk of losing clients.

> Amy told me that clients ask for a particular gender or ethnicity in a clerical worker. She said that this has been problematic since the EEOC seems to be cracking down on temp agencies. Then she showed me the card that she reads from when this happens. Basically,

it says they send the best qualified candidate. I asked what the clients think of that. She said some are okay, some push it, some get mad and want to order what they want to order. She says they try not to lose clients but sometimes it happens even though she's as nice as possible. [field notes 10/20/94]

Well, that's why there's clients that we won't work with, you know. Because they'll specifically ask for something and you'll say over the phone, "I don't know if you can tell, but I'm a brown-skinned person too." You just pass on the order. Or if you need the money, work on the order and swallow what you've gotta swallow. [Manny Avila, temporary agency representative]

Therefore, the organization of temporary work brings changes in the labor process that exacerbate cleavages between temporary workers, with more favorable results for those workers who can "do" race and class in a way to meet the "needs" of the agency and client. While the depiction of temporary employment in this research is not favorable, the type of work (clerical) may represent a more desirable alternative to poor women and women of color whose occupational choices have been greatly limited to "back room" service work (Glenn and Tolbert 1992).

Divisions between workers are worsened by the alignment of the interests of the temporary agency with the client, at the expense of the temporary worker. Stronger divisions between workers mean less resistance in the form of collective action by temporary workers who are already separated from each other spatially and temporally (Rogers 1995a). Thus, temporary work also represents a restrictive strategy for achieving flexibility in that it weakens workers' position in the workplace.

PRODUCING CONSENT

Given the deskilled, devalued, and uncertain nature of temporary work, how do we account for the fact that temporary workers work hard at their assignments on a daily basis? Temporary workers consent[4] to their own exploitation in a number of ways. Ideologies employed by the temporary agency, combined with the structural and material constraints described above, produce the consent necessary to keep temporary workers in line and working hard. The position of the temporary agency and the client are thus legitimated to the temporary worker, who is already constrained by changes in the organization of work that shift uncertainty to the worker and then utilize that uncertainty as a mechanism of control. The ideologies I will discuss are ideologies about skill and ideologies about upward mobility.

Ideologies about Skill

The temporary agency is central in creating a definition of the situation through the use of ideologies about skill. The first way in which this is accomplished is through an emphasis on the matching of skills. The temporary industry insists that it is matching skilled workers with skilled jobs.

> The education and skill levels of temporary employees of today qualify them for more jobs than ever before. Through the use of state-of-the-art technology and sophisticated procedures, a temporary help company can thoroughly test and accurately match skilled temporary employees with customers' needs and requirements. [National Association of Temporary Services].

This view that conceives of the temporary industry as benevolent matchmakers misrepresents the experiences conveyed by the temporary workers interviewed for this research. If anything, temporary workers shared the experience of feeling mismatched for their assignments. Regarding "state-of-the-art technology and sophisticated procedures," most temporary workers report being given spelling, math, and typing tests along with a brief interview even in many of the larger agencies. The extent to which workers feel temporary agencies are incapable of evaluating and properly utilizing their skills is reflected in a comedy skit that one temporary worker wrote based on her experiences.

> That's where I got the idea for the Absolute Power Temp Agency. You know, how does somebody at Kelly Girl know what Idi Amin's credentials meant, you know. Just that he could type. [He says] you know I can kill people and I can administrate a country. You know it didn't matter, but uh, can you type? [Ludy Martinez]

In addition, the language of quantification aids in constructing a definition of skill for temporary workers to internalize. Temporaries are told that they are paid according to the skills they will use on a particular assignment. If the assignment is general office, it pays a certain amount. Word processing pays a higher amount. Executive secretary pays even more.

> Once you have been evaluated, interviewed, and approved for hire, you are immediately eligible for assignments. Your rate of pay for each assignment is determined by the specific skill level required for the job, so you know you will always be paid fairly. [pamphlet from temporary help company]

Such quantification puts skills assessment in the realm of science (see Acker 1990 for a similar discussion involving job evaluation), thus legitimizing pay changes from assignment to assignment. The employment of "scientific" skills and computer testing software further supports the position of the agencies. However, workers do not always experience their pay as correlated with the skill of the job. In fact, sometimes temporaries feel that their pay rate is arbitrary (Gottfried 1991) or a product of what the temporary agency knows is the minimal acceptable rate for an individual temporary.

> And what they do is kind of play with the temps and give them what they think they'll take. I know they do that because you write down what's the lowest you'll take. [Cindy Carson]

> If I accepted it, that means I'd have to accept jobs from now on at that pay scale. And I didn't want to go down that far. [Jean Masters, thirty-four-year-old African-American woman]

Thus, notions of matching skills and the quantification of skill are attempts at creating ideologies about skill that elicit consent from temporary workers. As is evident from many of the preceding quotations, temporary workers do not always readily accept the agencies' viewpoint because of the disparity between the ideology and workers' immediate experiences. However, we should consider the potential impact of these ideologies on those in the position to make changes that affect temporary workers. Without direct experience in temporary employment, decision makers may more readily embrace these ideologies. Therefore, the operation of this ideology outside temporary employment may prove more important than its operation inside temporary employment because of its potential to reinforce material constraints on temporary workers' actions through inaction on behalf of legislators and other decision makers.

Upward Mobility

Yet another more powerful ideology operating on temporary workers regards temporary employment as a means to upward mobility. Temporary agencies advertise skill development as a benefit of temporary employment that will surely bring upward mobility for the hard-working temporary.

> . . . the temporary help industry acts to increase the skills and real wages of the workforce through its training and upgrading programs, and through the productive experience it provides [press release, National Association of Temporary Services].

> As workers compete in an ever changing and complex workplace, temporary help offers numerous benefits that give temporary em-

ployees an inside track to more advanced skills and better jobs. [press kit, National Association of Temporary Services]

However, in cases where temporary workers continually perform deskilled work, they are inhibited from acquiring or utilizing skills on the job. Further, while temporary industry representatives espouse the in-house computer training they offer to temporary workers, the reality seldom matches what is advertised. Not all temporary agencies have computer training available. The hardware, software, and space required represent a substantial investment for a smaller agency. In those agencies that do have computer training available, the "training" most often consists of the worker following an on-screen, computer-led tutorial. Temporary workers who have used these tutorials have found them to be inadequate because they offer little opportunity for the student to practice in a meaningful way.

> They advertise that they have the tutorial. And it's not really a tutorial that anyone teaches you. It's something that you, you hit the button on the computer and it says, [speaking slowly with emphasis] "Welcome to tutorial. We will now learn about a computer. This is your keyboard. This is the screen." And it takes you step by step by step. And the software is geared specifically for that and you type up the little thing they give you to type up or whatever. You don't have the option to write your own letter or whatever. [Bernice Katz, thirty-four-year-old Jewish woman]

At the temporary agency where I worked (a large regional agency) computer training consisted mainly of tutorials in WordPerfect, Microsoft Word, WordStar, DisplayWrite, MultiMate, Wang, and Samna Word. Also offered were Lotus 1-2-3 (version 2.2) and dBASE III Plus. Many of the tutorials were for outdated versions of the software, and tutorials for Lotus and dBASE are not adequate to produce proficiency in those who use them. Exceptions exist to this configuration and they are well publicized. However, the experiences of temporary workers reflect how rare the ideal portrayed by the temporary industry actually is.

In addition, not all temporary workers are eligible for computer training. Agencies sometimes require a certain number of hours worked before a temporary can use these tutorials. For example, at the agency where I worked, temporaries are required to have five hundred hours of work (almost three months full-time) before they are eligible for computer training. Since most temporaries work through more than one agency in order to secure enough hours of work, eligibility for such programs becomes more remote the more agencies a temporary worker utilizes.

Yet many temporary workers who do qualify and would like to acquire additional computer training are inhibited from doing so because of the fact that they are temporary. Temporary workers are constrained by the uncertainty of their situation and do not have the free time or flexibility many believe they do (Martella 1991; Negrey 1993). Many temporary workers are working full-time and are not able to take advantage of computer training at the agencies that typically have the same hours as the business they service.

> I try to go, I say I like to go once a week. That would be ideal. Truth is maybe I'm lucky if I can do it twice a month for an hour or so. But I like to go to keep up my skills and to be seen as a presence—that I'm doing something to improve my skills. [Jean Masters]

When temporary workers are not working full-time, they are involved in looking for work or taking their time cards to the different agencies they use. These activities can take a substantial amount of time. In addition, temporaries must be available immediately to the agencies should an assignment arise. For many, this means waiting by the phone or calling all "your" agencies to find work. As most temporary workers will tell you, if an agency calls with an assignment, you'd better be accessible or you will lose the assignment. Some temporary workers have gone so far as to carry beepers. Nevertheless, very few of the temporary workers I interviewed who desire to upgrade their skills have ever taken advantage of computer training offered by temporary agencies because of the constraints placed on them by their status as "temporary." Thus, the picture of temporary workers gaining upward mobility from skill development is not accurate.

Another fashion in which agencies utilize the ideology of upward mobility is through portraying temporary work as a good way for workers to get into a desirable organization or occupation. Temporary work is said to be a vehicle for workers to demonstrate their skills so that their talents can be discovered. The industry portrays itself as providing good jobs in tough economic times.

> Working as a temporary can be a meaningful and useful bridge to full-time employment by providing . . . an opportunity for workers to showcase their talents to a wide variety of potential employers. [press kit from National Association of Temporary Services]

> But the temporary help/staffing services industry can act as a "jobs bridge" to full-time employment. Temporary work offers workers, who may have been displaced during current workforce restructuring, a critical safety net of income, benefits, and skills training which often provides access back to full-time employment. [pamphlet from temporary help company]

Indeed, the most common reason temporaries consent to deskilled or devalued work is because they may gain a "permanent" job through temporary employment.

> After working three months there I'd probably have the references from the people I work with to get a permanent job there. And I guess that's kind of a starting gate. That's pretty much what I looked for. It's just too bad because the company is moving to Sacramento or something like that. [Mark Cranford, twenty-year-old white male]

> And that's why I'm temping is because eventually somewhere I will get an offer. And I won't have to go through the interview process in the same way everyone else does. They go, we love you, this is a formality. And you know you've got the job basically. [Michael Glenn]

> It's temporary and there's a possibility. The key is here, something maybe I haven't touched on too. There's that possibility that someone might see me and say, "Hey, he would be able to do this job." Maybe not the one I'm doing, but another job. And the possibility of acting too. [Doug Larson]

Thus, the ideology of upward mobility to permanency pushes temporary workers to work hard (at deskilled or devalued work) and stay with temporary employment because of the perceived possibility that it will lead them out of temporary employment to their dream job, whether it be inside or outside the corporate world. Temporary workers are workers-in-waiting, waiting for their reward, which is a "good" full-time job. Some workers take this view to the extreme as did one man who told me that by working in the kitchen at an entertainment company, he might be discovered for his talents as a sound engineer.

> If you do well, I mean if you're doing something in the kitchen and they really like you, and you say well I work on audio, they may pull you over and say here we've got this or something like that. You know, you can, it's easier to find out about jobs at a particular place if you're already in the place than it is to submit like unsolicited resumes. [Arnold Finch, twenty-three-year-old white male]

Unfortunately, Finch was not hired by this company. Still other workers feel that their writing skills or management skills will be recognized and they will be offered a permanent job that differs significantly from their temporary assignment. In fact, when the temporary workers I interviewed were offered permanent jobs, it was almost exclusively the same as their temporary assignment. Thus, temporary workers often turned down permanent offers because they did not represent upward mobility through temping. Rather than take a

permanent position that resembles a temporary position, temporary workers
waited in hopes that the next offer would be more in line with their expectations. They felt that they could perform deskilled or devalued work if it was a
means of upward mobility, but not as a permanent job.

> During the time I temped I must have been offered at least eight or
> nine permanent jobs at places like I didn't know how to tell them I
> would never consider working for them, not full-time, not at the
> same job. They'd have to give more than that. [Ludy Martinez]

> And I was offered a lot of full-time positions from the temp jobs. But
> I really, I was fortunate that I didn't have to take a job right away just
> to make ends meet. I could wait for the job I really wanted, one that
> I could use my degrees and talents for. [Ellen Lanford]

Thus the characterization of work as temporary represents an effective
strategy for eliciting workers to do work they would otherwise not perform
because they felt it was "beneath them." This scenario is reminiscent of
women college graduates feeling they could get into the management of an
organization through the secretarial pool. However, temporary work alters
internal labor markets in such a way as to significantly separate temporary
from permanent workers and their internal labor markets. To the extent that
the secretarial pool was ever a successful route into managerial positions, it is
even less so in temporary clerical employment. Temporary employees act as a
buffer around permanent employees to secure their jobs and cushion them
against monotonous work. As such, they find a considerable distance between
temporary employment and access to the internal labor market of a company.

When temporary workers perform work that lacks skill content, they are
unable to demonstrate their capability for performing a more skilled, permanent job. Temporary industry figures reflect that 35 percent of temporary
workers are offered permanent jobs. Of course, this leaves 65 percent who are
not offered jobs. In addition, the industry does not provide data regarding the
type of jobs offered, or whether these offers are ultimately accepted by the
temporary worker. In my research, those offered permanent jobs recounted
that they did not take the jobs because of low pay or low skill requirements. In
other words, temporary workers who filed for eight hours a day are not typically offered a position in the management training program. Jobs offered to
temporaries more often resemble temporary work in skill and pay level.
Nevertheless, many temporary workers remain hopeful for their shot at
upward mobility.

> I didn't want to go into an agency you know with a lot more, with
> being really overqualified and going to do clerical work. I felt that
> would be too devastating to me. Now I just don't care. I'll take ten

bucks and keep my mouth shut and go home. And you never know who you're gonna meet [while temping]. [Cindy Carson]

This is not to say that temporaries never find their perfect job through temping. Indeed, this must happen often enough to perpetuate and legitimate the scenario and in turn secure a docile temporary workforce. Cases of "temp finds wonder-job" are paraded out by temporary agencies to the media and their own workers.

In 1993, George Williams accepted a temp assignment with Ethereal Gas Company where his cheerful smile, reliability, and willingness to work made a good impression. Within a few months, he was offered a full-time position with the gas company and has since received a promotion and an opportunity for additional training. [temporary agency newsletter]

One agency even ran a contest soliciting "temp stories" from temporary workers in Los Angeles. The ad gave examples of the kinds of temp stories they were looking for. Prominently featured are the examples of temporary workers finding great jobs through temporary employment.

The client falls in love with you and you get offered a regular, full-time position with a company you've come to know and like. . . . IT REALLY HAPPENS. Just listen to [April's] story. She started off as a temporary receptionist at a literary agency in Century City, and now she heads up the entire TV literary department! [full-page, back cover, color advertisement placed by temporary agency]

Thus, both ideologies of skill and upward mobility help secure temporary workers' consent and labor in an environment of economic and structural constraints due to changes in the organization of work. Despite the limits on consent produced through direct, contradictory experiences, temporary workers often embraced these ideologies at least initially in the interviews perhaps partially as a way to justify their position to me. However, continued discussion revealed a measure of control that was far from complete. Indeed, the extent to which workers embraced a particular ideology seemed to be intertwined with the extent to which they perceived themselves as having other options. In this way, structural constraints and ideologies act as mutually reinforcing means for producing consent in temporary workers.

CONCLUSION

The picture of skill in temporary work is a complex one. Employers, in conjunction with permanent employees, can divide clerical tasks in order to insulate "core" workers from routine jobs, resulting in material deskilling of jobs for temporary workers. The overall technological labor process remains unchanged, while material skill is reallocated based on status as periphery or core. Alternatively, companies can hire temporaries into clerical jobs that are clerical in name only (upgrading the content of the job while leaving the pay intact) resulting in the ideological deskilling (devaluing) of temporary jobs. This research has shown that temporary work is both deskilled and devalued, with some temporary workers experiencing both material and ideological deskilling tendencies.

In addition, the social aspects of the labor process are dramatically changed for temporary workers, resulting in their loss of power, control, and opportunity. One significant alteration is in the operation of internal labor markets. Although represented by the temporary industry as "a foot in the door," temporary jobs do not provide the route to upward mobility as promised. Those temporaries who are relatively unskilled are structurally inhibited from developing the very skills that may help them in acquiring less marginal work. Many highly skilled temporaries are constrained from demonstrating their capabilities on the job because they are required to do relatively deskilled work. Yet even those who are able to demonstrate their skills on the job feel potential employers have little motivation to hire them permanently because of added benefit costs and the hiring fees charged by temporary agencies, and because they are already doing the job at a relatively low rate of pay. In this sense, temporary jobs are dead-end jobs regardless of the human capital temporary workers bring with them.

Consider the high-wage, high-skill workforce touted by the Clinton administration (see also Reich 1991). Given this research and trends in temporary employment, we need to consider the likelihood of such an optimistic outcome. Temporary employment seems to be resulting in a further bifurcation of the workforce into higher-wage, higher-skill "winners" and lower-wage, lower-skill "losers." Considering the overrepresentation of women and people of color in contingent forms of employment should warn us that continuing increases in temporary employment will likely exacerbate already existing gender and racial inequalities in employment. The "winners" and "losers" are likely to be divided by race, class, and gender as they are in many other aspects of social life. Indeed, we have seen that within temporary work, rewards such as better assignments are often dispersed with regard to these social categories.

Furthermore, what can be the meaning of affirmative action in a contingent economy? Temporary workers fall outside the purview of affirmative action because of the alteration in internal labor markets and the lack of responsibility incurred by temporary agencies. Temporary work is the epitome of the "at will" employment relationship in the United States because temporary workers can be terminated for any reason or no reason at all. Outright discrimination against temporary workers remains a problem that can be only partially addressed by EEOC "spot checks" of temporary agencies. Employers can cut short assignments or remove temporary workers without justification to anyone, obscuring clients' racial and gender-based "preferences" for workers. Therefore, civil rights legislation loses its impact for temporary workers, who, no doubt, find it difficult to pursue a legal remedy.

Management by uncertainty creates (or widens) cleavages between workers, reducing the potential for collective action. And to be sure, the existence of temporary employees in the workplace complicates issues of organization and representation. Yet, it is ironic that the growth of temporary employment is proceeding apace at the same time politicians are debating the elimination or drastic reorganization of affirmative action, as well as antilabor legislation such as the "Teamwork for Employees and Managers Act." As noted by Callaghan and Hartmann (1991), the reorganization of work wrought by temporary employment renders much hard-won labor legislation irrelevant. Those who work as temporaries know that eliminating such labor legislation only makes official what they experience on a daily basis.

NOTES

1. Technical and social labor processes are discussed here as distinct processes; however, the distinction is a reflection of the need for analytical clarity rather than an empirical reality. Social and technical labor processes are often intertwined so that it becomes difficult to judge whether a particular change in the organization of work constitutes a change in the technical or social labor process (or both). Furthermore, changes in technical labor processes certainly impact social labor processes, which changes in social labor processes impact technical labor processes.

2. We can all recall a secretary without whom the office would cease to function. Yet the skills that make her or him indispensable are seldom recognized or rewarded as such.

3. Compensation is not simply equivalent to the hourly wage, although temporary workers do typically earn lower hourly wages than their permanent counterparts (Callaghan and Hartmann 1991). Compensation includes material and nonmaterial benefits such as sick time, vacation, health and life insurance, job training, and consideration for promotion.

4. While this section focuses on the production of consent in temporary employment, I must note here that temporary workers are aware of many of

the conditions that produce consent. In addition, temporary workers do muster resistance in the workplace; however, their actions are highly constrained by the specific structure of work relations in temporary employment. For a full discussion of resistance, see Rogers (1995b).

5

Spread over Time and Place

Redivided Labor and the Role of Technical Infrastructure[1]

JOAN GREENBAUM

The late twentieth century was to be the age of white-collar work—of jobs that were dependable, well paid, clean, highly skilled, and in nice workplaces. But the age of large, centralized offices, with traditional, well-defined jobs, appears to be far shorter than the industrial era that preceded it. In the United States, and now increasingly in Europe, more and more office jobs are being spread over time and space, as the work gets done at all times of the night and day by people working from scattered sites, including their homes. This redivision of labor not only occurs across the time and space continuums, but also revises definitions of contractual working relations, with increasing numbers of workers parceled out in part-time, temporary, and otherwise contingent relations to employers (Greenbaum 1995).

This chapter focuses on office work that since the 1950s has been considered the backbone of the service sector. In the United States, office work represents 56 million people or about 46 percent of the workforce in jobs that include managerial, professional, technical, and administrative support occupational categories. While administrative support is the largest category—with over 18 million workers, even larger than the factory or sales workforce—it has begun to shed staple job groups like secretaries and bank tellers. Technical and related support occupations are touted as being critical and fast-growing, yet they make up only 3.8 million workers, or less than 7 percent of the white-collar workforce. Professional occupations, with 17.5 million workers, and managerial and administrative, with over 16 million workers, have been growing categories, although the number and range of new occupations, such as security guards, which have been added to these groups muddies the waters about collecting data along the lines where managerial and professional jobs could be more clearly separated from administrative support categories (Bureau of Labor Statistics, January 1995). The analysis presented here paints a picture which shows that while white-collar work has been based on rationalization and patterns of division of labor established by the 1970s, it now breaks out of the old patterns into new forms of redivided labor. It shows that the newer forms of divided labor bring together different occupational groups and job categories as tasks are being integrated and job categories broadened. These recombinations fuse old lines that once divided jobs between skilled and unskilled, and where labor processes generally were manipulated along this dimension.

In principle, the arguments laid out by Braverman (1974) and others about managerial control over the labor process are still in the center of the stage, because control over the labor process is the baseline for lowering the overall wage bill and increasing production. In practice the mechanisms for accomplishing this have shifted so that upper-level managers—what corporations like to call "strategic planners"—have more tools in their repertoire. One of the tools available now is the design of information systems that are more reliable and predictable and far less expensive than those developed in the mainframe era. Not only the predictability, control, and cost of these information systems support new divisions of labor, management's change in technical design principles has shifted from an emphasis on automation—a hallmark of the period when rationalization was the dominant strategy—to design principles of "coordination and communication," which foster faster changes in labor process management. The arguments I present here show that management strategy and technical systems designed to support it have little by little laid a foundation of what the computer field calls infrastructure. I describe the ways in which this technical infrastructure—including the media favorite, the Internet—reinforces patterns similar to rule-based bureaucratic practices established by management in the heyday of corporate dominance, yet fosters a broader redivision of labor along with intensified labor processes.

Clearly upper management's use of technical infrastructure in its battle for control over the labor process is not new, nor is it a deterministic one. New forms of technology do not spring out of the minds of Silicon Valley scientists as the popular press would have us believe. Rather, they have been built, piece by piece, and often mistake by mistake, on the basis of prior periods. Technology, like jobs, does not get reorganized overnight. What is happening now builds onto the base of the prior periods in the following ways: (1) *integrating* tasks rather than *separating* them can now be done based on the rationalization of office work in the period from 1950 through the 1980s and on a foundation of available software and procedures for developing software;

and (2) *broadening* job responsibilities rather than *specializing* them is like-wise built on prior waves of standardization and simplification of procedures and products. Both imply that workers have more skills, particularly more computer-oriented skills, but neither could have been accomplished by management if the basic strategies of rationalized work, including separation of conception from execution, had not been put in place. Moreover, the new, so-called flexibility of workers to do more tasks and use more skills does not imply increased wages or improved working conditions. Indeed, indications are that integrating tasks and broadening jobs have done what specialization and separation tried to accomplish before them: increase the pace and intensity of work and decrease the cost of labor (see Head 1996). Both of the major changes feed into the (3) *redivision of labor* at a global level, as well as redividing workers between those with contractual or employee status and those outside company walls. This shift in dividing lines also builds on the base of software and hardware available to support and induce rapid shifts in place and status of labor—what management literature likes to call "flexible labor."

The next section begins with an analysis of this third point, illustrating the ways that management practice and technical design have been used to spread work and workers over time and space, basing the arguments on a brief historical overview of how information technology has been designed to increase the pace and intensity of work and at the same time keep the wage bill down by getting more labor out of fewer workers. This is followed by an analysis of the first two issues, demonstrating through examples in professional, technical, and administrative support work how (1) tasks are being integrated and (2) job responsibilities broadened without corresponding increases in pay, and with intensified and often deteriorating working conditions. The last section takes up these points to examine the ways the new divisions, coupled with new integration of tasks and supported by technology designed for "coordination and communication," redefines the issues and contradictions we need to explore for further research and action.

SEPARATING WORK FROM PLACE

Rationalized labor processes were, from a managerial viewpoint, economically and socially effective in an industrial period when economies of scale were the norm and capital was rooted in one place. Indeed, at first mechanization, and later automation, were based on the fact that work would be supervised in a factory that was located as much as possible *under one roof*. Not surprisingly the early postindustrial systems of automation and management tried to make office work follow the same pattern, since these types of rationalized work procedures had been effective in factory production. Now the necessity for economics of scale is loosened by both managerial and technical changes and the rootedness of capital is seen as a deterrent to global competition. Thus control over labor processes, both managerial and that embedded directly in technology, has had to change.

By the end of the 1980s management theorists were complaining that bureaucratic practices were too slow for decision making in newly uprooted markets. Similarly, centralized decision making, extensive division of labor, as well as narrow job definitions and promotional ladders in hierarchical form were deemed "too inflexible" (see Peters 1992). In addition to management changing its tune on centralized control strategies, it also began to request information technology that would be more flexible in response to hurried market and organizational changes. For example, instead of large, specialized mainframe accounting and inventory applications, management began to rely on more general applications like spreadsheets and database packages for processing these *already rationalized* financial procedures.

The current period is marked by capital's ability to separate work from place, since newly integrated jobs can be redivided spatially rather than by specific functions. In the late 1980s this took the form of outsourcing the more routine back-office functions like payroll, accounts receivable, and transaction processing. In the 1990s as managerial practices, sometimes under the rubric of Business Process Reengineering, began to redefine entire products and industries even the front-office, formerly customer-based work, was prepared for outsourcing. In banking, for example, the service or 'product' that telephone-based customer service representatives provide is quite different from the face-to-face transaction or 'product' that customers experienced with branch banking. The same is true for computer services, where the customer liaison person on the "help line" is not expected to know or see the customer calling with the problem. In fact, almost every service industry from postal delivery to travel arrangements has changed their definitions of product so that the relations between customer and worker are not dependent on in-person services. What takes place of course is an increased standardization of the product, as, for example, in the types of "services" the banks handle online. And with increased standardization of product comes greater flexibility for management both to increase the range of tasks and responsibilities a single worker can do and to physically move the work.

The delinking of work and place has severe implications for the decoupling of labor from labor contracts, as more and more standardized products can be "produced" by outsourced workers, freelancers, and people who have only a contingent connection to the firm selling the "service." It is generally estimated that at least one out of four workers in the United States are contingent or supplemental—roughly 28 percent of the workforce (duRivage 1992). While the U.S. Bureau of Labor Statistics has just begun to collect data in this category, their 1993 estimates put the number of contingent workers at 39 million with another 21 million workers listed as part-time (Calem 1993). Both the contingent—that is, without employee status—and part-time nature of work has given rise to a huge "business services industry" that the government classifies as placing around two million workers every month (United States Bureau of Labor Statistics 1995). Manpower, Inc., the largest temporary (or as they are now called staffing) agency in the United States, is also the largest private employer, with over 600,000 "staffers" on placement at any given time (Fierman 1994).

The decoupling of labor from contracts is clearly noticeable in many areas of professional work where "products" or services can be sold as complete packages, such as lawyers preparing wills, systems analysts specifying program requirements, and textbook writers "producing" book chapters. In each instance the labor is sold not necessarily as time (although estimates are of course based on hours), but rather production of the final product. This represents almost a complete break from the industrial period of gathering workers under one roof and binding them to the work through labor contracts based on hours worked.

Information technology and telecommunications infrastructure, including fax machines, e-mail, voice mail, computer applications, and mobile phones, provide a base for reshuffling work and labor agreements. However, they could not, in and of themselves, bring about such changes without having been developed in relation to management objectives. Most significantly, the design of the current information technology applications has been developed on the basis of prior periods of standardizing work, computer processing, and products.

Management policies in the 1950s and 1960s seemingly were in love with the possibilities of computers and the temptations of creating office work in the image of factory automation. The automation image and the metaphors it conjured up were more image than reality. Despite the repeated attempts by large corporations to divide and redivide office work into streamlined, industrial-like routines, mainframe computers and their limited programmable capabilities lagged behind management expectations (see Greenbaum 1995). Nor was it clear to management that their reliance on rationalistic, step-by-step procedures and extensive division of labor was effective in terms of service quality and productivity. Even in the 1970s, when more routine, back-office functions had been almost completely severed from generally more skilled, front-office jobs, and computer programming had been made more effective (see Greenbaum 1979; Kraft 1979), management theorists and practitioners alike complained that office productivity was not increasing, and that automation was not solving the problem.

In the first half of the 1980s the newly minted term "office automation" was being actively marketed as a solution to white-collar productivity problems.

Yet as office employment and salaries were increasing, productivity remained a bone of contention in management circles. In 1986, *Fortune* magazine ran a cover story announcing the productivity crisis was coming to an end, for the issue was not that automation would solve the problem but that reorganizing work would provide management with the tools for cutting wage bills and increasing productivity (Bowen 1986). The second half of the 1980s was ushered in with both the mass acceptance of PC-based computing, instead of the centralized mainframes, and the beginning of reorganization of work along the lines of Michael Hammer's famous phrase "Don't automate, obliterate [work]" (Hammer 1990). The design of information systems shifted from the emphasis on sequential routine processing, which was the hallmark of "office automation," to setting standards for an infrastructure that would "coordinate and communicate" work processes.

It is not as if a management or a technical revolution occurred in the late 1980s, although the economic crisis of the late 1980s and early 1990s helped give management the upper hand in shaking out work practices and keeping wages down. Rather, the period was marked by the fact that prior sets of standardized labor processes could now be "cut and pasted" into new forms of integrated tasks and broader job categories.

INTEGRATING TASKS AND JOBS

Academic literature on upskilling in the 1980s held out promise that newer jobs with more integrated tasks and broader job responsibilities could bring about more job satisfaction (see Zuboff 1988; Adler 1986). Management literature added to this claim, also emphasizing that flatter organizational hierarchies would enhance many jobs with new decision-making power and enable "high-performance" workplaces—those where workers benefited from their increased productivity (see Nine to Five 1992). While we lack studies on job satisfaction among workers in current white-collar jobs[2] in the United States, case studies and anecdotal stories indicate that wages, working conditions, and job security in new job categories are being pressed under intensified labor processes that certainly do not meet the optimism of the 1980s advocates (see Herzenberg et al., forthcoming).

Telephone-based jobs offer a good example of integrated labor processes. The banking industry, for example, under pressure from changing regulations and massive 1980s loan losses, has pushed for what one executive called "the end of brick and mortar banking."[3] Instead of the former network of street corner branches staffed by tellers, assistant representatives, and varying levels of branch managers, larger banks are moving more of their operations to regionalized service centers where customer service representatives answer telephone queries and conduct transactions. Entry-level positions in the customer service field require more training and more knowledge of bank operations than entry-level teller jobs. Indeed, in one center that I studied, representatives took four weeks of classroom training followed by a comparable period of close supervision before they were expected to be responsible for calls on their own. Both classroom and on-the-job training focused on complexities and details of banking regulations, and representatives are expected to quickly familiarize themselves with three different types of computer applications. Given the labor market conditions of the area where the service center is located, the bank personnel department can recruit from a supply of available college-educated white-collar workers, even though starting salaries are only $19,000, with peak wages around $28,000. Although unemployment in the region stood at only 5.3 percent, the rate had doubled in the past two years; most of the increase was among white-collar middle managers and engineers laid off by large employers in the area.

The vice president in charge of service operations says that the jobs require a high degree of skill, particularly in problem solving, and that they are both high-stress and high-performance. The representatives are expected to handle around twenty calls an hour, with calls ranging from bank balances (although most of that goes through "voice response units") to lost funds and foreign transactions. Monitoring takes place on three technical levels—audiotaping, computer-based statistics, and telephone distribution statistics—each of which is backed up by quality-control "trainers" who meet with the representatives, review their performance, and report to their supervisors. The span of supervision is broad and flat, with one supervisor to approximately twenty representatives and no levels of middle management above that—a fact that frustrates the representatives because there is little room for promotion or new opportunities.

The center is supported by a web of computer systems that link each customer service representative with a variety of bank databases, including data from a large bank that was recently bought. Operations began in the late 1980s, with frequent updates and modifications to the overall computer system since then. Now, monthly changes to the applications and computer interface are common. In general the representatives were pleased with the window-oriented computer system, having the flexibility to access and review information in the order they choose, rather than being regimented into sequential procedures required by the older systems. Often they say they have to "be one step ahead of the customer," and switch to screens before the customer finishes explaining her or his query. The computer system supports this and could be considered a good example of information technology designed for "coordination and communication" rather than "automation," since the representatives do not have to step their way through hierarchical menus. The linking of the databases and the establishment of the bank's global network system also mean that the bank has the flexibility to shift work to another service center instead of hiring more staff in this one when peak periods occur. Another large bank recently announced that it had the capability to shift operations from its U.S. office to its United Kingdom based center, where representatives were trained to handle the same work (Uchitelle 1994). Implications are clear that the work can be shifted with the switch of a network, wherever the labor costs are lower, or the balance between high skill and comparatively low wages keeps the operation running.

Both the integration of computer systems and the integrating of tasks are built on a base coming from the 1970s and 1980s, where bank work was thoroughly rationalized so that even highly complex procedures like foreign currency transactions, which used to be handled by people with bank officer titles, have been more clearly defined and specified. Thus, the new labor process, while integrating tasks and broadening responsibilities, and indeed enhancing skills, has been designed to move jobs down to the lowest level, bringing former managerial and supervisory tasks into administrative assistant pay ranges.

BROADENING TECHNICAL AND PROFESSIONAL JOBS

Integration of formerly separated jobs and broadening of responsibilities also is evident in technical and professional work. The computer field, for example, once the target of rationalized work practices is being reorganized so that workers in all job categories are expected to know more and do more. Here, too, the formerly specialized and divided labor, such as the separation of programming and systems analysis, while never really considered effective was a step toward defining programming practices and developing software tools to enable more routine programming and systems functions.[4] Now, management can get mileage out of programmer-analyst-project managers, who cover a range of responsibilities, from meetings with customers to coding programs, but who are generally lumped into technical titles and do not earn high professional or managerial salaries. The large number of computer science graduates, as well as students with business degrees and general computer knowledge, means that employers in the United States have available an abundant pool of technically trained labor. In 1994, several regional studies showed college graduates receiving starting salaries at the lowest level in fifteen years, with the average entry positions in the $23,000–$24,000 range (Kilborn 1994).

Two trends are noteworthy in the labor process of computer work: the increase in telephone-based "help desk" and technical support jobs; and the growth of outsourced and often freelanced computer services, including programming, operations, and system development.[5] The first, the expansion of telephone "help desk" jobs, represents a semi-entry level position with a wide range of integrated tasks and broad responsibilities. People who answer technical queries about software support and network questions need to have strong problem-solving skills, as well as vast technical experience, when linking questions together and answering them within expected time frames. Increasingly these jobs, like their counterparts in banking, are located in regions out of urban areas, where labor costs tend to be lower. Companies are able to recruit college graduates, as well as existing employees who have played informal roles as "expert users." Training is usually on the job, and while the jobs pay relatively well for entry-level positions—usually in the high $20,000 to low $30,000 range—the level of experience and knowledge would have qualified for a higher position in the past. Indeed, with the collapse of mainframe programming and the demise of entry-level programming jobs, these new positions represent a rather high jump for entry into the computer field. Between 1990 and 1994, 49,000 programming jobs were lost in the United States, a trend that is still under way, as corporations have cut their mainframe programming staff, outsourced programming and operations functions to small shops, and sent traditional program coding tasks to countries like India and the Czech Republic, where wages are far less.

Computer services, once thought of as an essential part of corporate practices, have been increasingly outsourced to firms that handle everything from routine mainframe processing (such as bank transactions) to maintenance and redesign of PC-based applications. These secondary suppliers of services, while playing a specialized function, usually operate with a relatively small staff who function as all-arounders or generalists. Smaller PC-oriented applications development, custom modification, and maintenance are often contracted out to individual freelancers, many of whom originally started in the "parent" firm. The freelancers function as generalists, but usually within more specialized areas. They do everything from writing contracts to coding programs and build their practice by modifying pieces of existing standardized applications, using network and industry-wide software standards that have been agreed upon in the past few years. In effect, this work does not need to be as standardized as a decade ago because the new software used to produce it is already standardized. The next section will discuss the growing reliance of this virtual army of freelanced and outsourced labor.

The results of the newer integrated labor processes seem to be similar to those of the separated and specialized ones. Workers are induced through a variety of mechanisms to work more intensely, and in the case of technical and professional workers, for longer hours (see Schor 1991). The new mechanisms for intensifying the work, embedded in software and information technology infrastructure, mean that levels of management and supervision can be removed. Additionally, the newer forms of work organization, emphasizing group work and interchangeability of workers and teams, move management's problems with supervising individuals to the easier process of applying pressure to teams. Thus management of the labor process becomes built into the technical infrastructure, replacing the rule-based bureaucratic policies with preauthorized and preprogrammed procedures. Of course bureaucratic practices live on, as anyone who has worked for a large organization knows and as the success of the Dilbert cartoon illustrates, but such practices are able to be carried out with fewer middle managers and supervisors.[6] The corporate rule-based behavior, which emphasized internalization of company policies (see Edwards 1979), can now also be carried out by individuals who internalize intensified work practices under the rubric of professionalism. Labor market pressures and the labor process intensification serve as strong disciplinary measures, since maintaining the current piece of contract work, while lining up another, discipline the workforce.

A NEW VIRTUAL RESERVE ARMY?

In 1993 *Time Magazine* carried a story which proclaimed "by now, these trends [downsizing, outsourcing, etc.] have created an 'industrial reserve army' to borrow a term from Karl Marx—so large that a quite extraordinary and prolonged surge in output would be required to put all its members to full-time, well-paid work" (22 November). Now, several years later, it is becoming clear that with further outsourcing of work, and with increased technical infrastructure standards, this reserve army can be spread across time and space, so that workers no longer need to be in a physical workplace. The labor process of office work is increasingly a labor process designed for virtual workers—working from a variety of places and under a variety of contractual and noncontractual arrangements.

The separation of work from place, like that of labor from labor contracts, represents pressure points for workers as well as for capital. I believe that our task in analyzing labor process change is not to *predict* its future shape, but to highlight pressure points for change. In the 1970s the labor process debates inspired by Braverman's analysis focused on the degrading and deskilling aspects of labor process change. In the 1980s, particularly growing out of sociology, studies tended to favor a view of an "upskilled," more integrated labor process where "knowledge workers" would, particularly with desktop computers, do more interesting work (see Burris, this volume). Obviously, if we are to avoid this type of "talking past each other," the larger issues—not the specific trends—need to be put back into context.

Controlling the labor process in order to extract profit is top management's primary focus. Essentially, in the industrial period through early postindustrial time detailed divisions of labor had three main benefits for capital: it heightened productivity through specialization, repetition, and routine; it created divisions in the working class that kept people apart; and the first two served to hold wages down, keeping the overall wage bill in check. Up until the 1980s the industrial labor process with its detailed division of labor and technology of sequential automation was applied to office work along with the mechanism of bureaucratic control. During the 1980s it became clear to upper-level management that detailed division of labor, office automation, and bureaucracy were mechanisms that functioned too slowly in the rapid changes of deregulated international trade. While throwing out the specific industrial mechanisms of control, top management did not cast away the larger issues. Redivided labor by time, place, and contract status tends to keep the labor force divided, and while integrated and broadened jobs increase the range of skills people may have, the value of these skills is less when measured in terms of wages (see Steiger, this volume). Yet, as in the past, these newer mechanisms of control are laden with contradictions. In the following, I return to the issues of redivided labor, integration, and broadening of jobs, interweaving the contradictions in these mechanisms with a discussion of the way the technical infrastructure is designed.

Global and local redivisions of labor, whether they fall along the fault lines of contingent versus employed status, workplace versus virtual space, or part-time versus full-time, play the role of divide and conquer in heightening competition among new groups of workers, thus driving wages down and intensifying work practices. They also blur the older class and gender lines as jobs from administrative support through professional work get contracted out of the traditional office. Clearly, the divorce of job from place, as well as the outsourced and temporary status of more and more work, contributes to those jobs becoming known as " women's jobs." The feminization of clerical work refers to a strategy of labor market segregation used to push wages down. The same mechanisms are apparent in technical support jobs where pieces of work, such as programming and technical problem solving, are outsourced or contracted out, as well as in professional work where editing, writing, and legal services can all be bought and sold as individual "projects" or piecework. There has always been an emphasis on contingency status in that part of the labor market reserved for women. As Applebaum (1992:4) explained, the results of a study on contingency work: " . . . suggest that women are taking the growing number of temp agency jobs because employers are creating more temporary positions in the fields where women typically work, and not because temporary employment better meets their flexibility

needs." It should come as no surprise that this strategy, one of divide and conquer, plus suppression of wages by creating temporary and contingent positions, should be applied to male workers and formerly male-dominated occupations as well.

The integration of tasks and the broadening of job categories are labor
process changes that clearly expand the range of skill workers need to have.
Nevertheless, skill has always had many components and the match between
skill and compensation was never a direct one, as the case of clerical work so
clearly shows (Szymanski 1989). Clerical workers, particularly secretaries,
always exercised a wide range of skills, including problem-solving and technical
ones, along with broad job definitions, but their wages did not reflect this.
Thus, the integration and broadening of tasks and jobs, and its consequent
enhancement of skill, is as it has been, an issue of power and control over the
labor process and the labor market. Skill is better reflected in wages when the
groups possessing the skill have enough power to define their status and wages.

Indeed the redivisions of labor and the broadening of skill categories
could bring about new pressure points for change if they are used to shift the
balance of power. Workers who are in noncontractual or some form of contingent status, whether they come from administrative support or professional
occupations, are facing more uncertain job futures and wage increases. There
is common ground for collective organizing here, for just as industrial unionism grew from workers being united under one roof, so can postindustrial collective bargaining be sparked from the virtual and quasi-reserve status of
greater numbers of workers. This of course requires shedding the threads of
professionalism that are used to cloak the fact that work intensification is not
being linked with increased wages. It also requires recognition of the fact that
the commonalties among the workforce fall along different lines than during
earlier times. And significantly, it means understanding at least the design
behind the technical infrastructure used to reinforce the changes.

Most new information technology systems are now designed according
to principles of "coordination and communication"—two functions that have
previously resided in management. These newer applications and the networks they serve have been based on the idea that work that is divided in different places and is being done at different times can be *coordinated back
together* through communication media such as the Internet, the World Wide
Web, as well as e-mail, fax machines, and mobile telephones. This replaces
design strategy fashioned after the notion of automation, which was based on
the assumptions that work was rooted in one place, was routine, and could be
"automated" following sequential processing procedures. Current systems
designed for coordination acknowledge that work tasks may not necessarily be
routine or sequential, and therefore the coordination functions of the software
are designed to put the processes back together. Applications like Lotus Notes

and Windows Office reflect this thinking. Like the computer system used by bank customer service representatives in the case study I discussed, the software makes no specific requirements about the order of the processing or the steps people need to do in order to get their broader jobs done.

The design of the technical infrastructure, like the mechanisms of labor process control, also raises some new contradictions. While bureaucratic management practices placed coordination and communication under a top-down hierarchy, information technology is now being designed as a multiple-path mechanism. Indeed, attempts to force top-down strategies over the use of technology have proved ineffective: for example, in a case where a large industrial company felt that its staff was spending too much time on e-mail and declared that only internal e-mails would be allowed, management failed to recognize that their external customers were dependent on e-mail. Trying to stop the flow of communication in this instance almost stops their business. In a number of instances where calendar programs have been modified so that top managers can "see" the calendars of workers, but not vice versa, workers have responded with blank or filled-up calenders on their screens.

The coordination and communication functions of information systems can be seen as a double-edged sword: just as it gives management the ability to put pieces together, it also gives people in their roles as workers, citizens, and customers the chance to tell each other what they are experiencing and what might be done about it. As the potentially virtual reserve army of contingent workers spreads out in different places, it has some room to maneuver in the battle for control over the labor process. It has more skill, integrated job knowledge, and the support of communication technology, along with possibly blurring traditional class and gender lines. Thus, the flexibility that management has gathered from redividing labor and introducing new technical infrastructure, can also, if used in the context of power relations, be seen as flexibility for workers.

NOTES

1. The Bank Case Study cited here was conducted under a grant from the National Commission of Employment Policy, Contract No. 41 USC2552C3, U.S. Department of Labor. I participated in this study together with Cydney Pullman and Sharon Szymanski of the Labor Institute in New York City, whose work on designing and carrying out the study was, as always, inspirational. In addition I would like to thank the editors, whose comments and suggestions were extremely helpful in pulling together the arguments presented here. This was written when I was on leave as Visiting Professor, University of Oslo, Norway (1995–96).

2. An exception is Leidner's (1993) excellent study.

3. The following is based on a case study conducted for the National Commission on Employment Policy, 1995; see acknowledgments.

4. Programming applications like database packages, along with higher-level languages called Fourth-Generation Languages (4GLs), and system development support tools, including Computer-Aided Software Engineering (CASE) packages, are designed to speed up the software development process.

5. The U.S. Bureau of Labor Statistics has not as yet a specific occupational category for tracking technical support jobs; according to economists with the Bureau, some of these jobs are included under computer programming while others get mixed into various "technical" specialist categories. The analysis of technical and professional jobs presented here, as well as the discussion of technical infrastructures is based on the research conducted for my recent book, *Windows in the Workplace*.

6. In 1995, *Fortune, Forbes, Business Week*, and *Newsweek* all ran cover stories on downsizing. In March 1996, the *New York Times* ran a featured series of articles as well.

6

Dialectics of the Labor Process, Consumer Culture, and Class Struggle

The Contradictory Development of the American Automobile Industry

DAVID GARTMAN

Harry Braverman tried to explain the labor process of capitalism without taking into account the consciousness and culture of the workers involved. I hope to show in this case study of the American automobile industry that this is impossible. As other scholars have argued (Aronowitz 1973; 1978; 1979; Burawoy 1978; 1979), objective production and subjective cultural legitimation are wrapped in a contradictory, dialectical totality in which class conflict plays the role of mediator. Because Braverman ignored this dialectical unity, he failed to anticipate recent trends in the organization of capitalist production that go beyond his unilinear model of deskilling and degradation.

The American automobile industry is a strategic case for exploring the dynamics of production and culture because it helped to pioneer not only the economy of mass production but also the culture of mass consumption that came to legitimate it. Braverman himself recognized the industry's crucial role, although he did not realize the complexity of its contributions. He cited Ford's assembly line as an example of the division and pacing of work by management in order to centralize control over workers. And the auto industry also provides the pivotal case in Braverman's analysis of how managers win workers' compliance with the degraded labor process. Again taking the Ford Motor Company as his example, he argued that managers overcame workers' revulsion to the new assembly line through competitive advantage and higher wages. The incredible productivity of Ford's degraded labor process forced

93

competing automakers to emulate it or go out of business, effectively eliminating the less repressive forms of labor organization to which workers could
escape. In particular, Ford's Five Dollar Day program, which doubled the
daily wage of many workers, bought off the opposition and drew a vast labor
surplus of compliant workers to his alienated production process (Braverman
1974:146–50). Braverman argued that this high-wage policy, "that permit[ted]
a certain enlargement of the customary bounds of subsistence for the working
class," became institutionalized in the agreements between organized labor
and large corporations after the Second World War and was the key to legitimating the degraded labor process (Braverman 1974:151).

A close examination of the automobile case reveals, however, that
Braverman's account is simplistic, for two main reasons. First, he did not fully
explain how and why the high-wage policies of large corporations were insti-
tuted. Although he did mention the "natural resistance" and "natural revulsion" of workers to the newly degraded labor process, he did not explain how
workers rendered so thoroughly powerless found the resources to mount a
campaign of struggle that forced high wages from employers and eventually
organized the industry. In other words, Braverman did not explore the contradictions within the automotive mass production process that made class struggle possible.

Second, Braverman did not tell us how increased quantities of money and
means of subsistence legitimate degraded work in the eyes of workers. He took
for granted one of capitalism's most hard-won and dubious accomplishments—
the commodification of all human needs. He did not closely examine the
process of struggle through which people were cajoled to substitute their most
basic species-needs for the material commodities of capitalism and their rei-
fied mediator, money (Marx 1975). This required not merely larger quantities
of money and mass-produced goods but also a qualitatively different consumer culture that allowed workers to forget their degraded work and gave
them superficial satisfactions of their needs. Braverman's failure to examine
the cultural exigencies of mass consumption ultimately undermines his analysis of the deskilled labor process of mass production. For although initially
compatible, eventually the two came into contradiction, touching off renewed
class struggles that forced capital to pioneer new methods of labor control
unanticipated by Braverman.

The following case study of the American automobile industry seeks to
remedy these simplicities by tracing the contradictory relationship between
the labor process and consumer culture. The study is divided into four historical periods or conjunctures, each with its peculiar dialectics of class conflict,
mass production, and mass consumption. In this first period, extending from
about 1910 to 1925, the contradictions within the emerging process of automotive mass production gave rise to an incipient worker revolt that forced

auto corporations not merely to raise wages but also to pioneer the grounds for working-class consumerism. The demands of workers for beautiful, distinctive goods in this consumer culture threatened to contradict the standardization of mass production. But in the second conjuncture, beginning about 1925, auto corporations found ways to reconcile the deskilled labor process with consumer culture through superficial product styling, which gave consumers the look of escape, individuality, and progress on a mechanically standardized machine. This reconciliation produced the industry's heyday, which extended to the mid-1950s. But by the late 1950s, contradictions within this obviously excessive consumer culture began to expose the sameness hiding beneath the dazzling surfaces of automobiles, leading to the third conjuncture. A consumer revolt against Detroit's products forced manufacturers to offer more structural and mechanical diversity of models during the decade of the 1960s. This real diversity, however, wrecked havoc with the deskilled labor process, giving auto workers more discretion with which to struggle against employers. Escalating worker militancy and falling profits precipitated the fourth conjuncture, beginning in the mid-1970s. At this time auto corporations began to abandon the social contract with unions and explore new forms of labor organization that offered greater flexibility to meet consumer demands for individuality but simultaneously maintained control over labor. A careful examination of these periods reveals that the capitalist labor process does not develop unilinearly but dialectically, through the contradictory clash of the economic imperatives of production and the cultural imperatives of consumption.

CONJUNCTURE 1: THE CONTRADICTORY EMERGENCE OF AUTOMOTIVE MASS PRODUCTION

Elsewhere (Gartman 1979; 1982; 1986; 1993) I have analyzed in detail the early history of the labor process in the American automobile industry. I generally concluded that Braverman's model of the deskilling and degradation of work describes the broad historical trajectory of work in the industry. But contrary to Braverman, this history was not a smooth, inexorable expansion of capitalist control. The degraded labor process in the auto industry was fraught with contradictions that gave workers the power to struggle against it, both individually and collectively. These contradictions pointed beyond the labor process to the culture of mass consumption as the site of their transcendence.

The division, mechanization, conveyorization, and automation of automotive work were consciously intended to and actually did deskill labor and otherwise transfer its control from the workers to the managers and capitalists of the industry. But auto workers did not passively accept these changes as inevitable. Individually they walked out and stayed away from degraded, deskilled auto work in droves. In 1913, the year in which Ford introduced the moving assembly line and other work-intensifying and -controlling methods, labor turnover in his factory reached an annual rate of 370 percent, with absenteeism averaging a daily rate of over 10 percent.

Collectively auto workers resisted the new technology by restricting its output. In many shops workers banded together to set and enforce production quotas to prevent managers from intensifying labor to inhuman levels. Finally, workers organized walkouts, strikes, and stoppages of production to combat the increasing control that managers wielded over them through the new methods. At first spontaneous and small-scale, these efforts quickly escalated into full-scale drives to organize industrial unions that could protect auto workers from unilateral managerial authority and recapture some control over their work.

If the new labor process had rendered workers as powerless and acquiescent as Braverman often depicted them, then such struggles as occurred in the auto industry and elsewhere would have been impossible. He neglected to recognize, what Marx (1967:348–50) had, that although the divided and mechanized production process rendered individual craft workers powerless, it inadvertently strengthened the collective power of the largely unskilled workers who replaced them. First, the large investments in fixed capital required by the new technology concentrated and centralized auto production into a few huge factories, bringing discontented workers into close communication with one another and stimulating class consciousness and collective action. Second, the deskilling of work homogenized both the wages and working conditions of auto workers, eliminating previous divisions and creating a broad base of common interest in collective action. Finally, the minutely divided and mechanically linked labor in the new factories made auto production highly interdependent and consequently vulnerable to disruption, allowing a militant minority of workers to shut down a factory (Gartman 1986:164–78).

Early automakers realized that mass production methods would not be profitable unless worker resistance was contained, so they began to experiment with new forms of labor control. Out of the struggles of this period one policy gradually emerged as most successful in cajoling workers to abandon any claims to control the labor process and submit to the machine-mediated discipline of management—high wages and generous benefits. Automotive managers grudgingly conceded to struggling workers that which least threatened their sacrosanct "managerial prerogatives"—money. Henry Ford led the way in 1913 with his Five Dollar Day program. As Braverman recognized, Ford's doubling of the daily wage of many of his workers was a conscious attempt to buy off the mounting resistance to the degrading technology of auto production. But Braverman did not recognize that to achieve this effect, capitalists and managers had to do more than merely pay workers more money. They also had to persuade and cajole them to spend it in a way that supported rather than undermined the new mass production process. As Antonio Gramsci (1971) recognized long ago, the Five Dollar Day was a *cultural* as well as an economic offensive, an attempt to school the working class in the bourgeois lifestyle of privatized, rationalized consumerism.

Ford was worried that workers imbued with the distinct working-class and immigrant cultures of the day would not spend their new wages "wisely" but "squander" them in traditional activities stressing mutuality, collectivity, and reciprocity. So he undertook to school workers receiving the new wage in individual, privatized, home-based consumption, which he believed supported the fragmented, individualized work in his shops. With the introduction of the new wage, Ford created the Sociological Department to encourage his workers to create a refuge of home-based consumption to compensate for the inhumanities of factory production. The employees of this department investigated the leisure lifestyles of Ford workers, discouraging "harmful" practices like smoking, drinking, living in extended families, and sending money to relatives in the "old country." They encouraged workers to cultivate the bourgeois traits of saving, owning single-family homes, and purchasing major consumer durables (Gartman 1986:203–28; Meyer 1981). Ford's offensive was part of the general cultural program of middle-class reformers and corporate capitalists during this period to break up what they perceived as the rowdy and unorganized culture of the working class, which often provided the basis for collective struggles (Rosenzweig 1983; Goldman and Wilson 1977).

The emergence of working-class consumerism in the late 1910s and 1920s was not merely, however, the product of cajoling bourgeois reformers but also the outcome of the conscious choice of working Americans from among available alternatives. Worker efforts to regain some of their lost control in the workplace were met with heavy-handed resistance by both corporate managers and state managers. Under these circumstances not of their own choosing, workers settled for what they could realistically achieve— higher wages with which to construct a home-based refuge of consumerism that allowed them to momentarily forget the dehumanization of mass production factories (Fox 1983). By the mid-1920s Robert and Helen Lynd (1929:80–81) wrote in their influential ethnography of Middletown (Muncie, Indiana) that workers increasingly defined their lives in terms of consumption: "Frustrated in this [work] sector of their lives, many workers seek compensations elsewhere, . . . if no longer in the saloon, in such compensatory devices as hooking up the radio or driving the 'old bus' . . . ."

This trade-off of workplace control for home-based consumption was pioneered in the 1920s, but it did not become institutionalized until the early 1950s. By this time, corporations in cooperation with state managers had successfully contained the larger political and economic ambitions of organized industrial workers within a narrow framework of bureaucratic collective bargaining. Enshrined in laws like the National Labor Relations Act and the Taft–Hartley Act, this bargaining structure combined with Keynesian demand management and state support for auto use and home ownership to ensure American workers the wherewithal to participate fully in the compensatory consumerist lifestyle, which became the primary ideological bulwark of contemporary American capitalism (Piore and Sabel 1984:49–104; Aglietta 1979:179–208, 328–79; Davis 1986:102–53).

CONJUNCTURE 2: OVERCOMING THE CONTRADICTIONS BETWEEN MASS CONSUMPTION AND MASS PRODUCTION

Construction of a legitimating culture of mass consumption was not as simple, however, as merely ensuring workers enough income to buy commodities. Not just any old goods could blot out the inhumanities of alienated mass production and provide superficial satisfaction of the needs denied there. Workers entering the expanding culture of consumption demanded products of a specific design and style to meet these needs, and this stylistic demand threatened to undermine the very mass production process that required legitimation.

Braverman's analysis of the capitalist labor process does not take into account this dialectic of aesthetic and production imperatives. He mentioned product design in passing, but argued for its complete subordination to the imperatives of the deskilled, mechanized labor process. Braverman (1974:208–9) argued that products not originally amenable to production on specialized machinery were altered in design to adapt them to this deskilling technology. He gives examples from the housing and baking industries, in which the imperative of mechanization necessitated the degradation of their products into shoddy, tacked-together "manufactured homes" in the first case and spongy, nutritionally empty bread in the second. This model of product design as dictated by the imperatives of the degraded capitalist labor process fits only the early automobile industry. Henry Ford and other early mass producers of automobiles did alter considerably the aesthetic appearance and design of early automobiles to facilitate their production on specialized, automatic machines and assembly lines operated by largely unskilled detail workers.

The earliest American cars were luxury objects designed and produced by skilled workers in a craft production process. The bodies of these vehicles were meticulously constructed and finished sculptures in wood, designed and built by skilled bodybuilders. A draftsman laid out the original design following long-established traditions. Then workers constructed a wooden frame and fitted it with wooden or aluminum panels, which were bent or beaten by hand. Bodybuilders often effected flowing, elaborate curves in these panels to produce curvilinear, organic motifs. Finally, the body was meticulously finished by the hand-application of up to twenty coats of slow-drying paint and varnish. The visual impression created by these finely crafted auto bodies was one of aesthetic unity and cohesion, which was the direct consequence of the craft labor process under the conscious control of skilled workers themselves. Because these workers controlled the entire process of construction, with little division of labor or supervision, they could coordinate the different steps and carefully adjust them to one another. The aesthetic cohesion and organic unity of these early cars bore direct testimony to a nonalienated, human-centered process of production in which conception and execution of work were embodied in the same intelligent source. This unified labor process also allowed individuality of design, for both machines and workers were flexible and unspecialized. Manufacturers could consequently turn out a wide variety of body styles (McLellan 1975; Oliver 1981).

The labor processes responsible for producing the mechanical parts of these cars were also skilled and flexible, yielding results that were similarly varied, distinctive, and visually appealing. But the expensive labor and materials lavished on these early cars meant that they were outrageously expensive, far beyond the means of the average American. Possession of such cars thus was a direct symbol of the great wealth required to appropriate the labor of so many others (Donovan 1965:1–14).

Mass production of automobiles required increasing the volume of production and lowering the unit price. To do so under the antagonistic relations of capitalism, Ford and other automakers had to get rid of the craft production process, for its powerful workers resisted producing as quickly and cheaply as capitalists demanded. But in order to revolutionize the labor process with deskilling machines and assembly lines, the first mass producers also had to revolutionize automobile design. Because the specialized machinery of mass production was rigidly inflexible, capable of producing only one type of part, manufacturers had to drastically reduce model variety, leaving one or perhaps two standardized cars like Ford's Model T. The aesthetic consequence of such product standardization was the increasingly homogenized appearance of cars—the individuality and distinction of craft-built cars gave way to the cookie-cutter sameness of mass-produced ones (Nevins and Hill 1954:240–41, 260, 332–34).

Exacerbating this homogenized appearance of early mass-produced autos was the almost complete absence of color—nearly all were finished in a thin coat of black enamel. The monotonous monochrome of mass production was again the direct result of the imperative of displacing skilled workers with deskilling machines. In order to mechanize the process of painting a car, Ford and other mass producers began to replace slow-drying varnish paints with enamel. Parts were dipped in tanks of enamel and then baked in conveyorized ovens, completing in a few hours a process that previously required weeks. The only problem was that the high baking temperatures changed most color pigments, except black (LaFever 1924:17–19; Arnold and Faurote 1972:360–83).

The use of skill-displacing machinery in the production of automobile bodies also transformed the flowing, organic lines of the craft-built cars into the stark rectilinearity of the mass-produced jalopies. In the late 1910s and early 1920s the hand-formed wooden bodies were replaced by all-steel ones, whose parts could be quickly stamped out on automatic presses and welded together by electric resistance machines. However, due to the primitive nature of the press technology at this time, body panels and parts had to be almost completely flat, resulting in cars that were extremely square (La Fever 1924:15–17; Schipper 1921). Use of deskilling technology also sacrificed the unity and integrity of mass-produced vehicles. With the conception now separated from the execution of work, it was impossible for workers to integrate the auto into a cohesive whole through the adjustment and fitting of separate parts. The engineers and technicians who now planned the entire production process could not possibly take into account all the contingencies of imperfect machines, materials, and people. Thus, parts were often not close-fitting or aesthetically compatible. For this reason, these early mass-produced cars looked, in the retrospective words of some auto designers, as if they "had been assembled from a variety of pieces, all designed independently of each other and then put together without much thought to their interrelationships" (Chrysler 1963:6).

The design and aesthetics of these early mass-produced cars were obviously and visibly determined by the deskilling and control imperatives of mechanization, as Braverman claimed. The standardized, square, fragmented appearance of cars like the Model T bore direct testimony to the fragmentation, standardization, and rigidification of the production process and human labor that produced them. And driving one of these cars directly testified to one's subordination to dehumanized labor. In contrast to the craft-produced automobiles whose possession testified to the ample means to command the expensive labor of others, the cheap mass-produced cars testified to the owners' modest means and degraded class position. Cars like the Model T thus became socially stigmatized and were the butt of many demeaning jokes. One quip asserted that you can go anywhere in a Model T, except society (Lewis 1976:121–25).

Because of Braverman's exclusive focus on the objective production process, he did not recognize these cultural connotations of mass-produced goods and the problems they created for the legitimating ideology of mass consumption. As long as consumer goods like automobiles bore the stigmatizing signs of mass production, they could not provide Americans with the compensating sense of individuality and progress that they were denied in production. During the 1920s, workers with higher wages began deserting such products in favor of those with more style and beauty that allowed them to forget the harsh degradation of factory life. The market share of Ford's socially stigmatized Model T fell from 50 percent in 1923 to 15 percent in 1927, while the share of General Motors' Chevrolet Division more than doubled during this period. GM's success was the result of a product policy developed by its president, Alfred Sloan, who understood that consumers wanted a greater variety of constantly improving cars that testified to progress and individuality. But how could such cars be manufactured without undermining the standardization and high volumes necessary for mass production? The answer, in a word, was styling (Sloan 1972:63–77, 171–75).

In the mid-1920s, General Motors discovered that its mass-produced cars could be made to *look* individualized and high-quality by obscuring their connection to the mass-production process with the superficial style characteristics of the craft-produced cars. And standardized cars could appear to be constantly improving by incremental alterations in appearance. In 1925 GM officially adopted the policy of annual model changes. Every year a new model was introduced with incremental changes in appearance: new headlights and taillights, more (or less) chrome trim, differently shaped body panels. Harley Earl, who was hired in 1927 as the chief stylist at General Motors, stated: "The thing is to tool them into coming out with a car that has so many changes in little things, it looks entirely new" (Holliday 1969:16). Beneath the dazzling kaleidoscope of automotive surfaces, however, the same old standardized technology was kept for years, producing the high volumes that made mass production possible (Sloan 1972:187–93).

Similarly, the variety of automobiles that GM offered consumers to compensate them for standardized Fordist jobs was achieved in style alone. During the 1920s Sloan ordered the corporation's previously independent carmaking divisions to begin to standardize and share components to allow their mass production. But he did not want GM car lines to *appear* the same, for he recognized that "People like different things" (Sloan 1972:207). He struck upon the idea of differentiating GM's six car lines mainly in appearance through superficial body styles and features. But this policy of stylistic differentiation ran into problems during the 1930s, when the Depression imposed cost-cutting exigencies on all manufacturers. GM initiated a body-sharing program in 1933. To increase the volume and cut the costs of body production, all of the corporation's cars were built upon one of three standardized body shells, which were designed in the Body Development Studio of the GM Styling Department. But then these shared shells were turned over to a series of divisional styling studios, where stylists applied the details that made them appear unique: bumpers, grills, headlights, trim. GM stylists eventually developed a series of superficial styling cues distinct to each division that made its products immediately recognizable to consumers (MacMinn and Lamm 1985:75–81).

Other automakers followed GM's pioneering policies during the 1930s, allowing the industry to reconcile the standardized, deskilled mass-production process with the consumer demand for individuality and progress in goods through superficial styling. And during the Depression years the style trend that best offered consumers compensation for these denied needs was streamlining. As the economic collapse destroyed hopes of any real progress, Americans sought solace in the corporate promise of an imminent technological utopia. The machines that made this promise seem real were streamlined ocean liners, airplanes, and trains, vehicles whose advanced design symbolized a new age of abundance to be achieved not through social change and struggle but through the cooperative application of science (Meikle 1979).

Under consumer pressure, automakers, like manufacturers of other mundane goods, began to adopt the superficial aesthetics of streamlining, producing several important ideological effects. First, by adopting the rounded, curvilinear look of the most advanced transport machines, the unchanging automotive technology was made to appear advanced. Second, the extension of the streamlined body over previously exposed mechanical parts like frame members and the gas tank, ostensibly to reduce wind resistance, obscured from sight all the crudely finished, rectilinear parts that reminded consumers of their standardized and heteronomous work lives. Finally, the streamlined mass-produced cars of the 1930s looked increasingly like the rounded, integrated bodies of the expensive makes, which previously could be produced only by costly craft labor. Consequently, in the realm of consumption Americans could escape the reminders of the class inequalities of the workplace (Meikle 1979; Pretzer 1986).

The fruition of this automotive ideology that obscured and legitimated class differences would await the postwar prosperity of the 1950s. With American manufacturers dominating world markets and the state underwriting consumption through Keynesian demand management and bureaucratized collective bargaining, America exploded in a frenzy of exuberant consumerism. And 1950s automobiles were the main support of this consumerist ideology. The prosperity lead automakers to upgrade the cheaper models in size, power, and gadgetry until they closely resembled the more expensive makes. In an era in which the working man's Chevrolet was distinguished from his boss's Cadillac by merely incremental amounts of chrome and horsepower, America's claim to classlessness seemed credible. Building upon themes pioneered in the 1930s, auto styling in the 1950s also cultivated images of escape and progress. Both were captured in tacked-on aeronautical symbols like tail fins and air scoops, which promised consumers an escape from the mundane realities of the workaday world into the realm of freewheeling supersonic flight.

CONJUNCTURE 3: CONSUMER DISCONTENT AND THE CONTRADICTIONS OF FORDISM

Although the cultural demands of legitimation drove auto design beyond the simple production-determined aesthetics postulated by Braverman, superficial styling initially reconciled these demands with the imperatives of mass production. But eventually the dynamics of this consumer culture produced contradictions that undermined the satisfactions of automotive dream machines and pushed their design beyond the foundations of deskilling mass production. In the 1950s the trend toward bigness, power, and convenience in all car lines leveled the traditional differences between cars in the price hierarchy, making it more and more difficult for consumers to satisfy their crucial desires for individuality and distinction. And in their desperate attempts to distinguish their company's homogeneous dream machines from their competitors', auto stylists pushed the superficiality of design to outrageous heights. Tail fins, headlights, chrome, and accessories proliferated in an obsession with quantity that soon had cars struggling under the weight of this useless ornamentation (Flink 1988:277–93).

With everyone's dream machines looking exactly alike, Americans began to awaken to the superficiality of their consumer visions. A trickle of consumers began to desert Detroit dream barges for the distinction of small, light, sporty imports. By the end of the 1950s, this trickle had become a flood. Another contradiction of Fordist consumption also had a sobering effect on Americans. The attempt of everyone to find individual fulfillment through autos led to unintended social consequences that prevented anyone from attaining fulfillment. The millions of Americans seeking to escape from the industrial city in their dream machines soon found themselves trapped in a nightmare of traffic congestion. And the countryside to which they escaped quickly turned into a wasteland of choking smog and environmental devastation (O'Connor 1984:179–87; Bosquet 1977).

Compounding these contradictions of mass consumption were the contradictions of mass production, which also became increasingly evident as the 1950s turned into the 1960s. The escalating civil rights struggle and the discovery of poverty revealed that Fordist prosperity was purchased at the price of superexploitation of marginalized secondary workers. And even the privileged primary workers in the high-paying corporations became increasingly restive throughout this period, for prosperity undermined the incentives that

induced them to trade workplace autonomy for monetary rewards. Low rates
of unemployment and increasing social-wage programs took the sting out of
the managerial threat of firing, giving these workers the freedom and power
to reexamine the workplace issues that they had been forced to bargain away
earlier (Bowles, Gordon, and Weisskopf 1984).

These contradictions fell especially hard on the decade's youth, the first
generation to grow up under the full sway of Fordism. Because they took
prosperity for granted, the rewards of America's boring and standardized consumer culture hardly seemed worth the sacrifices they were asked to make to
accommodate to increasingly degraded Fordist work. Consequently, middle-
class youth rebelled against the oppressive apprenticeship in authoritarian
schools that was the admission price for standardized white-collar jobs. And
working-class youth questioned the sacrifices required in Fordist factories for
the privilege of purchasing shoddy, standardized goods. Both began to
demand more meaningful gratifications and increased control over their institutions (Ehrenreich 1989; Aronowitz 1973).

Faced with the revolt of consumers against monotonous products and the
social costs of consumption, as well as the growing discontent of workers
within Fordist production, capitalists responded by offering Americans merely
larger doses of the same old consumer opium. Blacks and the poor were given
higher social wages, while discontented primary workers were given higher
market wages and benefits. And manufacturers offered these consumers with
more money a growing array of goods finely differentiated for the purse and
personality of each individual. No longer able to rely on superficial diversity,
companies began to differentiate their goods by essential characteristics like
size and function to appeal to markets specialized by age, gender, region, and
lifestyle. Automakers offered consumers an astounding array of distinct automobiles during this decade. While all cars offered in the 1950s were big
sedans, by 1970 consumers could choose among subcompacts, compacts,
intermediates, and full-sized cars. The number of distinct models increased
from 244 in 1960 to 370 in 1970. And each model was generally available with
a broad range of consumer-specified options. John Gordon, the president of
General Motors, stated in 1963: "Our objective is . . . a car for every purse,
purpose, and person" (Sloan 1972:520).

But this increased dose of individualized consumption only intensified
the contradictions of mass consumption. When each individual sought to
express his or her identity through a personally tailored vehicle, America's
roads became even more crowded, dangerous, noisy, and polluted. There
emerged, as the *Wall Street Journal* noted, "a growing rebellion against the
car," as the image of the automobile in the popular consciousness changed
from a vehicle of freedom to a menacing, malevolent force (Mossberg and
O'Donnell 1971:17).

The escalation of automotive individuality undermined not only the cultural legitimation of mass consumption but also threatened the foundation of mass production. Model proliferation threatened the standardization of products upon which the deskilled, automated, and specialized process of production rested. As the number of auto engines and models grew during the late 1950s and early 1960s, both engine and assembly plants became more specialized (Abernathy 1978). But because sales did not increase as rapidly as product variety, the increased costs of these specialized plants were amortized over a smaller number of units, driving up unit production costs (Wright 1979:104, 118–19).

Further threats to standardized mass production were created by the wide array of options available on each model. Factories were forced to keep huge inventories of parts and schedule them to arrive at the assembly line at just the right time in just the right combination. The increasing variety of options also undermined the precise balancing of the minutely divided tasks along the assembly line. Cars of widely varying options requiring different amounts of time and effort were assembled on the same line. This variation and uncertainty gave auto workers power to contest the incessant speedup and reassert some control over their own work, for managers could not precisely determine the assembly time for each combination. Lippert (1978) reported that in his Cadillac body plant the workers most militant in fighting line speed were those engaged in installing one of the most infamously troublesome design accessories of the period, the vinyl top.

The problems of coordinating product variety combined with worker slowdowns to increase production costs and halt productivity growth in the industry (Rothschild 1973:48; Abernathy 1978:156–59). Because increasing foreign competition prevented American automakers from merely passing these increased costs of production along to consumers, as they had been accustomed, they suffered falling unit profits. Thus, the product proliferation required to satisfy the cultural demands of Fordist mass consumption undermined the economies of scale and balance of power in Fordist mass production in ways wholly unanticipated by Braverman. In the 1960s selling more cars required producing more different types of cars, destroying standardization, creating uncertainty, and giving auto workers the power to struggle against unilateral managerial control of work intensity.

Automakers met these new contradictions in the Fordist constellation of mass production and mass consumption with a series of deadly traditional responses that only made them worse. Beginning in the mid-1960s, top managers at the Big Three launched campaigns of parts-sharing between cars to cut down the costs of product diversity and render assembly operations more standardized. The automakers also slowed down the cycle of annual model changes, stretching out the life of body shells and major components. Finally, managers resorted to the traditional industry panacea of speedup, or increased production pace (Wright 1979).

But these traditional Fordist solutions to declining profits and productivity only served to exacerbate the deep contradictions of the system. Increased parts-sharing made corporate models look more alike, undermining the individuality that consumers demanded. And with cars changing little from year to year, consumers could no longer find progress and excitement in new cars. But the biggest impact of these measures fell on the industry's workers. Empowered by low unemployment rates and high social wages and chaffing under the old inequities of degrading production, America's auto workers were not willing to accept the new intensification of labor. Quit rates among employees rose steadily in the decade and by 1969 reached levels unknown since the postwar labor turmoil. Absenteeism also skyrocketed, doubling and tripling in auto plants. And strikes and stoppages rose sharply, with many unauthorized by the union (U.S. Bureau of Labor Statistics 1972:117; Rothschild 1973:123–25).

The strike that came to epitomize the new militancy occurred at GM's Lordstown, Ohio plant in 1971 (see Isaac and Christiansen, this volume). When the corporation rebuilt the plant the previous year to produce the Vega minicar, it carried the deskilling and degradation of auto work to new heights. Skilled assembly work, especially welding, was transferred to robots, and the pace of the manual jobs left behind by automation was set at a furious pace by the speeding machines. Old-fashioned time and motion study intensified the pace of assembly lines to an unprecedented 102 cars an hour. And to compel workers to submit to the inhuman pace, management of the plant was turned over to the tough-minded GM Assembly Division, organized in 1965 to standardize and rationalize corporate assembly operations. The first step GMAD took at Lordstown was to fire seven hundred assembly line workers and crack down on worker discipline.

These draconian measures led the local union, which represented the plant's relatively young workforce, to strike, not over wages and benefits but over control issues like line speed and unilateral managerial authority. The president of the Lordstown local, Gary Bryner, implied that the strike challenged the very structure of the degraded labor process: "Many feel that the industry is going to have to do something to change the boring, repetitive nature of assembly line work or it will continue to have unrest in the plant" (Aronowitz 1973:43). Braverman himself took note of this Lordstown strike in his discussion of job dissatisfaction in the 1970s (1974:33–34). But he interpreted the attention given to such worker discontent as merely a faddish rediscovery of "one of the fundamentals of capitalist society" (1974:38). In a totally ahistorical manner, Braverman refused to acknowledge the unique conjuncture of contradictions that gave rise to this renewal of workplace struggle, preferring instead to give a static account that reduces it to an eternal repro-duction of the basic structures of capitalism.

But contrary to Braverman, the historic position of these young auto workers was unprecedented. Never before had a generation entered Fordist factories with little experience of the hard times that encouraged their fathers and grandfathers to trade off workplace dignity and autonomy for economic security and heteronomy. And never before had a generation learned to expect much more out of work from the system of mass education through which most had passed. Braverman is right to have argued that the struggle over workplace control is as old as capitalism itself. But in the early 1970s this age-old struggle occurred in the context of contradictions of production and consumption that strengthened and allowed it to shake the foundations of Fordism. Escalating consumer demands for individuality generated by the contradictions of Fordist consumption led to changes that contradicted Fordist production and gave workers both the motivation and power to strug-gle against its abuses. Fordism, that combination of mass production and mass consumption, had reached its limits (Aronowitz 1973:21–50; Garson 1975:86–98; Terkel 1975:256–65).

CONJUNCTURE 4: THE STRUGGLE FOR POST-FORDISM

The decline of Fordism touched off a renewed struggle that has pushed the labor process in the auto industry beyond Braverman's narrow, unilinear model. This is not to say, as some pundits of post-Fordism postulate, that all the imperatives of Fordism are being reversed in a rush back to a future of neocraft production in small shops by multiskilled workers who control their own labor. Indeed, the capitalist imperative of controlling labor seems as strong as ever. Yet, in the face of changing demands of consumption, capital-ists are beginning to find new ways to realize this control imperative that Braverman did not anticipate.

If Fordism is the vague term used to characterize the system of mass pro-duction pioneered by the auto industry—high-volume production of a stan-dardized product on specialized machines operated by unskilled workers orga-nized by bureaucratic collective bargaining—post-Fordism is the equally imprecise term used to describe production systems that depart from this model. The most popular vision of post-Fordism is "flexible specialization," a concept developed by Piore and Sabel (1984) to describe and prescribe a sys-tem of low-volume production of differentiated products on general purpose machines operated by highly skilled workers organized by decentralized, enterprise-based bargaining. As critics have pointed out, this concept leaves much to be desired as an empirical description of the direction of American industries, especially automobiles. American automakers are seeking, under the pressure of consumer demand, to develop more differentiated products and to change them more often (Womack et al. 1990:119–26). In order to do so, they have been seeking to adopt more flexible forms of technology and labor organization. But such flexibility does not seem to require small firms producing in small batches. Mass production in large firms may also be rendered more flexible without great sacrifices of volume (Sayer 1989). This model may also exaggerate the skills required by workers operating the more flexible technology. Thomas (1994) suggests that it is not the technology that determines the level of skill exercised by workers but the social struggles over its control.

A more realistic model of post-Fordist production is provided by Japanese automakers, whose system has been labeled "lean production." As practiced in Japan, this form of mass production does depart from Fordism by producing a greater variety of rapidly changing car models through more flexible technology and organization (Womack et al. 1990; D. Friedman 1983). Contrary to popular belief, however, the system is not predicated on the most advanced microelectronic technology—in many cases the Japanese seem to prefer older, more manual machinery over expensive computer automation (Sayer 1989: 673–74). The key to their success is the human, not technical, organization of their factories. The major Japanese automakers break with the rigid occupational division of labor of Fordism and "transfer the maximum number of tasks and responsibility to those workers actually adding value to the car on the line" (Womack et al. 1990:99). Line workers are responsible for and must learn the skills of simple machine repair, quality-checking, housekeeping, and materials-ordering. They are also expected to learn all the jobs in their work groups and participate in quality circles to anticipate and solve production problems. Such an organization not only eliminates lots of indirect labor— hence its "leanness"—but also renders workers more flexible and able to adapt to new products introduced regularly. Pay systems are also more flexible, based more on seniority than job, and determined more by enterprise-based bonuses than industry-wide formulas.

American automakers are seeking in many ways to reproduce the relations of Japanese lean production. In recent years they have pushed the union, under threat of plant closure, to abandon centralized industry bargaining and work and seniority rules based on narrow job definitions in favor of decentralized enterprise bargaining and broader, more flexible occupational categories. As part of this reorganization, most companies have also introduced programs of participatory teams that give workers greater responsibilities and discretion in their own work (Altshuler et al. 1984; Katz 1985).

Critics have rightly challenged the idea that lean production and teamwork in either American or Japanese plants leads to any significant increase in worker skills. What this really entails is forcing workers to do a number of rather simple, plant-specific jobs that require manual dexterity, stamina, and an ability to follow directions (M. Parker 1993:270–72). Although lean production does not reverse Braverman's deskilling dynamic, it does seem to challenge his postulated imperative for managers to centralize all discretion in their hands. Even critics have recognized that to achieve flexibility workers are required to be cooperative and voluntarily impose high standards of productivity on themselves (M. Parker 1993:264). But how, then, do managers ensure that workers use this discretion and initiative to speed up production rather than slow it down, as American auto workers did in the late 1960s and early 1970s? This involves control measures of a new type that Braverman ignored.

The Japanese solution, which American automakers have tried to emulate, involves team pressure and internal labor markets. Since workers receive part of their pay in bonuses based on plant production and profitability, team members have an interest in pushing each other to work harder (M. Parker 1993). And workers also use their discretion to increase production in order to obtain promotions in the firm's job hierarchy. This is an especially important incentive in Japan, where strict policies of filling jobs by internal promotion mean chances for advancement are tied closely to the firm (Cole 1979). But it has also become increasingly salient in the United States due to the high rates of unemployment in the early 1990s that discouraged labor market mobility. Also important in making workers in Japan dependent on firms is the lack of social welfare programs that provide nonmarket income. The American industry's attempt to approximate Japanese conditions has not only led to efforts to weaken unions like the United Auto Workers but also to roll back programs like welfare and unemployment insurance so as to make American workers similarly dependent solely on wages for a livelihood (Piven and Cloward 1982; Bluestone and Harrison 1982).

The jury is still out on whether automakers will be able to impose lean production techniques on American workers. In the end their success will be determined by the strength of labor's resistance to these measures. But what is not in doubt is that the consumer demand for a diversity of changing products that culturally legitimate the workplace rigors of capitalism have driven employers to search for labor control methods that go beyond the minute division of labor and centralization of discretion postulated by Braverman. Unless we recognize the contradictory totality of production and consumption, economics and culture, those of us who consider ourselves Braverman's heirs will lack the understanding to realize his admirable goal of truly liberating work and leisure lives for all.

7

Degradations of Labor, Cultures of Cooperation

Braverman's 'Labor,' Lordstown, and the Social Factory

LARRY W. ISAAC AND LARRY D. CHRISTIANSEN

To speak the words "labor process" is to at least imagine the name of Harry Braverman. Following the appearance of *Labor and Monopoly Capital (LMC)*,[1] it became the touchstone for two decades of research on work and has contributed to reshaping other substantive domains. Before *LMC*, postwar industrial social science studied workers and workplaces from perspectives that emphasized managerial viewpoints and objectives. These approaches embodied a one-sidedness that situated the social scientist on the side of capitalist management and work systems design architects. Braverman did much to critically illuminate that particular political stance. He emphasized that the capitalist labor process was the core dynamic that enveloped and permeated the most fundamental social structures of the monopoly capitalist era. Instead of viewing capitalist management as the technical essence of industrial progress coupled with politically neutral workplace administration, Braverman emphasized the domination and control of capitalist managerial design. In particular, "scientific management" was the key to capitalist domination that led to an "averaging down" of human labor. Contrasted with the pollution of industrial modernization orthodoxy of the time, Braverman felt like a breath of fresh air.

But Braverman's thesis also had unfortunate consequences. We argue that several key features of *LMC* embody a very definite one-sidedness rooted in the orthodox treatment of the commodity-form. In particular, we critically assess his conceptions of labor, time, culture, and workplace as emblematic of this tendency. Singularly, but especially in concert, these elements give

111

Braverman's account of monopoly capitalism an unwitting conservative ring
that seriously constrains labor-power. As such, Braverman is an excellent
example of a long tradition of critical theory that has often produced very
powerful critiques of capitalist society without also showing where working-
class power has been exercised in the past and where its potential might exist
under currently emerging conditions.

We develop this essay in two major sections. First, we center a critique on
five key elements of *LMC*, namely, its political economy approach to labor,
one-dimensional linear teleological view of time, one-sided culture of capitalist cooperation, and unidirectional reductionist view of the workplace; the
fifth element is methodological—the use of a generalizing interpretive case
method. The purpose of the critique is the juxtaposition of an alternative set
of founding premises. In the second section, we employ these alternative
premises to guide our reanalysis of an important case—the General Motors
(GM) Lordstown struggle of 1971–72.

THEORETICAL CRITIQUE AND
ALTERNATIVE FOUNDATIONS

There have been many excellent critiques and extensions of Braverman's
LMC.[2] Our purpose is not to rehash that extensive literature, but rather to use
LMC in a critical dialogical fashion to lay an alternative theoretical and
methodological foundation. We begin with a critique of Braverman's conception of labor because it forms the basis for and shapes several other key features of the theory of untrammeled, linear, universal degradationism—that is,
temporality, culture, and place of production. We follow with a critical assessment of the methodological principle used to link the theory of labor degradation to data (case materials such as the Lordstown strike). This methodological section serves as a bridge between Braverman's Lordstown and our
reanalysis of that case of labor–management struggle. An abstract of these key
dimensions of critique and our alternative founding premises is presented in
Table 7.1.

Braverman's theory of labor is based on a reading of *Capital* that uncriti-
cally embraces several key premises of *Capital*'s antagonist; it is an approach
that reads back into Marx key elements he had criticized in classical political
economy (Cleaver 1979). For Braverman, this normalization of capital and
labor as economic objects corresponds primarily to a separate "economic"
sphere with its own special "laws of motion." In short, it accepts an "economic
base-political/ideological superstructure" separation and, giving primacy to
the former, allows an "objectivist" strategy to seem reasonable. But there is
more to his objectivist approach. This economism is characteristic of much

Table 7.1. Key Dimensions of Critique and Alternative Directions

Dimension	Braverman	Alternative Direction
Labor	One-dimensional political economization of labor as object	Twofold character of labor in the commodity-form; emphasizing the simultaneous subjective and objective character of labor
Time	Ahistorical teleological time	Contextual time and event-based time
Culture	One-dimensional culture of labor cooperation with capital	Multiple workplace cultures— labor cooperating with capital and labor producing cultures of solidarity against capital
Workplace	Reduces place of labor to capitalist firm; privileges workplace in all social determinations	Social factory with multiple sources of labor degradation and multiple social movements of labor
Method	Interpretive case approach	Extended case approach

orthodox social science as well as much Marxist theory that has a legacy extending back through Western Neo-Marxism into the Second International (Cleaver 1979).

Braverman's political economy understanding of capital and labor contained the core of his theory of social relations. He began with a clear distinction between labor-power and labor, but these are not presented as categories of social relations that embody *both* objectivity and subjectivity, simultaneously abstract and concrete labor. Instead, Braverman proceeded to build his theory of class relations on a one-sided *principle of subjectivity* and derivatively, a one-sided *principle of potentiality*, namely, one that is predicated on the possibility and realization of physical separation of subject and object. In an attempt to show what monopoly capital did to the working class and to justify his "objectivist" analysis against conventional social science "questionnaire subjectivity," Braverman located subjectivity exclusively in capital personified as total managerial control of conception. By focusing exclusively on capitalist management's always successful conception and deployment of work system design, technology, and organization, Braverman, in effect, fractures class relations internal to the commodity-form, thereby producing class in which one side appears as the active subject (capital) and the other as the activated object (labor).

Although Braverman did not begin with a one-dimensional labor premise, he did manage to end up with an image of labor as an abstract object processed exclusively and almost effortlessly in the image of capital. The key to this accomplishment in Braverman is the premise that human labor-power special not only because of its infinite potential but also because "conception" (sub-jectivity) and "execution" (objectification) can be physically separated from each other; that is, workers can have their subjectivity engineered out of them. So the labor process can be reduced (and has been in much sociology of the labor process) to workplace technical requirements in which workers are acti-vated as "factors of production," objects of capitalist will.

Consequently, in the *LMC* story, the antagonistic social relations of com-modified labor become thoroughly domesticated. Of course, that was (is) the engineering objective of Taylorist scientific (and other) management strategies that permeated much production theory and practice yet never achieved the capitalist ideal as fully realized surplus value extracted from a docile labor force. We can agree that capital accumulation does, indeed, subordinate increasing amounts of human labor-power (and life-time) as it converts it into labor for capital without also accepting that it does this automatically, smoothly, just as it pleases. And this is Braverman's principle of potentiality that derives from his one-sided principle of subjectivity: it is the stance that ignores the fact that labor-power is not solely the power or potential to work for capital in the pro-duction of surplus value; it, too, is the potential to subvert (reshape) that process and thereby the social relations and conditions that make it possible in the first place.

For Marx, on the other hand, the commodity was the point of departure because it forms the elementary unit of capital as a set of social relations. Labor-power and labor do not appear as separate entities (i.e., things) in Marx, but rather social relations (namely, value relations) that constitute the two-sided, antagonistic character of capital. To the capitalist buyer, labor-power is the general form or depository of potential value, abstract labor, including its surplus forms. The movement from labor-power (subjective potential) to actual labor as "output" (objectification of the subject) is the "problem of man-agement" in the capitalist labor process. But it is labor-power (the power, potential, capacity of labor) in the commodity-form that holds both principles of subjectivity and potentiality for Marx. The labor process, in general, is always the act of the objectification of the subject. Within the capitalist labor process, objectification of the collective subject can be *more or less* for capital at any given moment, hence the term "variable capital" in Marx. To bracket subjectivity in analyzing the commodity-form of labor (as Braverman does) is, in effect, to assume that human labor is an object like any other, or that it can be converted into such an object. Ironically, this is the sort of premise central to classical political economy that drew scathing critique from Marx (in general, see Marx [1857] 1973). The key in Marx is the twofold character of labor. Each of Marx's categories that unfold in and as *Capital* are presented as social relations, simultaneously "objective" and "subjective" terms (e.g., Postone 1993).

In *LMC*, the final picture is one in which *labor* is framed as an object. Subjectivity has not been thoroughly extinguished (Wardell 1990); Braverman (1974:151) let it show, for instance, as working-class anger and hostility contained beneath the surface of daily habituation to alienated work. Sometimes he even alluded to worker militancy (Braverman 1974:31-34). But none of this is from a working class that is understood as even a partial producer of history. Thus, the principle of potentiality is what becomes extinguished in Braverman—wage labor as an appendage to a superior subject simply has none. The working class is locked away as an impotent, if sometimes hostile, victim of degradation within the "iron cage" of monopoly capitalism. In *LMC*, the only possible, albeit implicit, potential transformative imagery might be a generalized labor degradation and immiseration process. But just how the victimized working class is ever able to play the savior's role is unclear given the extremely effective prison constructed in Braverman's grand narrative. In 1844, Marx (1975:280) pointed out that "political economy starts from labor as the real soul of production; yet to labor it gives nothing, and to private property everything. Confronting this contradiction, Proudhon has decided in favor of labor against private property." In 1974 Braverman, too, confronted this contradiction in favor of labor, but gave everything to monopoly capital.

This one-dimensional, objectivist economism has important implications for other key features of his argument. Below we concentrate on how this particular labor premise shapes Braverman's use of *time*, *culture*, and *workplace*, and is complemented by his particular use of *method*.

Time

Much social science theory, especially that composed as grand narratives of modernity (Antonio 1990), has often been tied to a particular philosophy of history animated by a special conception of temporality (Sewell 1996). Typically it is one in which the future is the perfection of the present, and the present is the inevitable culmination of the past. History is endowed with teleological temporality—what *was* is what *had to be*—a form of "ahistorical time" in which history is conceived to be a continual seamless unfolding of the same underlying commonality (Isaac and Griffin 1989). Explanatory accounts based on teleological time consist in causal attribution of a historical occurrence resulting from abstract transhistorical laws that lead to some future end-state. Neither the actions or reactions that constitute a historical occurrence, nor concrete conditions that shape and constrain such actions, are given causal power. Concrete actions and events, when acknowledged, are "actually explained by events in the future" displaying a monotonic historical trajectory produced by "long-term, anonymous causal forces" (Sewell 1996). What exists is inevitable.

LMC embodies a teleological temporality coupled with a fixation on one key practice—Taylorist "scientific management"—that produces a type of "big bang" theory of the origins of monopoly capitalism. Around the turn of the century, in what Braverman called the "scientific-technical revolution," the needs of especially large corporate industrial firms were married with the technical power of physical sciences. The offspring, industrial engineer, spawned a new breed of management. Frederick W. Taylor was, of course, emblematic of that breed, and a leading figure of the corresponding "industrial efficiency movement." Taylor, too, harbored a teleological view of the world expressed in the common notion of progressive industrial modernity. As he saw it, there were two obstacles to the fulfillment of America's industrial destiny—worker habits coupled with traditional management practices. "Systematic soldiering," as he called it, was in fact the informal workgroup cultural practice of maintaining some worker control over the pace of the labor process and product quality. According to Taylor (Braverman 1974:98) soldiering was "done by the men with the deliberate object of keeping their employers ignorant of how fast work could be done [and is] by far the greatest evil from which both workmen and employers are suffering." Both universal and inevitable among workers, soldiering by workers and traditional managerial inability to eliminate it were the major obstacles to completing the industrial progressivism of the modern workplace.

In Taylorist industrial progressivism, the antimodern practices of traditional worker and management would be overcome by the application of scientific management principles. Braverman's contemporary antagonists—the post–World War II industrial modernity theorists—similarly emphasized a teleological trajectory of scientific expertise, skill, and general work upgrading. In both versions, science was the key to industrial modernization, generalized upgrading, and even emancipation offered by industrial society. Braverman turned the tables. He told the compelling story of how the inexorable insertion of "scientific management" into more and more workplace operations actually reversed the orthodox master narratives of emancipatory industrial modernity. While the trajectory is reversed relative to both oppositional scenarios, the teleological conception of time is retained. Hence, Braverman achieved a directionality for capitalism by a radical inversion of industrial modernization theory's teleological time.

Critical conjunctures of events that form turning points are certainly important in historical analysis (Isaac and Griffin 1989; Sewell 1996). But the construction of historical arguments containing teleological time in which some key past event acts such as the "big bang" can lead to problematic consequences: that is, a "pure origin that contains the entire future of the social system *in potentia*, and which the partially contingent events that occur subsequently are robbed of their affectivity and reduced to the status of markers on the road to the inevitable future" (Sewell 1996:251). For Braverman, the story of the development and implementation of Taylorist scientific management was the decisive moment that changed capitalism forever, setting labor on a declining evolutionary trajectory of degradation inside an *imprisoning* monopoly capitalism. Braverman supplants the telos of orthodox emancipatory industrial modernity with a telos of an imprisoning degradation.

There are many different forms of temporality (e.g., Aminzade 1992) that might be juxtaposed to Braverman's singular, linear ahistorical time. At minimum, an alternative grounding should pay attention to both contextual and event-based time. *Contextual time* refers to time that serves as a broad boundary or frame for relatively constant (within context or period) social conditions that change in important ways between contexts or periods. For example, differentiating between (periodizing) multiple historical regimes of accumulation across twentieth-century U.S. history (e.g., Isaac et al. 1994) might be considered more justifiable historically than Braverman's uniform "monopoly capitalism."

Event-based time (or "eventemental time" in Sewell's terms) refers to the dimensions of temporality that are integral to how events unfold and is crucial to the process of social structuring. Events contain the tracks of structurings and are grasped by how the actions that constitute the event are sequenced (e.g., Griffin 1992). Historically grounded, event-based temporality treats time as a form of social organization, a social product with multiple forms of sequences that are nonlinear and contain multiple temporalities—for example, significant tempo variations, timings, and turning points. Such time relies on path dependence in historical process—that is, prior actions establish or shape the possibility for future actions—but not as uniquely determinative of future occurrences or exact unfolding of an event. Integrating event-based time with path dependence precludes any simple linear evolutionary or teleological time path for a social process. It leads to a path dependency that is thoroughly contingent on time–space (historical) conditions.

Cultures of Cooperation

Braverman's objectivist economism leads to the neglect of the cultural dimension (see Swidler 1986) of class relations in the labor process; that is, there is no concern with social meanings, conscious strategies and tactics, collective solidarities, and loyalties produced by working-class communities (see Fantasia

1988). This position is the direct result of a conscious choice: Braverman simply believed that there was little that might be learned about the working class at this level (see Braverman 1976:122–23). Alternatively, for Marx the labor process simultaneously creates both material and symbolic culture. This labor process is contingent on conditions produced by past labor and these inherited conditions include that which we understand as culture (see Marx [1852] 1978). The point is twofold: culture is a product of human labor and labor is itself culture-constituted. Thus, we use culture here as a referent for historically specific meanings, conditions, and products of concrete human labor, not as a separate sphere or realm of social life.

It is not entirely true that culture is ignored by Braverman. But its character, like that of the active subject itself, is thoroughly one-sided. Capitalist culture, and especially managerial-technical cultures of work system design, are depicted as always unilaterally triumphant over other possible meanings and practices. Working-class culture, as generally embodied in practices of artisan/craft knowledge, skill, and control is what Braverman saw being destroyed by monopoly capital. As Taylorist scientific management redesigned the capitalist workplace to eliminate worker control of the production process, it transferred knowledge in the form of productive arts from skilled artisans to capitalist managerial departments and their technical property. Consequently, Braverman's working class appears drained, cultureless, lacking collective conscious capacity or resources for struggle, resistance, insurgency, or revolt. It may be an alienated, angry working class, but within monopoly capitalism it appears to be disarmed, and increasingly so, as linear teleological time carries scientific management practices (and its technical extensions) smoothly over its victims and into the future.

Integral to this imagery in Braverman is his one-sided premise of cooperation. Cooperation is not explicitly theorized, although it does play an important implicit role in his argument. In particular, it shows up as the Taylorist success story, the purchase of obedience-escalated productivity in return for monetary wage increases. The Taylorist work-system design engineers presuppose a work culture of mercenaries. So, too, does Braverman. Thus, cooperation appears as collective labor-power activated as labor for capital; it operates quietly, smoothly in rather automatic, mechanical, nonproblematic fashion through the vessels engineered by scientific management.

In *Capital* we find cooperation to be a critical two-sided category. In the formal subsumption of labor under manufacture, simple cooperation is required as the worker drives the implements of the labor process. But in the transition from manufacture's formal subsumption within the regime of absolute surplus value production to machinofacture's real subordination of labor within the regime of relative surplus value production—Braverman's key historical moment—the presupposition of or need for cooperation becomes transformed qualitatively, not eliminated. Machinofacture makes it possible for large industrial capital to more completely and "efficiently" drive or consume labor-power. But this domination presupposes labor's cooperation with capital. True, features of cooperation are more thoroughly integrated into the design of massive production technologies, but the need for labor's cooperation is still present; in fact, its *social* character becomes magnified. The cooperative character of the labor process becomes more thoroughly a "technical necessity dictated by the instrument of labor itself" (Marx [1867] 1967:386). As capitalist production becomes increasingly fragmented, serialized, and therefore social in character, cooperation becomes more valuable to the capitalist and "constant capital" itself grows more vulnerable to the lack of worker cooperation.

Precisely for this reason the collective class capacity of labor, collective labor-power, expands with the technical power of large-scale industrial capital. So the paradox: the contradiction of labor-power under these conditions of capitalist development shows up as increasingly degraded work, while the power of labor to thwart those very conditions also expands. Thus, the social power of labor increases in a twofold fashion, both for capital and as alternative to capital (Marx [1867] 1967:386). For Braverman, once the real subsumption of labor takes place, capital is the sole possessor of agency. For Marx, on the other hand, capital in this phase of development "*appears* [emphasis added] as the dominant subject and owner of *alien labor*, and its relation is itself as complete a contradiction as is that of wage labor" (Marx [1857] 1973:471). This appearance is the product of inverted social relations, a form of estrangement of subject and object; that is, a fetishism of gigantic proportions in which the very source (working-class subject) of tremendous wealth and power comes to (appears to) be dominated by it (capitalist object).

Contrary to Braverman, within all social strategies, forms, and conditions of capitalist organizational cultures of adherence and cooperation, there is always another side; namely, a cooperation among workers for purposes other than the mechanical expansion of surplus value. Marx ([1857] 1973:272) indicated that two-sidedness when he observed that labor was a use-value for capital but also "the only use-value that can form the opposite pole to capital." In Braverman's work, labor appears simply as use-value for capital.

If cooperation has two sides, then we can speak of at least two generally corresponding cultures. One meaning of cooperative culture is that which Braverman presupposed, a culture of labor compliance for capital under increasingly degrading working conditions. Its otherness is a worker cooperative oppositional culture that is always present to varying degrees within the former. Fantasia (1988:14–17), for instance, speaks of this side as a "culture of solidarity" that is constructed by participants during the course of collective struggle as a "map of meaning," in which class consciousness is understood as a dynamic cultural expression. Fantasia eschews the conventional social science approach to "class consciousness" as a "static ideational attribute or posses-sion." Instead, he treats "class consciousness" as an "active cultural 'process' that is complex, shifting, and problematic" (Fantasia 1988:107). It is symbolic action and sequence-dependent, presupposing a variable temporality that is conducive to taking seriously the events and contingency of struggles.

Braverman's objectivism is, of course, one source of his unidimensional culture of cooperation. But there is another source: his implicit premise of cat-aclysmic social change—revolutionary transformation through the ultimate breakdown of capitalism.[3] This romanticized "all or nothing" conception leads to political devaluation and theoretical neglect of working-class organization, movements, resistance, and oppositional cultures. Oppositional cultures devel-oped in relation to forms of domination and degradation do spawn, depending on historical conditions, diverse tactical forms of resistance that vary jointly along a covert–overt confrontational dimension and along an individual–col-lective action dimension.[4] Overtly dramatic forms of labor struggle and revolt constitute only a fraction of this antagonistic reality (e.g., Scott 1990; Kelley 1994). And organized labor, both local and international leaderships, can play important conditioning roles in forming cultures of cooperation; but worker militancy and labor unions are not necessarily isomorphic through time and space. Militant worker cultures have developed in the absence of unions, with the support of unions, and sometimes even despite unions.

As new forms of scientific management proliferated in industry, so, too, did worker cooperative oppositional cultures that resisted and thereby reshaped them in various ways. Cultures of insurgent solidarity produced not only resistance to the contemporary use of scientific management and intensi-fication of production (e.g., Olssen and Brecher 1992), but also contributed enormously to the cultural repertoire of strategies and tactics that would be reproduced, handed down, modified, and used in subsequent movements and struggles.[5] While Taylorism did succeed in containing or destroying some worker culture, it simultaneously created new grounds for subsequent strug-gles. In this sense we can speak of sabotage, in a wide variety of forms, as the key lexicon of insurgent worker cultures of opposition.[6] Braverman's one-sided labor process, on the other hand, depicts a working class victimized because it is divorced from its own cultural productions.

Workplace

Braverman's labor process has very definite spatial boundaries; that is, he reduced the place of work to the sphere of the capitalist firm. This is a factory reductionist labor process premise that also stems from the broader political economy tradition of Marxism (see Cleaver 1979). In the monopoly phase, capital totalizes all social life, subordinating all spheres of society to the "gigantic marketplace" where all come to "serve the needs of capital." Domination and degradation are rooted at the "point of production" (as capitalist firm) but extend outward through the separation of conception and execution in general, and scientific management in particular. Workers are engineered to passivity in the workplace; all others become passified by the powerful forces of the "gigantic marketplace."

Braverman was correct to posit the social extensiveness of capital. However, his spatially delimited conception of the place of labor, coupled with a unidirectional flow of domination and degradation from "the point of production," is much too limiting. Once capital accumulation generalizes the commodity-form of social organization, the classical equation that capital equals the "place of employment" or even the "economy" is inadequate. The place where labor happens, where the working class is located, where class relations are constituted, where class struggle is waged is simply not just the special location of the "shopfloor." Instead, a more adequate spatial image is acquired in the social relational matrix that constitutes the capitalist social formation in which wage dependency is imposed on both the directly waged as well as the unwaged to work for and sometimes against capital (e.g., Marx [1857] 1973:304; [1867] 1967:763; Cleaver 1979; Frank 1994). This allows us to see capital as a set of social relations that entails labor in (re)-production, circulation, and movements of value distribution that stretch throughout society. The production/reproduction of the working class, its degradation under and resistance to conditions of capital accumulation encompass not only work in the capitalist factory but also work in the home and the community. Thus, the "factory" where the working class works is the society as a whole, the "social factory" (Cleaver 1979:57). National productivity targets, institutionalized social wage packages, and related extensive social crises (e.g., national/global wage relations, slumps, etc.) signify the material reality of the "social factory." Contrary to Braverman, the creation of the social factory is very much the outgrowth of the contradictions, crises, and working-class power realized in struggles internal to the society shaped in the image of the commodity-form. The Fordist-Keynesian regime of accumulation and its corresponding expanded state erected during the crises of the long "New Deal" of the 1930s and 1940s is a crucial case in point (e.g., Van der Pijl 1984; Isaac et al. 1994).

Several key implications follow from this line of reasoning. First, the broad conception of labor process, so crucial to Marx, emphasizes that human labor exists outside the direct wage relation of the capitalist workplace; significant portions of the working-class labor even when their toil may not be remunerated with a wage (e.g., household labor). Second, capital accumulation implies the expanded reproduction of the wage-dependent population, whether directly waged or not; thus the working class consists of both waged and unwaged labor-power that includes, but extends beyond, the capitalist "workplace." Third, class struggle is not limited to the shopfloor, but is generalized throughout the entire social factory in the form of social movements of labor that resist various capitalist impositions, degradations, and exploitations. Fourth, this means that social movements, ostensibly rooted in conditions other than factory productivity[7] (e.g., race, gender, environmental degradation), should be analyzed as, not simply reduced to, class struggles. Finally, this implies that a critical question for the analysis of working-class struggles is the qualitative character of relations between social movements throughout the social factory. One hypothesis is that oppositional worker cultures that may be played out in various ways on the "shopfloor" are sometimes shaped in important ways by social movements emerging in other departments of the social factory. This is a fundamental question of intraclass struggle so pivotal to working-class (de)-formation.

METHOD

If the reciprocal relation between theory and data is the province of methodology (not simply narrow technique), then we would expect that methods are differentially theory-compatible. And so it is here. Braverman's theory of labor and its chief implications (discussed above) are reinforced by the manner in which he used empirical case materials. In particular, his approach is consistent largely with the "interpretive case method."[8] This is a reductionist method in the sense of failing to differentiate between the general and macro, on the one hand, and the particular and the micro on the other; the latter couplet is simply taken as an isomorphic expression of the former. The central consequence of this approach is to treat empirical cases as exemplary expressions of the master macro-general process—in Braverman's work the key processes that uniformly and evenly encompass work and worker in a spiraling descent of degradation. There is no serious attempt to be temporally or spatially comparative; historical variation, difference, contingency are of little interest because causality is understood to be transhistorically homogeneous and universal.

Braverman's treatment of the famous Lordstown strike of 1972 is paradigmatic. The text surrounding the discussion of Lordstown offers it as evidence of two distinct but disturbingly related trends: the unjustified focus on subjective conditions of work by most writers in the early 1970s; and the persistent application of modern principles of scientific management and its corresponding degradation of work and worker (Braverman 1974:33; 178–79). But more important, Lordstown also plays a subtextual role for Braverman. Minimization of worker subjectivity and homogenization of historical process allow him to either (1) mostly ignore events of worker struggle and their outcomes, or

(2) denude context and process by treating all such events as exemplars express-
ing the same transhistorical determinations and consequences of degradation.
Historical contingency is lost. Lordstown is simply the latest, well-known
instance of the universal, seamless unfolding of monopoly capitalism's degradationism at work.

We contrast major elements of the interpretive case method as it appears
in *LMC* with the general terms of an alternative—the extended case method—
in Table 7.2. The implications of our alternative theoretical grounding and
the principles of the extended case method (in Table 7.2) guide our subsequent reanalysis of the Lordstown strike. A closer look at Lordstown will permit us to highlight concretely those alternative theoretical foundations that
were discussed above in an abstract manner. In particular, the analysis will
show that the Lordstown event was not simply an expression of labor degradation; that was only one side of the story. When the twofold character of labor,
historical temporalities, multiple cultures of cooperation, and a field of social
movements are taken seriously in a comparative case approach, that event
looks quite different than it does through the lens of *LMC*.

THE LORDSTOWN GENERAL MOTORS STRIKE OF 1971–72

We concentrate on Lordstown for several basic reasons: (1) Braverman made
explicit reference to it in *LMC*; (2) it occurred during the years when
Braverman was writing *LMC*; (3) it took place in the auto industry—the "clas-
sicus locus" (as Braverman put it) of alienated, degraded labor processes; and
(4) it stands as one of the more notable strikes in post–World War II U.S.
labor history.

Our analysis begins by placing Lordstown in historically contextualized
time. After, presenting a brief narrative of the temporal sequence of major
actions that constituted the Lordstown event, we discuss several distinct but
interrelated cultures of cooperation that appeared in the struggle. Finally, we
compare key features of the Lordstown with another GMAD-initiated strike
and three wildcat strikes in older Detroit auto plants that occurred about the
same time. In all cases substantial degradation of work and worker is present;
in all cases, workers resisted in significant ways; yet the shapes and outcomes
of these auto-struggles varied in important ways.

Contextual Time: Lordstown in Historical Context

As the foundations of the postwar Fordist-Keynesian regime began to erode,
the general rate of profit began to slow about 1965 and by the late 1960s and

Table 7.2. Comparative Summary of Key Features of "Interpretive" and "Extended" Case Analytic Methods

Feature	Braverman's Interpretive Case Method	Extended Case Method
Mode of situation	Constitutes monopoly capitalist	Constitutes the social
Generalization	Society as the obverse of industrial modernization theory	Society as anomalous with regard to some preexisting theory, then reconstitutes that theory
Object of analysis	Macro-societal evolutionary process in which degradation is omnipresent and one-dimensional	Time–space event specific relations that shape domination, resistance, and differential outcomes of struggle
Explanation	Constructs deductively generic explanations	Constructs genetic explanations of particular outcomes
Comparison phenomena	Noncomparative in time/space	Focuses on similar and attempts to explain differences in time–space coordinates
Causality	Homogeneous anonymous general forces of monopoly capitalism	Multiplex and conjunctive involving indivisibility of elements that all tie a social situation (event) to its determinative context; historically specific causation
Empirical case significance	Derives from what it says about a population of similar cases	Derives from what it indicates about society
Totality	Expressive totality—cases are treated as exemplary instances	Historical uniqueness results from mutual determination of context and event process
Macro/micro	Reductionist—micro appears as expression of macro principles; the particular is folded into an expression of the general	Seeks to locate the macro foundations of micro by drawing on general economic arguments to understand how the micro event shapes and is shaped by macro processes

Table 7.2. Comparative Summary of Key Features of "Interpretive" and "Extended" Case Analytic Methods (continued)

Feature	Braverman's Interpretive Case Method	Extended Case Method
Social change	Eventual automatic breakdown in macro system structure	Centers the role of social movements

Source: Basic core elements of "interpretive" and "extended" case analytic approaches are adopted from Burawoy (1991).

early 1970s, it was dropping sharply. But the squeeze on profits was uneven across sectors of capital; losses in manufacturing dominated the general pattern (Van der Pijl 1984:278–80). One of the key pillars of the postwar Fordist growth surge was the dominance of U.S. capital in mass production consumer durable markets. Internationalization of Fordist markets began to undermine that position. Penetration by foreign auto capital into U.S. markets rose gradually from the late 1950s into the 1970s. By 1970, imports had captured almost 15 percent of the passenger car market (Rae 1984). Throughout the early 1960s, GM was able to maintain control over roughly one-half of the U.S. market. But that, too, started to fall off after 1965, plummeting to slightly under 40 percent of the market in 1970 (Zetka 1995a:Table 8.1). Earnings on investment were also becoming more volatile for all U.S. automakers throughout the 1960s. GM, for instance, went from an industry high of almost 26 percent return on equity in 1965 to 6.2 in 1970 (Zetka 1995a:Table 8.5).

Throughout the postwar Fordist-Keynesian years, U.S. auto producers competed for mass market volume through product differentiation, generating a frenzy of exaggerated designs and a constellation of options (Gartman, this volume). This marketing strategy—attempting to hyperdifferentiate a highly standardized product—had significant consequences for auto companies and their workers. For the companies it contributed to increasingly specialized engine, parts, and assembly plants; but since sales did not keep pace with increased product variety, the rising costs of tooling and technical layout for a growing number of specialized plants had to be spread over fewer cars. Consequently, unit production costs rose (Abernathy 1978). Declining productivity figures for the industry reflected this fact (Rothschild 1973; Katz 1985) despite the proliferation of "labor-saving" technological innovations; and because of the growing penetration of foreign capital into U.S. markets, these increased unit costs could not be so easily passed on to consumers. Marketing strategy contributed to the profit squeeze in the U.S. auto industry (Gartman this volume), but it was not the only cause.

The auto labor process bore the imprints of both the increasingly special-ized plant division of labor and the agreement made by the UAW in the "Treaty of Detroit" not to contest "labor-saving" technological innovations (Davis 1986). By 1959 the auto industry in general and GM in particular reor-ganized many plants based on type of labor process (Zetka 1995a). The strat-egy separated supplier production facilities (with more solidary and militant work groups) from final assembly plants (with their classically atomized work-ers pushed by the drive system). In short, this dual strategy produced a hege-monic regime in supplier plants and a despotic regime within final assembly, ostensibly designed to limit wildcats in the latter. Ironically, the product dif-ferentiation market strategy tended to produce cracks in final assembly despo-tism. The staggering array of assembly combinations and permutations trans-lated into a wide range of time and effort variations in work tasks. On one hand, this variability magnified uncertainty for management in the translation from abstract to concrete labor; on the other hand, it created an opportunity for workers to enlarge the pores in the working day as they expanded their capacity to contest speedups.

Lordstown was part of a larger wave of worker militancy between the mid-1960s and the mid-1970s that displayed a variety of interesting dimen-sions. In 1969–70, general strike activity hit a peak wave (Dubofsky 1995:128). Midcontract strikes grew rapidly after 1965, peaking at 758 in 1969 for manu-facturing sector; for all industries, the peak appeared in 1972, when nearly 2,000 midterm stoppages were registered (U.S. Bureau of Labor Statistics, various years). And there were no fewer than 50 local wildcat strikes within autos between 1965 and 1973 (Zetka 1995a:Table 2.1).

Militancy took forms other than authorized strikes or even recognizable wildcats. Workers flooded the grievance mechanisms. The grievance level at GM alone more than doubled between 1960 (106,000) and 1969 (256,000) (Weller 1974:2). For the industry, the grievance rate surged between 1970 and 1973, while the industry absenteeism rate continued to climb throughout the decade (Katz 1985:112). When militancy is gauged in a multidimensional manner—that is, the grievance rate, unresolved grievance rate, quit rate, unauthorized strike rate—auto worker militancy truly exploded between 1964 and 1973, then subsided in the 1974–75 recession (Norsworthy and Zabala 1985). Moreover, industrial worker militancy was not accidental or isolated militancy; rather, it was contextualized, enveloped, and nourished by a host of other insurgent movements that magnified its potential subversive capability. The captains of auto capital worked diligently to contain it.

GM, and to varying degrees the other auto companies as well, responded to the crisis in profit distribution, circulation relations, and labor process with a formidable arsenal of weapons. First, they fought on the terrain of *product line*, and did so in two ways. One was to compete in the subcompact market. To stem the tide of creeping internationalization, all U.S. producers came out with their own "subcompact": Ford "Maverick" and American Motors "Hornet" in 1969; the next year the Ford "Pinto," American Motors "Gremlin," and GM's Chevy Division's "Vega" (Rae 1984:127). The other product line strategy was designed to contain rising unit costs resulting from proliferation in model variations and options by rationalizing component modularity, extending the temporal length of model design, and reducing the number of parts comprising models (Weller 1974:3).

Second, they fought with *plant location.* During the 1960s corporations increasingly resorted to the spatial logistics strategy pioneered by General Electric during the 1950s (Davis 1986; Moody 1988). They attempted to decentralize production by geographically dispersing plants into "fresh" rural or semi-rural areas where the workforce might have less militant traditions. One of the keys, too, was the impact that these relatively isolated complexes would have on worker community-based solidarities as employees would commute, sometimes long distances, from small and large communities, reducing the level of co-worker contact away from the plant. As Moody (1988:100) put it, the hope was that "Workers in the new plants would be hundreds or thousands of miles away from the old centers of CIO strength and light years from the culture of its radical early years."

Third, automakers imposed *technical reorganization of production and the labor process.* Contrary to popular impressions, the final assembly plant operations were among the last major phases—within a long line of serialized production—to be extensively and intensively mechanized. Many still relied on relatively large quantities of direct labor (Abernathy 1978:26). Ford's Lorain, Ohio (Econoline) plant and GM's Lordstown complex were pioneers in minimizing direct labor in final assembly during the 1960s squeeze. For instance, at Lordstown when the redesign for Vega production was completed in 1970, it included eleven "Unimate" welding robots that performed 95 percent of the 3,900 body welds (Abernathy 1978:137). The revamped Lordstown Vega line also sported state-of-the-art "line balancing" and "product mix scheduling" that allowed different models and model variations to be produced on one line (Abernathy 1978:202).

Fourth, they deployed *specialized paramilitary management to administer and reorganize final assembly production facilities.* The General Motors Assembly Division (GMAD) was formed in 1965. During the late 1960s and early 1970s, GMAD took over eighteen assembly plants, leaving just four "home" plants in Detroit untouched (Weller 1974). The formation and operation of GMAD had been based on the belief that a specialized managerial unit wielding a "get tough" approach could boost GM's sagging productivity and profitability and, in the case of Lordstown, effectively compete with the Japanese and German producers in the subcompact market (Russo 1990:284).

GMAD established its "get tough" reputation by employing administrative takeovers, cutting the workforce, speeding up production lines, and imposing a "paramilitary approach to discipline" (Russo 1990:284). UAW International President Leonard Woodcock described the unit as "the roughest and toughest in GM" (Weller 1974:8). GMAD was hell-bent on a mission to impose a new managerial definition of a fair day's work within each plant, irrespective of any past customs, precedents, or contractual restrictions (Zetka 1995a). Shopfloor and plant particularities were to be leveled to a newly imposed general, abstract standard. GMAD's philosophy was the quintessence of Taylorized-Fordized conception of time and labor, and it wielded all of its formidable resources to accomplish those aims.[9]

When GMAD took over a plant, all previous agreements—formal and informal—were nullified. Typical practice would include: (1) elimination of dual plant managements (i.e., one for Fisher Body Plants and one for GM car assembly division, such as Chevrolet); (2) removal of dual UAW locals and dual contracts; (3) workforce reduction; and (4) overriding work agreements to produce a speedup (Weller 1974; Zetka 1995a). GMAD had their own version of "making out" (Burawoy 1979). A competition operated among the eighteen GMAD-administered assembly plants that centered on daily auditing of each plant's efficiency and quality via a centralized computer. GMAD officials' bonuses and promotions were tied to this internal competition, generating a pressure-cooker for home-plant management and workers (Herman 1975). Aiming to massively increase productivity while "downsizing" its workforce, GMAD cut total production workers by twenty-one thousand in the first quarter of 1972 alone (Weller 1974). In every plant taken over, labor–management conflict escalated to major proportions and the issues were almost always the same. The UAW/GM department reacted to GMAD-initiated speedups with major strike waves launched in 1969 and 1972 (Zetka 1995a). What was so special about Lordstown?

The Lordstown complex, located in the semi-rural countryside of the Ohio Mahoning Valley, extending over a mile along the Ohio Turnpike between Cleveland and Youngstown, was built in 1966 at a cost of over $100 million. It is a relatively remote location, removed from high-density working-class communities. Many workers lived in small towns or commuted long distances from larger cities (Garson 1984). At times, the facility employed more than thirteen thousand workers producing primarily Chevrolet Impalas until 1970. In the spring of that year, the facilities were renovated and retooled to build the Vega, GM's weapon against the small imports, with production targets set at four hundred thousand per year (Weller 1974). By 1970, the complex consisted of two separate GM plants—the Fisher Body Plant and the Chevrolet Division Plant assembling the Vegas and van trucks. Each was run by separate management teams; each had their own UAW locals with separate contracts: Local 1112 for the assembly workers and Local 1714 representing the body plant employees. The workforce at Lordstown was unusually young, with an average age of twenty-four, eighteen years below the national industry average (Russo 1990:283). Moreover, the workforce had the highest level of formal education of any GM assembly plants and was mostly male—only three hundred to five hundred women were employed on the production lines. Ten percent of the workforce were African-American, fifteen percent Puerto Rican; some were self-labeled "hippies," and some were Vietnam veterans, some were both (Terkel 1974). These workers were drawn from two different working-class stocks: (1) industrial urban youth from the surrounding areas, many of whom came from families and communities that were part of a long industrial tradition; and (2) migrant youth from rural West Virginia and Kentucky, mostly from families and communities of coal-mining tradition. Wages and benefits at Lordstown were highly competitive and plant jobs were considered among the best employment opportunities in the area. In mid-1972 the average wage rate was $4.56 per hour indexed to the cost-of-living. With overtime, some workers were making more than $13,000 per year. Fringe benefits also were among the best in the U.S. automobile industry (Aronowitz 1973). Despite favorable wages, a GM management offensive set the stage for a major showdown.

Event Time: The Lordstown Strike Sequence

To illuminate event time, we trace the sequence of the movement–countermovement actions among the key players at Lordstown: the rank-and-file workers; the UAW International, Local 1112, and GM/GMAD. This brief narrative highlights important phases, actions, and turning points that formed the internal dynamic of the strike.

GMAD Takes Over. In September 1971, the plan to move GMAD into Lordstown was announced, instantly sparking a wildcat stoppage at the Fisher Body facility (Herman 1975). On 1 October the GMAD entered the Lordstown complex and began an immediate restructuring. Major changes followed GMAD's modus operandi: (1) amalgamation of the two separate managements and local unions; (2) immediate layoff of 350 workers; (3) increased production line speed from approximately 60 to 102 cars per hour (almost twice the industry standard of 55); (4) the introduction of additional "Unimate" robotic welding machines; and (5) the negation of shopfloor plant agreements installed during a contract strike the previous year, resulting in harsher enforcement of new work rules and compulsory overtime. GMAD's restructuring history had produced a trail of strikes: since 1968–69, of the ten total GMAD reorganizations, including Lordstown, eight resulted in strikes. But it was Lordstown that had attained national notoriety. Even before the 1971–72 conflict Lordstown had gained the dubious distinction of being the fastest, most automated, "advanced" assembly line in the world. For production workers, GMAD's reorganization represented a clear speedup—there was more work for fewer workers and less flexibility in how that work was done. The stricter work rules and methods meant banning the practice of "doubling-up" and other forms of worker task self-organization that were protected by a local culture of agreements between workers and foremen. The new changes meant that each worker was now responsible for performing a single operation approximately eight hundred times daily.

Wildcat Warfare with GMAD. Workers responded to these initial changes in diverse ways representing multiple, flexible forms of militancy. In addition to general resistance of orders from foremen, workers frequently forced "slow downs" of the assembly line and used "working to rule" (carefully adhering to pre-GMAD production methods/standards) as typical resistance strategies. Absenteeism increased to comparatively high levels. Other forms of sabotage were used—product sabotage against automobiles and machinery with periodic eruption of outright in-house "wildcat strikes." GMAD's response to these layers of resistance was simply more of the same—active disciplining and discharging of workers, often furloughing workers without pay. In one instance, 1,400 workers were disciplined.

In the first weeks of December, GM laid off an additional 350 workers as part of its restructuring plan. By this time, the plant repair lot—with a two thousand vehicle capacity—was being filled on a daily basis with damaged or incomplete automobiles. With the repair lot overflowing with damaged cars, the assembly line was forced to stop production, and "short shifts" became a daily occurrence. Grievances had mounted to more than three thousand since GMAD entered Lordstown, most of which challenged the new work methods. National press coverage grew with reports of defective Vegas being returned to dealers.

Just before Christmas, GM sent a letter to all employees, blaming the dispute and its destructive effects on frequent acts of individual sabotage perpetuated by a few disgruntled and isolated workers—a sort of "few bad apples" spin on the situation. UAW Local 1112 quickly countered that the dispute was a result of the more than seven hundred layoffs and the sheer acceleration of the assembly line.

GMAD Softpeddles Its Offensive. Little changed over the next month until GM posted a notice warning workers of another increase in disciplinary actions and outright discharges. By that point the number of unsettled grievances exceeded five thousand, more than 20 percent specifically charged work procedures. GM was refusing "short shift" allowances, which meant that most workers were being compensated for an average of only seventeen hours per week. Local 1112 decided on formal action and the International eventually gave approval. The strike authorization vote was set for 1 February 1972.

On 24 and 25 January, the Lordstown plant experienced its first full days of production since December 1971. But that was not a signal of improving relations; one week later, the members of Local 1112 cast an almost unanimous vote in favor of a strike: an exceptionally high 85 percent of workers eligible voted 97 percent in favor of walking out. On 18 February, Local 1112 set a deadline: unless negotiations reconciled the dispute, the strike would begin on 3 March.

UAW Authorizes an Official Strike. Apart from these threats by Local 1112, nothing changed throughout the remainder of February. As promised, the strike began at 2:00 A.M. on 4 March, idling over 7,700 workers. The next day, despite pleas from both GM and the UAW, twenty-five picketers blocked all plant gates, refusing to allow five hundred nonstriking "white shirts" into the plant. Soon after, GM and the UAW began negotiations. Local 1112 was informed by the International leadership that strike benefits would not last long as a result of a bankrupted strike fund from the GM strike in 1970. On 6 March, negotiations produced a significant job-elimination resolution—most GMAD-eliminated jobs would be restored. For its part, Local 1112 agreed to drop approximately four thousand grievances; seniority rights and shift preference remained the primary issues to be resolved. After the UAW demanded a new contract, talks deadlocked and negotiations collapsed on the afternoon of 7 March. The next day negotiations resumed, and reports leaked that UAW threatened to shut down a fabricating plant by the end of the week, potentially idling an additional 2,200 workers.

Weeks passed with little national coverage. On 24 March the National Labor Relations Board (NLRB) regional office in Detroit filed unfair labor practice charges against GM, citing its negotiating methods. The day following the NLRB decision, GM and the UAW agreed to end the strike. Within two days and only hours after 30 percent of eligible Local 1112 members voted 70 percent in favor, the twenty-two-day official strike came to an end.

Balance Sheet. For workers, the settlement included reinstatement with back-pay for most of those laid off and the assembly line was restored to the pre-October 1971 pace. In exchange, Local 1112 withdrew over four thousand grievances. The struggle that extended from October 1971 into the spring of 1972 was a defensive action by the workers. In the aftermath of the strike, even Local 1112 President Gary Bryner admitted as much. But, as

Bryner later reflected, the strike gave workers "a measure of control," as it forced GM to honor the existing contract and, by doing so, it curbed the march of labor degradation at that time and place.[10]

Together the wildcat struggle and the authorized strike cost GM approximately $150 million in lost production. The question of longer-term losses (due primarily to publicity over inferior product quality and lingering worker militancy) is more difficult to estimate, but certainly more substantial. But, then too, the gains to workers were greater than the explicit terms of the strike settlement, for they had forged a solidary culture of cooperation in struggle.

Labor's Cultures of Cooperation: Management, Union, Sabotage. The battles at Lordstown were, in many ways, as old as the auto assembly lines, and the weapons with which capital fought were often ingenious, usually formidable. Yet for all their power, these organizational strategies could not remove equally ingenious worker militancy, although they certainly increased the level and changed its form. Instead of always relying on open strikes—whether authorized or not—Lordstown workers resorted to a wide variety of tactics, including covert sabotage actions.

The youthful Lordstown workers operated in a workplace culture that did have militant ties to past working-class generations, despite the efforts of GM plant logistics experts. But exposure to the militant culture produced in the concurrent wave of social movements was probably even a more significant politicizing force.[11] This wave of insurgent social movements (e.g., civil rights/Black Liberation, antiwar, student, feminist, consumer, environmental) coupled with relatively tight labor markets put workers in a more powerful position to resist workplace impositions and degraded working conditions. More significantly, there were signs of cross-movement convergence with potential for far more. At Lordstown it took the form of generalized radicalism and more specifically a convergence of auto worker control struggles with issues of product quality and rhetorics of the consumer movement. By countering with integrated concerns of product and worklife quality backed by a "producer ethic" (Moberg 1978; Garson 1984), workers resisted the imposition of work as deskilled mindless cogs wrapped in a "job ethic" that GMAD had planned for them. Actions and rhetorics emphasizing product quality were deployed as weapons against full-tilt mass production capitalism that valorizes quantity over quality.

The context of a growing wave of worker militancy did not go unnoticed. Both business management and business union leadership saw it as a major problem. Malcolm Denise, vice president of Labor Relations at Ford, spoke frankly about the matter when he addressed a group of Ford executives in November 1969. He indicated that UAW leadership had lost control of the rank-and-file and he knew why (quoted in Weller 1974:4):

The reason is a big influx of a new breed of union member—*a younger, more impatient, less homogeneous, more racially assertive and less manipulable member*—whose attitudes and desires admittedly are not easily read by a sixty-two year old labor leader. . . . As many of you are only too aware, the new workforce has had a costly and unsettling impact on our operations. *More money, time and effort than ever before must now be expended in recruiting and acclimatizing hourly employees*; quality control programs have been put to severe tests; large numbers of employees remain unmoved by all attempts to motivate them; and order in the plants is being maintained with rising difficulty. (emphasis added)

Denise knew what he was talking about. After only three months of guerrilla warfare with GMAD at Lordstown, GM estimated that they had suffered lost production of some twelve thousand Vegas and five thousand trucks at a cost of $50 million (Russo 1990); by the time the authorized strike ended, the losses would grow by another $100 million. The impact of labor militancy ("the bad attitudes of the new breed of worker") was even more staggering for the industry as a whole.[12]

Worker militancy that takes the form of wildcat tactics is often undertaken as much in protest against union leadership as against management (Fantasia 1988), and we examine examples of such wildcat strikes below. While worker dissent against the union certainly existed at Lordstown, the thrust of the rank-and-file action was not in open defiance of the union. Worker cooperation with management, on the other hand, was simply contradictory: workers cooperated and they did not. Certainly after GMAD arrived, they cooperated far less than before, illustrating that collective worker militancy is typically a partial product of management militancy (Fantasia 1988: 233). Worker cooperation with the union also appeared to be contradictory. The union itself, as a formal industrial relations entity, occupied a contradictory position: during the struggle it simultaneously *expressed* and *contained* worker militancy. The Local and International clearly understood the GMAD actions as a brutal speedup with accompanying contract violations, but the union also had to legally guarantee "management's right to manage." The dilemma was expressed, on one hand, by tremendous pressure (from GMAD and the International UAW) on Local 1112 to get control of the workers; on the other hand, the Local had to deal daily with and represent a solidary and militant rank-and-file that was in no mood to roll over for GMAD (Herman 1975).

Local 1112 took a complex, multifaceted stance toward militant tactics. It contained militancy in the form of public wildcat strikes as walkouts, openly urging in the most strenuous terms that workers avoid such action. At the same time, the local also openly directed a "normal pace" (or "working to rule") strategy—a form of sabotage against the illegitimate speedup; that is, workers were to follow the pre-GMAD pace even though line operations were being driven at the new (faster) pace. The concern for product quality was central to this approach by the workers. Finally, the union publicly disavowed (as legally it must), but tacitly allowed and supported more intermittent individual and small group forms of sabotage—that is, sabotage that restricts output and that deliberately degrades product and production equipment as it degrades the worker. Gary Bryner publicly claimed that the wildcat warfare against GMAD's offensive was due to rank-and-file initiatives, not the union's.

Such sabotage was important at Lordstown and, more generally, represents part of workers' collective voice. While sabotage can be delivered as an individual act, the saboteur must usually have indirect support or active cooperation of the work group if management's reprisals are to be thwarted. The efficacy of worker sabotage depends on the strength of both formal and informal work groups. It also is conditioned by tacit support from the union when it defends accused workers in confrontations with management (Zabala 1995).

At Lordstown, it was the militant rank-and-file tactics (in part) that pushed the UAW and GM to a settlement. The five months of guerrilla tactics and sabotage served as a form of extralegal, noninstitutionalized conflict that augmented and strengthened the formal institutionalized collective bargaining procedures set in motion by the authorized strike. It is equally important not to forget that the union presence produced the conditions that allowed the wildcat tactics to be wielded with some effectiveness for several months; the union's role was not that of a simple management tool for disciplining the rank-and-file. Such simple instrumental views represent "a facile and dangerous form of myopia" (Montgomery 1979:156). In sum, the important preconditions for effective worker sabotage in resisting degradation reside in a culture of cooperation among the rank-and-file and union to formally represent workers in disputes with management. Sabotage in the absence of these solidary conditions, however, can backfire, imposing high costs on insurgents (Zabala 1995).

MOVEMENTS IN THE SOCIAL FACTORY: DIFFERENTIAL SOURCES AND CONSEQUENCES OF LABOR DEGRADATION

Following the basic direction of the extended case approach, we can expand our understanding of the Lordstown strike by comparing it to several other significant auto industry struggles that took place about the same time. We aim to illuminate how local variations in the social organization of production, labor degradation, and social movement relations contributed to differential (not uniform) trajectories and outcomes of both intraclass and interclass struggles.

GMAD Strikes in Ohio

The first comparison with Lordstown focuses on the second most famous GMAD-provoked strike—the Norwood clash that followed on the heels of the Lordstown settlement in April 1972. While Lordstown received far more attention than any of the other GMAD strikes, Norwood was often mentioned too. Braverman (1974:179), for instance, refered briefly to characteristics of both strikes. Moreover, the Norwood strike is noteworthy if for no other reason than its length—174 days—marks it as the longest authorized local strike in U.S. auto industry history (Zetka 1995a:234).

We summarize several important characteristics of these two strikes in Table 7.3. Note that there are more similarities between these two strikes than differences. The precipitating event in both instances was the GMAD reorganizational offensives, and this incursion produced a host of virtually identical strike grievances. Important differences, however, most certainly account for the variability in strike outcomes—modest success (defending the pre-GMAD status quo) for Lordstown and failure at Norwood. The key distinction resided in the product market positional power that exclusive Vega production afforded the Lordstown workers. Due to the crucial role the Vega played in GM's strategic attempt to compete in the small-car market, both the company and the UAW International leadership were willing to negotiate a quick settlement. Also, International UAW officials emphasized that Local 1112 needed to settle quickly because the strike fund had been largely depleted by the UAW national strike in 1970.

The story at Norwood was different on the dimension of market power. That facility produced Fisher Bodies and assembled Camaros, Firebirds, and Novas. Although it was the exclusive production site for the Camaro and Firebird at the time of the strike, GM inventories were swollen with these models. Consequently, GM management refused to negotiate over the strike issues at Norwood,[13] preferring a strategy of allowing the UAW strike fund to pay workers while the company sold off the excess inventory. Unlike Lordstown, the union leadership did not urge quick settlement because of a small strike fund (Weller 1974); rather, "the UAW International did little but stand by and watch" (Zetka 1995a:234).

Zetka (1995a; 1995b) has demonstrated that the reorganized auto regime of 1959–73 tended to generate more authorized strikes while depressing the

Table 7.3. Comparison of the Two Most Famous GMAD-Provoked Strikes

Characteristic	*General Motors Lordstown Strike, 1972*	*General Motors Norwood Strike, 1972*
Precipitating events	GMAD offensive launched October 1971	GMAD offensive launched July 1971
Strike issues	Dehumanized work conditions Labor discipline and control speedup Respect for existing contract	Dehumanized work conditions Labor discipline and control speedup Call for new contract
Worker actions	Prestrike: in-house unauthorized wildcats and sabotage; authorized "normal pace" or "working to rule" strategy	Prestrike: signs of some work sabotage—excessive absenteeism on occasion, but not the same intensity as Lordstown
Significant workforce characteristics	Mostly white males; younger than most plants	Mostly white males
Local union leadership	Supported worker militancy Counseled against wildcat walkout Urged "normal pace" strategy Called authorized strike vote	Counseled against wildcats and eventually called for authorized strike vote
International union leadership	Eventually supported strike vote Urged quick settlement because of limited strike fund	Eventually supported strike vote Did not urge quick settlement
Social movement relations	Generalized movement militancy spillover—esp. Vietnam vets, also consumer movement dovetail; some IS and SWP members	Had a longer history of shop-floor militancy than Lordstown
Community	No substantial involvement	No substantial involvement
Plant type	Fisher Body & Chevy Assembly	Fisher Body & Chevy Assembly
Market power	Substantial: sole production site for Vega, the key weapon in the GM small car market	Little: sole production site for Camaros and Firebirds, but GM had large backstock of both

Table 7.3. Comparison of the Two Most Famous GMAD-Provoked Strikes (continued)

Characteristic	General Motors Lordstown Strike, 1972	General Motors Norwood Strike, 1972
Strike outcome	Authorized strike lasted twenty-two days; produced a rollback to pre-GMAD conditions	Authorized strike lasted 174 days; produced no major change for workers; total loss

Sources: Major sources cited in text plus news clipping files acquired from: Cleveland State University Library, Akron-Summit County Public Library, and Cincinnati Historical Society.

frequency of wildcats. But the form of wildcats also changed: rather than following an occupation- or department-based mobilization (as in the pre-1959 period), they were typically plantwide mobilizations supported and often led by UAW local leaderships. Solidary work groups were important in pushing local union officials to pursue grievance resolution outside institutional collective-bargaining channels. Although workers in the more atomized assembly labor processes were less likely to wildcat, those that did so often had greater market positional power. However, when GMAD launched its reorganizational offensives it tended to reverse part of this process by recoupling Fisher Body facilities (with more solidary work groups) and GM assembly divisions (with more atomized workers). In other words, any wildcat militancy muting advantage that GM might have gained by physically separating plant-based labor processes and administering differential labor relations policies, tended to be at least partially negated in the GMAD reorganizations of multiplant facilities. Lordstown and Norwood are good cases in point.

The Lordstown–Norwood contrast highlights several significant points. First, workers deployed two forms of guerrilla or covert sabotage tactics: (1) "working-to-rule" or "normal pace" strategy openly backed by Local 1112; and (2) more individually driven, clandestine sabotage against product and facility that happened within the solidary cover of fellow workers and Local 1112 but not under the union's open direction. Second, this sabotage activity shifted the quality and quantity of cooperation, which in turn altered the quality and quantity of Vegas coming off the line. Third, the role of circulation relations—product market positional power—served to condition labor-power by altering the efficacy of worker militancy. Fourth, the militant tactics contained an important temporal dimension. The timing of the in-house wildcat activities at Lordstown for several months prior to UAW strike authorization contributed to the company's sense of urgency for a settlement. The sequence of resistance tactics interacted with product market position, expanding workers' power at Lordstown. Fifth, the growing number of defective Vegas shipped to dealers and subsequently returned by consumers generated a news story that allowed both GMAD and the UAW to air their opinions. Irrespective of where public sentiment came down on the issue, it was bad press for GM Vega sales. Finally, the comparison suggests the importance of distinguishing the roles played by local and international union leadership in worker struggles as part of the political regime of production (Stepan-Norris and Zeitlin 1991).

Detroit Chrysler Wildcat Strikes

We can gain additional analytic leverage by expanding the comparative scope of auto industry strikes (remaining within the years when Braverman was writing *LMC*) to include explicit, open wildcat actions. In particular, during the summer of 1973 wildcats shook three Detroit Chrysler plants in rapid succession—the Jefferson Avenue, Forge, and Mack facilities. We draw on Heather Thompson's (1995) analysis of these cases, summarizing key features of each event in Table 7.4.

All three wildcats developed from years of racism encased in disinvestment-based deteriorating conditions in the older inner-city plants. Since the mid-1960s, the union had been losing credibility with most African-American and more left-oriented white workers. Although elements of speedup were present (especially in the Forge and Mack disputes), each event was also a battle over the degradation accompanying blatant company and union racism in the shops.

Strike location, conditions, and issues were all quite similar but outcomes did vary to some degree. The Jefferson Avenue wildcat took place on 24 July and succeeded in gaining the limited demands of the strike: firing of an extraordinarily racist foreman and amnesty for all wildcatters. The Forge and Mack strikes, on the other hand, were disasters. The Forge uprising started on 7 August and continued for six days, culminating in behind-the-scenes UAW fratricide, with company representatives teaming up to break the strike and punish the leaders. By contrast, the Mack strike met with the most crushing blow. The wildcat began on 14 August with workers sitting down on the production line. That first phase was broken with the assistance of the Detroit Police. The next day the wildcats set up pickets at the four plant gates. They were subsequently confronted by one thousand UAW officials, wielding bats and other weapons, who put a bloody stop to the worker insurgency.

The key to explaining the variability in outcomes across the three Detroit cases—moving from modest success, to the UAW-Chrysler clandestine fratricide, to the UAW openly and violently crushing the strike itself—appears to

Table 7.4. Detroit Chrysler Wildcats, Summer 1973

Characteristic	Jefferson Ave. Plant	Forge Plant	Mack Plant
Precipitating events	Racist altercation between foreman and worker	Accumulation of unsafe working conditions and racism	Long history of accidents, safety protests, and racism
Strike issues	Shopfloor racism	Speedup Poor safety Racism	Speedup Poor safety
Worker actions	Two African-American workers shut down line and demanded discharge of racist foreman; majority of workers supported wildcats	Third shift refused to work; wildcat lasted six days	Workers sat down on production line broken up by police; wildcat pickets the following day
Significant workforce characteristics	Predominantly African-American men	Predominantly African-American men	Predominantly African-American men
Local union leadership	Denounced and exerted pressure to end	Denounced and pressured to end	Denounced and pressured to end
International union	Denounced tactics and mobilized leadership	Denounced and blamed on outside radicals	Denounced, then one thousand officials to break wildcat picket with violence
Social movement relations	Multiracial UNC	Some multiracial remnants of FORUM	Multiracial UJC & WAM

Table 7.4. Detroit Chrysler Wildcats, Summer 1973 (continued)

Characteristic	Jefferson Ave. Plant	Forge Plant	Mack Plant
Community	None known	None known	Detroit PD called in
Plant type	Final assembly	Forge & cast parts	Stamping plant
Market power	Unclear	Substantial parts link	Unclear
Strike outcome	Foreman fired Wildcatter amnesty	UAW helped company break strike	Wildcat crushed by UAW violence; no safety issues resolved; many wildcatters fired

Sources: Thompson (1995); *Wall Street Journal*, 9, 10, August 1973.

be timing or sequential order. The UAW leadership was sending a message about wildcats, especially those involving racial militancy, and the strength of the message escalated with each successive event in July and August: the position of the strike in the sequence of summer wildcats at Chrysler corresponds to escalating UAW leadership fear, anger, and desperation to end wildcats of this kind "once and for all" (H. Thompson 1995).

Thompson's analysis also contrasts these Detroit Chrysler wildcats with the GM Lordstown strike. She argued that both the Lordstown and Detroit events were ignited by similar underlying issues of workplace control and degradation of conditions under which workers were expected to labor. Yet UAW leadership responded quite differently to Detroit and Lordstown cases. The mostly white male workforce at Lordstown spoke shopfloor protest language that was familiar to the UAW leaders. The Chrysler wildcats, on the other hand, followed closely on the heels of militant Black Nationalist movement uprisings in the Detroit auto plants—especially the League of Revolutionary Black Workers (see Geschwender 1977)—in the late 1960s. The language of struggle was much more militant and rooted in the Black Power movement. Erosion of union legitimacy, which grew out of shopfloor racism and inhumane (highly dangerous) working conditions, created the space for black dissidents to maneuver. Even after 1971, when the Revolutionary Union Movements (RUMs) had been largely repressed, worker dissent continued, becoming more multiracial in composition. By this point, according to Thompson (1995:208), "it was very difficult for these [UAW] leaders to look at rank-and-file dissent objectively, even that which continued to surface as a result of management's flagrant abuse of the contract, and the insensitivity to black worker civil rights in the Chrysler plants throughout the early-1970s." In the summer of 1973, most national UAW officials saw black workers' militancy, even in solidarity with white workers, as a disruptive and threatening presence (H. Thompson 1995).

The primary implication of Thompson's analysis points to the significance of the interaction of social movement militancy with the political leadership in a regime of production. More concretely, the shape of class struggle, the form of strikes and their outcomes, depended heavily on intraclass struggle shaped by (1) the type of worker militancy (here racialized culture of opposition) in relation to (2) union leadership that was inwardly conservative on racial matters, as a key feature of the political regime of production. At Lordstown the union had credibility; protest demands were cast in familiar, nonthreatening language; and the local and international union leaders backed the strike. At Detroit Chrysler, the union had lost credibility among most workers; protest demands were cast in a racialized militancy alien to the union leadership; and the local and international leadership vigorously opposed and actually helped crush the wildcats (H. Thompson 1995).

LORDSTOWN'S SIGNIFICANCE

So what lessons should we draw from Lordstown? The implication of *LMC*—constructed with one-dimensional conceptions of labor, time, worker culture, workplace—and the interpretive method used in dealing with the Lordstown case suggest that increasing application of scientific management design would virtually mute worker militancy and thoroughly eliminate any consequential impact of such a struggle. For Braverman, Lordstown, Norwood, and other struggles were *expressive* episodes in a dual sense: on the one hand, they expressed the principles of thorough degradation of work and worker that was the inevitable fate brought by the crushing force of the monopoly capitalist totality; on the other hand, these were expressive actions by workers, merely serving to vent pent-up anger and frustration but not to be taken seriously as sources of material change. Braverman treats empirical cases like he treats the working class—in a thoroughly subsumptive manner.

At one level, Lordstown was significant because of the extraordinary volume of press coverage it received. This is, in part, why the case shows up in *LMC*. But the coverage was not accidental or random. Our analysis suggests several key elements that converged to make Lordstown a noteworthy case. First, Lordstown happened on the cusp of a major transformation in U.S. regimes of capitalist accumulation—that is, conditions were changing for companies and workers in the transition out of the "Golden Age of Fordism." Second, it was deeply embedded in an upsurge of auto militancy that resulted from a profit-squeeze induced speedup and this militancy was further exacerbated as potential threat by its contextualization in a multiplex social movement wave. The significance of workforce age composition (youth), military status (Vietnam vets), counterculture appearance ("hippies") only makes sense against this movement backdrop. Third, the Lordstown complex had previously achieved notoriety for its high-tech status as the fastest auto assembly line in the world. The GMAD offensive promised to break that record. Fourth, Lordstown points to more than just the "blue-collar blues" of alienated workers popularized around the event. More important, it illustrated the broader moments of capital in the joint interplay of: (1) the profit-distribution process (in the profit squeeze on U.S. manufacturing in general and autos in particular); (2) circulation/market relations (the role of the Vega in GM small-car market strategy); and (3) labor process changes and struggles on the shop-floor (among GMAD, Local 1112 of UAW, and the rank-and-file). Finally, Lordstown had elements of worker victory attached to it. Only if the "acid test" for agency is exclusively the growth of revolutionary class consciousness and the overthrow of capitalism—as in Braverman (1974)—would one conclude that the auto workers at Lordstown (or Norwood, or Detroit) had no agency. But these event cases of worker struggles were most certainly structured in important ways. Our comparative analysis suggested several key local conditions shaped the outcome of these auto struggles at that time, namely, product market power, the character of worker militancy cultures, and the role of union leadership.

BEYOND BRAVERMAN AND LORDSTOWN

What are the broader implications of both our critique and case analysis for post-Braverman labor process theory? First, *the trajectory of labor process theory is underpinned by a fundamental bifurcation of the twofold character of labor in the commodity-form.* From Braverman's "structuralist logic of capital" to various left functionalisms (e.g., R. Edwards 1979; Burawoy 1979), the emphasis tended to be on how the social organization of work was always structured to be functional for capital with little apparent objection by workers. More recently, resistance theories (e.g., Fantasia 1988) and Post-Marxism of various stripes have turned to quests for subjectivity (Knights 1990; Willmott 1990) and new sources of agency outside the working class (e.g., Laclau and Mouffe 1985). This structure-to-agency trajectory has been accompanied by a corresponding shift from pessimism and despair to optimism and hope (Tanner, Davies, and O'Grady 1992). All these currents are interesting and emphasize important elements, but the fundamental problem that all share, in various ways, is the separation of subject/object, ideal/material, agency/structure. It was precisely because Marx had appreciated (at least since "The Theses on Feuerbach") the dilemma presented by this estrangement, that he was so excited by unraveling the secrets of the twofold character of labor in *Capital*. None of the major currents in post-Braverman labor process theory have adequately comprehended this point. To be sure, Braverman has been frequently criticized for ignoring class struggle. Typically this has meant that a certain amount of worker agency or resistance must be wedded to capitalist control. But the deeper issue has always been why control? Why resistance? (Cohen 1987). The twofold character of all social forms in capitalism "mediate people's relations with each other and with nature, and are, at once forms of being and consciousness" (Postone 1993:22). In other words, there is no separate sphere of structure or distinct area of active agency. Moreover, the twofold character of labor in the commodity-form posits the process of social structuring that ensures class struggle; that is, at root, class struggle is a driving force in capitalist society because human life activity—labor—is structured by and embedded in the twofold social forms of value, commodities, money, capital. This is the key to the central challenge facing labor process theory, as Tanner et al. (1992:440) put it: "How does one simultaneously demonstrate that the imperatives of capitalism require management to assume responsibility for the design of work and at the same time show that, against all odds, the working class has not lost its appetite for combating these measures?"

Second, *labor process theory has largely ignored the importance of time.* Labor process theory could benefit substantially by taking time more seriously. There are two distinct but interrelated avenues that could be profitably pursued: (1) important insights could be acquired by appropriating developments on temporalities from historical sociology (e.g., see Griffin 1992; Sewell 1996); and (2) further theoretical development of dialectical time embodied in the commodity-form of labor (see Postone 1993).

Third, *labor process studies would benefit by paying more attention to multiple bases of labor degradation and cultures of resistance in the process of intraclass struggles.* Degradation may not be rooted simply in a deskilling of work current that flows in a uniform, secular descent through time and space. Nevertheless, capitalism does generate plenty of worker degradation based in the terms of class, race, gender, and other oppressions that sometimes produce militant subjectivities with the potential to alter the terms of capitalist development. Contrary to Braverman, degradations of work and worker tend to generate a counter-response, set within and partially determined by the twofold character of labor. The particular shape and strength of that resistance, whether seen in class terms or not, will depend on cultures of resistance shaped in intraclass struggles, not on an immanent teleological subjectivity that posits the essential anticapitalist consciousness of workers (see Tanner et al. 1992).

Fourth, *labor process theory has been hampered by a privileged workplace reductionism.* Post-Braverman labor process theoretical developments have almost exclusively assumed a narrow conception of "the point of production." We have argued that the workplace should be seen as more socially extensive and have used the term "social factory" to emphasize that point. The narrow factory reductionist approaches to the labor process neglect: (1) the broader significance of labor processes throughout the society; (2) the possibility that social movements—born of oppressions throughout the social factory—can penetrate the shopfloor, shaping both the character of labor degradation and politics of both intra- and interclass struggle; and (3) the fact that there are multiple moments of capital in Capital—for example, circulation relations and profit-distribution processes—that can shape the terms of the labor process and worker power.

Finally, *capitalism does have an immanent historical dynamic.* Some have argued that criticisms leveled against Braverman for his neglect of worker consciousness and struggles are misplaced because that was not the level at which he was working; Braverman was mapping the broad trajectory of capitalist development (e.g., Harvey 1982:106–19). We disagree with the implicit separation in such a position. In fact, our central message is that degradations of labor, corresponding cultures of cooperative resistance, and a broader receptivity to social movements as working-class struggles can be framed within a Marxist critical theory that contains an immanent historical dynamic; and it can do so without adopting problematic teleological time (Braverman 1974), teleological working-class consciousness (Tanner et al. 1992), or resorting to an amorphous pluralistic retreat from class (Laclau and Mouffe 1985). The global immanent historical dynamic of capitalism is the "productivity treadmill" that repeatedly transforms and reconstitutes the conditions and meanings of labor and time (Postone 1993:287–91). That dynamic is rooted in the commodity-form's twofold character of labor in which the level of "productivity" entails class struggle (e.g., over the *conditions, intensity, duration of labor*). These terms are central to understanding the Lordstown, Norwood, Detroit cases and, of course, numerous other struggles throughout the twentieth-century social factory.

NOTES

1. Most citations for Braverman are to *Labor and Monopoly Capital*; therefore, only page numbers will be given when necessary. The only other source used will be designated Braverman (1976).

2. See, for example, Jacoby (1985), Aronowitz (1978), Burawoy (1978), Clawson (1980), Meiksins (1984), Gartman (1986); and larger reviews in P. Thompson (1989), and Knights and Willmott (1990).

3. Braverman made explicit his principle of potentiality in an exchange after the publication of *LMC*: "I have every confidence in the revolutionary potential of the working classes of the so-called developed capitalist countries. Capitalism will not, over the long run, leave any choice to these classes, but will force upon them the fulfillment of the task which they alone can perform. This presupposes an enormous intensification of the pressures which have only just begun to bear upon the working class, but I think there is no question that it will happen. I have long tended to agree with those who think it will still be a long time in coming" (Braverman 1976:124).

4. On varieties of resistance forms in different settings, see: Genovese (1976) on subtle forms of slave resistance in the antebellum U.S. South; Van Raaphorst (1988) on forms of resistance among highly atomized domestic service workers in the late nineteenth and early twentieth centuries; Gartman (1986:Chapter 8) on resistance tactics in the early automobile industry; and Kelley (1994) on African-American working-class cultures of resistance.

5. For example, the IWW developed an "oppositional subculture" that was based on premises radically different from those of "institutionalized collective bargaining" (Davis 1975:88). And it was a rich culture including: the "sab-cat" and the "wooden shoe" as countersymbols to the Taylorist stopwatch

(Davis 1975), among many others (see Miles 1986; Salerno 1989); the sit-down strike, perhaps used first by Wobblies at a GE plant in 1916 (Miles 1986), was later to become a tactical weapon of choice under some circumstances, especially during the 1930s; and sabotage in the general sense was (and is) an integral part of the working-class "grieviculture" (Davis 1975:91).

6. In 1912, Frank Bohn, charter member of the IWW, explained *sabotage* in the following way: "Sabotage means 'strike and stay in the shop.'" Striking workers thus are enabled to draw pay and keep out scabs while fighting capitalists. Sabotage does not necessarily mean destruction of machinery or other property, although that method has always been indulged in and will continue to be used as long as there is a class struggle. More often it is used to advantage in a quieter way. Excessive limitation of output is sabotage. So is any obstruction of the regular conduct of the industry" (quoted in Kornbluh 1964:52–53). For more contemporary treatments of sabotage at work as class struggle, see: Montgomery's (1979:155-56) discussion of "communication-by-sabotage"; Jermier's (1988) assessment of the general rationality of sabotage in organizations; and Zabala's (1995) analysis of cases of worker sabotage in an auto plant.

7. In fact, terms of the U.S. post–World War II regime of accumulation were based on certain conditions of segregation and exclusivity in gender and race that had much to do with the movements that contributed to its demise (e.g., see Moody 1988).

8. See Burawoy (1991) for a more detailed discussion of this and several other case analytic methods—ethnomethodology, grounded theory, and the extended case method.

9. An example of the minute concern over tightening the pores of the working day was reported in the *Cleveland Plain Dealer* (23 January 1972): "GM calculated that if each worker at Lordstown worked one-half of a second more each hour, the Company would save one million dollars a year."

10. The first statement by Bryner in 1972 comes from Herman (1975:63): "When you look at it realistically, we set out to change nothing in the strike. We said, let's return to the condition of October '71, and we'll wait until 1973 to negotiate about all the other issues." The second point comes from a 1991 interview with Bryner cited in Asher and Edsforth (1995:36).

11. As Russo (1990:283) suggests: "The auto workers at Lordstown . . . were not isolated from the culture, values, and political turmoil of the 1960s. . . . The media, especially television, had further educated and exposed these and other workers to the social and cultural attitudes of the 1960s—attitudes characterized by a lack of automatic acceptance of authority. . . . Workers who had college experience . . . had been exposed to the antiwar movement and were often cynical and distrustful of hierarchy. The attitudes of the Vietnam veterans were even more militant."

12. For example, Norsworthy and Zabala (1985) estimated the effects of worker militancy on productivity and production costs in the auto industry for the period 1958 to 1980. Their evidence indicates that, on average for the years 1971–76, an annual 10 percent "improvement" in worker behavior (i.e., from management's point of view: reduction in overall militancy as gauged by grievances, unresolved grievances, quits, unauthorized strikes) resulted in a 3 percent to 5 percent decrease in unit production costs. For those same years, such an "improvement" would have yielded aggregate "savings" in the range of $2.2 billion to $5 billion! Although capital's drive for surplus value leads to calculations premised on abstract labor, there is no simple "technical" formula that determines or predicts whether Lordstown's line speed yields 40, 80, or 120 Vegas per hour. The pace at which labor-power is consumed, materialized as GM Vegas for instance, signifies the relative balance of power between collective parties as they confront each other on the line each day (Montgomery 1979).

13. "Unlike the Lordstown walkout, where there was an outcry from management of Chevrolet to settle quickly because the Vega was losing ground to the Ford Pinto, there was little pressure from within the company on the Norwood negotiations" (*New York Times*, 26 September 1972, p. A20).

8

Gender, Occupational Sex Segregation, and the Labor Process

JAMES A. GESCHWENDER
WITH THE ASSISTANCE OF LAURA E. GESCHWENDER

This chapter analyzes occupational sex segregation as a vehicle to aid our understanding of the relation between gender and earnings for persons employed full-time for the full year. The fact that women earn less than men has long been a subject of scholarly investigation. Attempts to explain gender differences in earnings have ranged widely from those who interpret gender inequality as the result of choices made by women, to others who focus upon patriarchal structures, to some who see it as a by-product of class struggle, to others who attribute it to capitalist oppression. It appears that all proposed explanations include occupational sex segregation as one of the central factors creating and maintaining gender earnings inequality, supporting Reskin's (1993) suggestion that the gendered occupational structure should constitute a central focus of any attempt to analyze gender earnings inequality. We in this chapter attempt to explore the origin of occupational sex segregation, its relation to the capitalist labor process, and the manner in which each impacts upon gender earnings inequality.

Reskin and Roos (1990) argued that the origin of occupational sex segregation can be seen in the interaction between employers' ranking of potential workers and workers' ranking of potential jobs. They state that, all other things being equal, employers exhibit a strong preference for white (Euro-American) male workers, will hire them if possible, and will set wage scales in such a manner that economic returns to human capital associated with any occupation will be positively associated with the proportion of workers in that occupation that are Euro-American males. Their analysis implicitly is based upon assumptions regarding sexist and racist beliefs held by employers, but their logic is not that far removed from the work of Braverman (1974), which returned the social organization of the capitalist labor process to the forefront of people's attention and revitalized a serious debate over the relation of capitalism to gender and racial or ethnic inequality.

Reskin and Roos focused their analytic attention on the social division of labor while Braverman focused his more on the technical division of labor. Nevertheless, both agree on the three following propositions. Occupations tend, to varying degrees, to be segregated by gender and by race or ethnicity. Earnings vary by gender and race or ethnicity. It is, therefore, logical to assume that a relationship exists between observed earning differentials and existing patterns of occupational segregation. This set of propositions constitutes the starting point of our analysis. We wish to explore the extent of the association between occupational sex segregation and earnings and attempt to ascertain the basis for any earnings differentials which it does not explain. We also wish to ascertain whether the technical division of labor is the sole or primary determinant of occupational sex segregation, whether the social division of labor is the primary cause, or whether we have to look toward some combination thereof.

THE LABOR PROCESS AND
GENDER EARNINGS INEQUALITY

Braverman's (1974) pathbreaking work rekindled an interest in research on the labor process. This work attracted uncritical raves, unremitting criticism, and a certain amount of balanced critical analysis. The latter has been valuable since it pointed to gaps in the analysis and simultaneously suggested improvements. We hope that this chapter will fall into the latter category. We will not attempt to cover all aspects of Braverman's analysis of the labor process but will particularly consider those portions relating to the interaction between the technical and social divisions of labor—especially the implications that this interaction has for the analysis of gender in the workplace. We explore racial/ethnic identity only to the extent that it interacts with gender in shaping various aspects of the work situation.

Fragmentation, deskilling, and the degradation of work are key ingredients in Braverman's analysis. He assumed that the systematic subdivision of work is a central aspect of production under capitalism. The need for skilled labor is diminished and the power of craftworkers undermined by the systematic breakdown of work into its constituent parts. Craft organizations are destroyed and higher-priced skilled workers are replaced by lower-priced lesser skilled workers. This process often involves the replacement of Euro-

American men with women and minority workers. The processes of fragmentation, deskilling, and degradation of work are accompanied by the contraction of sectors of work that typically employ men (especially majority men) and the expanding sectors typically employing women and minorities. Thus, the transformation of the capitalist labor process results in a diminished role and lower earnings for men along with an expanded role played by women without any necessary increase in their earnings capacity. The earnings of women and minority workers still tend to be lower than men's, even with the diminished earnings of the latter.

One of the earliest feminist critiques of Braverman came from Baxandall, Ewen, and Gordon (1976), who argued that Braverman's analysis was flawed because he failed to take into account the extent to which the capitalist labor process was embedded in, and partially shaped by, larger societal processes — most notably, patriarchy. There were two aspects to their criticism. First, they claimed that the focus on wage labor failed to incorporate the gendered relation between waged and unwaged labor and the central role that this relation played in the process of capital accumulation. Weinbaum and Bridges (1976) made a parallel argument in asserting that an exclusive focus on the labor process ignores the extent to which capital structures a conflict between women in their role as consumers and men and women in their role as workers. Reproduction of people takes place in the household and women are forced to become consumption experts in their effort to make the paycheck go as far as possible. In addition, capital continually restructures the social organization of the work process to shift as much of the labor as possible away from waged workers and onto the shoulders of women as consumers.

But this was not the sum of the criticism launched by Baxandall, Ewen, and Gordon. They further argued that even Braverman's analysis of the social organization of waged labor as such was flawed by his failure to take patriarchy into account. Women are channeled into a specific set of occupations because of a gendered set of expectations that derive from the manner in which gender is constructed in the larger society. The net consequence of this channeling is the construction of a labor force segregated by sex.[1] P. Thompson (1989: 180–209) provides a selected summary of empirical evidence supporting this line of analysis (see also Bradley 1986). While Baxandall, Ewen, and Gordon do not explore this issue, one of the consequences of this process of occupational sex segregation is a wage scale in which women are compensated at a lower level than men. One could interpret this gendered wage scale as resulting from capital's drive to maximize profits, working-class efforts to strengthen its bargaining power vis-à-vis capital, or attempts by men to maintain patriarchal privilege (see Geschwender 1992, for an attempted integration of these arguments). Geschwender argues for a class struggle interpretation which asserts that male workers organize to pursue their common class interests but that they do so in the context of a patriarchal society and, consequently, they opt for patriarchal solutions to class problems (on this point, see also Cockburn 1981 and Philips and Taylor 1980). Women's interests are sacrificed by men in the pursuit of shared class interests. It may well be the case that this sacrifice will prove to be far more expensive to the working class as a whole than anyone could ever anticipate, but that is the subject of a different essay.

No clear consensus exists as to the causes of occupational sex segregation but, regardless of theoretical interpretation, a direct relation between occupational sex segregation and gender differences in earnings is generally assumed. The principles embedded in Braverman's analysis of the capitalist labor process suggest that majority group male workers will be more highly concentrated in more skilled and better paid occupations while female and minority workers will be more highly concentrated in less skilled and more poorly paid occupations. We are not herein concerned with whether these "skill differences" are "real" or merely "socially constructed"—that is, illusionary (see West 1990 for a discussion of the literature on this topic) since either way, the impact would be the same. A second possibility is that both occupational sex segregation and higher earnings for men are the logical outgrowth of men having organized to protect their shared gender interests. In direct opposition to that perspective, one might argue that both result from capital deliberately manipulating race, ethnicity, and gender in order to divide the working class. Whichever of these theoretical perspectives is preferred, the implication logically follows that predominantly male occupations will be compensated at a higher level than predominantly female occupations and that there will be an earnings gradient between the polar types. However, we are not convinced that the empirical situation is that clear-cut.

This chapter begins with a review of what we know about the relation between occupational sex segregation and gender earnings inequality, evaluates the methodology used in the research on this subject, proposes an alternate approach to the measurement of occupational sex segregation, and examines the objective situation using 1980 and 1990 U.S. census data. This will enable us to assess both the actual situation and changes during the decade. This analysis hopefully will shed light on the relation between the technical and social divisions of labor. We include within our analysis the interaction between gender and race/ethnicity but we will not attempt to analyze all of the consequences of racial/ethnic variation because we believe that this would make our presentation too complex and would distract attention from the main thrust of our analysis. This chapter concludes with an exploration of the theoretical implications of our findings.

OCCUPATIONAL SEX SEGREGATION
AND EARNINGS INEQUALITY

Researchers have not always produced consistent findings but a moderate decline in the extent of occupational sex segregation seems apparent, though the rate of change appears to be somewhat snail-paced, and occupational sex segregation remains at a fairly high level. Albeda (1986) found relatively small changes in occupational sex segregation between 1958 and 1981, and King (1992) concluded that it remained relatively constant from 1940 to 1988. Carlson (1992) found that occupational sex segregation declined significantly during the 1960s and 1970s but that the rate of change slowed substantially thereafter. She concluded that more real progress has been made in reducing occupational segregation than indicated by the measures which yield lower values due to the number of new female entrants into the labor force. Jacobs (1989) estimated the index of segregation across detailed occupational categories to be about 68 between 1910 and 1970 but then dropped to about 60 in 1980. Cotter et al. (1994) found a 6.4 percent decline in occupational sex segregation during the 1980s. Reskin and Cassirer (1994) determined the index of segregation to be 53 for detailed occupations in 1990. It appears that, at a minimum, more than half of all employed men and women would have to change detailed occupational categories if men and women are to be similarly distributed across occupations.

This differential distribution of males and females across occupations contributes to the gender gap in earnings, estimated to be 69.9 percent in 1991 (Institute for Women's Policy Research 1993). Jacobs (1989) calculated that 25 percent of the gender gap in wages is attributable to the sex segregation of occupations. His estimate is slightly lower than Treiman and Hartmann's (1981) determination that 30 percent to 45 percent of the pay gap stems from occupational segregation. It is highly probable that additional segregation at the level of the firm and the job accounts for an additional portion of the observed wage gap (Baron and Bielby 1985; see also the summary of literature in Kilbourne, England, and Beron 1994:1151). Cotter et al. (1994) found that decreases in occupational sex segregation account for approximately 28 percent of the reduction in gender earnings inequality that took place between 1980 and 1990.

But, it is important to note that occupational sex segregation is not the whole story so far as gender inequality in earnings is concerned. Reskin and Padavic (1994) found that in most occupations women earn between 70 percent and 85 percent of what men earn. Kilbourne, England, and Beron (1994: 1151) summarized literature that argues that women receive lower rates of return to human capital. They also suggested that some characteristics of occupations held by women (e.g., nurturing) are associated with lesser rates of pay as are the secondary industries in which they are located and the fact that they tend to have less job experience (see also England et al. 1994). Kilbourne, England, Farkas, et al. (1994) concluded that occupational sex segregation explains between 5 percent and 12 percent of the gender gap in earnings while gender differences in work experience explains between 21 percent and 24 percent. O'Neill and Polacheck (1993:218) found that the closing of the gender gap in work experience accounts for 26.7 percent of the reduction in gender earnings inequality that took place during the 1980s. Some recent research suggests that the gender gap in pay may not be the same in male-dominated occupations as in female-dominated occupations. Reskin and Padavic (1994) summarized data produced by the U.S. Bureau of Labor Statistics (1991; 1992; 1993) that demonstrate that men outearn women to a lesser extent in predominantly female occupations than in other occupations. Earnings by gender are also more similar in lower-paying occupations (Reskin and Padavic 1994:107–9).

There is little question that occupational sex segregation is a major contributor to gender earnings inequality, but the relationship may not be as straightforward as commonly thought. The prevailing research-based opinion suggests a positive linear relationship between earnings and the proportion of male workers in an occupation (Baron and Newman 1990; Bridges and Nelson 1989; England et al. 1988; Jacobs and Steinberg 1990; Parcel 1989; Sorensen 1989a; 1989b). Increases in the proportion of female workers in an occupation usually are associated with decreased earnings. Some research (see Reskin and Roos, 1990) has attempted to explore whether the earnings decline precedes or follows gender desegregation but the existence of the association is not questioned.

There has been little research testing the possibility that the techniques used to measure occupational sex segregation help to shape the findings. Much of the previous research treats occupational sex segregation as a continuous variable by ranking individual occupations according to the percentage of females employed in that occupation. The index of dissimilarity, or a size standardized version thereof, is then used to determine the proportion of persons of one sex that would be required to change occupations in order to equalize gender distributions (see, for example, Jacobs 1989). The percent female in a given occupation is frequently related to other variables such as level of earnings or gender earnings inequality (see, for example, Abrahamson and Sigleman 1987 or Petersen and Morgan 1995). It may be the case that this is the best operational measure of occupational sex segregation but that is yet to be determined. The use of the measure without more substantive research has the defect of assuming what should be tested. The application of regression analysis to data sets measuring occupational sex segregation as a continuous variable produces results that tend to appear linear. It is difficult to detect a curvilinear relation, should one exist (for an exception, see Cotter et al. 1994).

A few researchers have used a categorical measure based upon the percent female in the total labor force but with little consistency in the categories constructed. Jacobs and Steinberg (1990) defined heavily white male occupations as those having 90 percent more white males in them and heavily female occupations as ones with 67.2 percent or more females. Peterson (1989) used 80 percent to 100 percent female as female occupations and zero percent to 30 percent female as male occupations with the rest being mixed. The norm has been to use three categories with "mixed occupations" being defined as a band of some specified percent on either side of the percent female in the total labor force with occupations having greater or lesser percent female workers labeled, respectively, as "female" or "male" occupations. Three categories might be too few to reveal a curvilinear relation. Further, some of the choices of cutting points between occupational categories result in labeling an occupation as mixed when substantially more than half of those working in it are male and labeling an occupation as female when almost 50 percent of the workforce in it are male. Besides being esthetically displeasing, that set of definitions may lead to misleading interpretations.

Gender appears to interact with race and ethnicity in determining earnings. Geschwender and Geschwender (1994) demonstrated that women from different ethnic groups differ significantly in their rates of labor force participation, in the types of jobs that they get, and in the level of compensation that they receive. The size of the gender gap in pay varies across ethnic groups. The earnings ratio between women and men is about 82 percent for African-Americans, 81 percent for Hispanic-Americans, and 69 percent for Euro-Americans (U.S. Bureau of the Census 1992b). A greater degree of earnings equality exists between minority women and men than between Euro-American women and men, in part, because minority men earn less than Euro-American men. For example, African-American men earn 75 percent of Euro-American men and Hispanic-American men earn less than 66 percent of what Euro-American men earn (Reskin and Padavic 1994:104–5).

The interactions among gender, race, and ethnicity have not been fully explored by research in this area. Indeed, there is reason to believe that sex segregation is more severe and long-lasting than racial segregation. Albeda (1986) found between 1958 and 1981 only small changes in occupational sex segregation but substantial decreases in racial segregation. She also found a trend toward convergence in the occupational distribution of Euro-American and minority women. Tomaskovic-Devey (1993) found that for a sample of North Carolina workers, the index of dissimilarity was 55 across race groups but 77 across sex categories. King (1992:33) found substantial declines in occupational segregation by race during the 1960s but that sex segregation remained relatively constant between 1940 and 1988. It also appears that the combination of race and gender exerts an effect different from either separately, as suggested by the fact that dissimilarity indexes are highest between African-American men and Euro-American women and between Euro-American men and African-American women. Bernhardt, Morris, and Handcock (1995) found that the gender earnings gap was closing between 1967 and 1987 but that it was closing much more rapidly for African-American women than for Euro-American women. Carlson (1992) concluded on the basis of her research that it was impossible to draw meaningful conclusions about gender or racial inequality when examined separately inasmuch as the two were inextricably linked.

Reskin (1994) has provided a more detailed analysis of how sex and race influence the allocation of jobs. Like other research, she also documented the fact that sex segregation occurs to a greater extent than race segregation but perhaps more striking is her finding of a lower degree of ethnic segregation among women than among men. Importantly, Reskin's research demonstrates that sex and ethnicity operate in tandem to affect job allocation. This research attempts to assess the impact of the interaction between gender and race/ethnicity upon occupational sex segregation and earnings, but it will not explore the extent of variation among racial/ethnic groups.

METHODOLOGY

Our analysis is conducted with data taken from the 1980 and 1990 U.S. Public Use Census tapes. We created a large population sample for each year by combining data found on the one percent sample (PUMS) tapes for each of fifty states and the District of Columbia. Our analysis is limited to persons, twenty-five to sixty-four years of age, working for salary or wages, employed full-time (thirty-five or more hours per week) for the full year (forty-eight or more weeks). The inclusion of persons employed either part-time or for less than the full year would have yielded some interesting information, but it would have confused the issue with respect to the direct impact of sex segregation upon earnings. We use twenty-five as our lower age limit because most people have concluded their education by then. We use sixty-four as our upper age limit because a large number of people have begun to reduce their work commitment or have dropped completely out of the labor force by this age.

We use a categorical measure of sex (gender) composition of occupations because we consider it likely that the relation between earnings and gender (sex) composition may not be linear. We use 100 percent census data on the sex composition of detailed occupations for the construction of five categories of sex-segregated occupations: heavily male (0 percent to 24.9 percent female);

moderately male (25 percent to 39.9 percent female); mixed (40 percent to 59.9 percent female); moderately female (60 percent to 74.9 percent female); and heavily female (75 percent to 100 percent female).

Census occupational codes are used to group occupations into nine classifications having a rough correlation to status groupings: Executive, Administrative, and Managerial Occupations; Professional Specialty Occupations; Technicians and Related Support Occupations; Sales Occupations; Administrative Support Occupations; Service Occupations; Farming, Forestry, and Fishing Occupations; Precision Production, Craft, and Repair Occupations; and Operators, Fabricators, and Laborers Occupations. The occupational codes changed very little between 1980 and 1990. One 1980 occupational code was made into three for the 1990 census and ten 1980 occupational codes were collapsed into five in 1990. We recoded 1990 occupations to correspond to 1980 occupational codes for comparative purposes. We used 502 detailed occupations for 1990 but the recoding required to make 1980 and 1990 categories comparable reduced this to 497 detailed occupations.

Age is measured in years. Wage and salary income is measured in dollars. Native-born Americans are the comparative referent when we control for immigration status. When analyzing the 1990 census data, immigrants are classified into those arriving prior to 1970, between 1970 and 1984, and between 1985 and 1990. The corresponding time periods used for the 1980 census data are prior to 1970, between 1970 and 1974, and between 1975 and 1980. High school graduates with no additional formal education serve as our comparative referent when education is controlled. All others are classified into persons dropping out of school prior to the completion of high school, persons with some formal education beyond completion of high school but short of acquiring a bachelor's degree, a bachelor's degree as the highest earned degree, and possession of an advanced degree beyond the bachelor's. Regional location is controlled with the use of nine census regions (the Northeast is used as the comparative referent) but, except for controlling for the impact of region, little attention is paid to region in our analysis. Our discussion of findings will generally be based on mean incomes but deviations between mean and median incomes will be noted.

Race/ethnicity is measured using self-identification data. The category used as a comparative referent is Euro-Americans (non-Hispanic whites). African-Americans are non-Hispanic Blacks. Native Americans include American Indians, Eskimo, and Aleut. All Hispanics are classified as Mexican-Americans, Puerto Ricans, Cuban-Americans, or Other-Americans. Asian-Americans are identified as Chinese-Americans, Filipino-Americans, Japanese-Americans, Asian Indian-Americans, Korean-Americans, or Other-Americans. Consequently, the category of Other-Americans is a mixed bag, including some Hispanic-Americans, Asian-Americans, and Pacific Islanders.

Table 8.1. Occupational Sex Segregation by Gender: 1980 and 1990

			Percent of Workers in Occupational Category				
Year	Gender Category	All	Heavily Male	Moderately Male	Equally Mixed	Moderately Female	Heavily Female
1980	Men	302,528	59.9	22.6	10.4	3.1	3.9
	Women	162,686	9.7	15.8	16.2	9.3	49.0
	Total	465,214	42.4	20.3	12.4	5.3	19.7
1990	Men	357,679	50.2	26.8	13.7	5.2	4.2
	Women	241,897	7.5	17.8	18.3	14.0	42.4
	Total	599,576	33.0	23.2	15.6	8.7	19.6

FINDINGS

Table 8.1 presents by sex the 1980 and 1990 distributions of full-time workers into occupations categorized in terms of sex composition. The decade was characterized by a small but meaningful reduction in the extent of occupational sex segregation. The most noticeable change was a 9.4 percent decrease in the proportion of workers in heavily male occupations. There was a very slight decrease (0.1 percent) in heavily female occupations and small increases (between 2.9 percent and 3.4 percent) in each of the other categories. The proportion of males working in heavily male occupations decreased by 9.7 percent and the proportion in all other categories increased by between 0.3 percent and 4.2 percent. The proportion of females working in both heavily female and heavily male occupations decreased (by 6.6 percent and 2.2 percent, respectively) while the proportion in all other categories increased by between 2.0 percent and 4.7 percent.

Table 8.2 presents mean and median earnings for 1980 and 1990 by gender and by occupations categorized in terms of degree of sex segregation. The relation between the sex composition of an occupation and earnings is not linear in either year. Workers in heavily female occupations earned the least of all categories. Mean earnings successively increase as we move through moderately female, mixed, and moderately male occupations but earnings in heavily male occupations fall between those in moderately male and mixed occupations. In 1980 they were closer to the former, while in 1990 they are closer to the latter. Both men's and women's earnings exhibit the same pattern of increases with movement from heavily female occupations through moderately male occupations but earnings in heavily male occupations vary by gender and year. Mean earnings for women in heavily male occupations fell between those in mixed and moderately male occupations in 1980 but were even higher than those in

Table 8.2. Mean and Median Earnings by Gender and Occupational Sex Segregation: 1980 and 1990

Year	Workers		All	Heavily Male	Moderately Male	Mixed Occupations	Moderately Female	Heavily Female
1980	All	Number	465,214	197,124	94,057	57,889	24,453	91,691
		Mean	$ 16,592	$ 18,371	$ 20,072	$ 15,339	$ 12,827	$ 10,995
		Median	$ 14,848	$ 17,152	$ 17,920	$ 13,824	$ 11,776	$ 9,984
	Men	Number	302,252	181,338	68,345	31,567	9,362	11,916
		Mean	$ 19,463	$ 18,879	$ 22,670	$ 18,398	$ 16,397	$ 15,189
		Median	$ 17,920	$ 17,920	$ 19,968	$ 17,152	$ 15,104	$ 13,824
	Women	Number	162,686	15,786	25,712	26,322	15,091	79,775
		Mean	$ 11,253	$ 12,258	$ 13,166	$ 11,669	$ 10,612	$ 10,369
		Median	$ 9,984	$ 10,752	$ 11,776	$ 10,752	$ 9,984	$ 9,984
	Gender Ratio	Mean	57.8	64.9	58.1	63.4	64.7	68.3
		Median	55.7	60.0	59.0	62.7	66.1	72.2
1990	All	Number	599,576	197,579	138,932	93,290	52,307	117,468
		Mean	$ 28,863	$ 30,528	$ 35,011	$ 29,778	$ 23,737	$ 20,349
		Median	$ 24,320	$ 26,880	$ 28,160	$ 24,832	$ 20,992	$ 17,920
	Men	Number	357,679	179,445	95,856	48,915	18,462	15,001
		Mean	$ 33,686	$ 31,039	$ 39,517	$ 35,412	$ 29,994	$ 27,023
		Median	$ 28,928	$ 27,904	$ 32,000	$ 29,952	$ 26,880	$ 23,808
	Women	Number	241,897	18,134	43,076	44,375	33,845	102,467
		Mean	$ 21,731	$ 25,469	$ 24,984	$ 23,568	$ 20,324	$ 19,372
		Median	$ 18,944	$ 21,248	$ 21,760	$ 20,992	$ 18,688	$ 17,920
	Gender Ratio	Mean	64.5	82.1	63.2	66.6	67.8	71.7
		Median	65.5	76.1	68.0	70.1	69.5	75.3

moderately male occupations in 1990. Mean earnings for men in heavily male occupations were slightly higher than those in mixed occupations in 1980 but fell between those in mixed and moderately female occupations in 1990.

There seems to have been a shift toward a greater degree of gender equality between 1980 and 1990 both for all occupations combined and for each of the categories of sex-segregated occupations. The shift was much greater among the heavily male occupations than in any other category. These trends could reflect, in part, the trend toward sex desegregation of occupations but something special seems to be happening with respect to the heavily male occupations. In 1980, the mean earnings of all workers in heavily male occupations was 110.7 percent of that for all workers, regardless of occupation, as compared to 105.8 percent in 1990. Male workers also experienced a relative decline in earnings for this occupational classification (from 97.0 percent to 92.1 percent of that for all workers) while female workers experienced a relative increase (from 108.9 percent to 117.2 percent). In either year, men in heavily male occupations earned less than the average for all men, while women in these occupations earned more than the average for all women.

We next explore the possibility that occupational status and patterns of occupational sex segregation interact in such a manner as to impact upon the relation of earnings to gender. Table 8.3 presents the data needed to evaluate this possibility. The decade saw small declines in the proportion of workers in clerical, craft, and operative and labor occupations coupled with increases in all other status classifications. The changes that took place within status classifications were not uniform. The two most heavily male occupational status classifications in 1980 were craft and farm occupations, each of which exhibited only a slight tendency toward increased female representation. The next highest proportion of male workers was found in the operatives and labor occupations, which did not exhibit any movement toward reduction in degree of sex segregation. In contrast, noticeable reductions appear in the degree of male domination of management, professional, technical, and sales occupations. Females had dominated the clerical occupations in 1980 and continued to do so in 1990 but almost one-twelfth of all clerical workers were in heavily male occupations in 1980 compared to fewer than one in one hundred in 1990. Service occupations also exhibited a dramatic reduction in the proportion of workers in heavily male occupations.

Table 8.4 presents mean and median earnings of men and women for each separate occupational status category for 1980 and 1990. The ratio of women's to men's earnings is more nearly equal in 1990 than in 1980 for each and every occupational status category. The movement toward greater gender equality is generally greater for median than mean incomes. It ranged between 2.3 percent and 8.3 percent for mean incomes and between 2.5 percent and 10.5 percent for median incomes.

Table 8.3. Occupational Status Classification by Occupational Sex Segregation: 1980 and 1990

Year	Occupational Status Classification		Percent of Persons in Status Classification in Segregation Category					Percent of Workers in Status Level
			Heavily Male	Moderately Male	Mixed Occupation	Moderately Female	Heavily Female	
1980	Management Occupation	N	7,992	48,120	8,988	130	0	65,230
		%	12.3	73.8	13.8	0.2	0.0	14.0
	Professional Occupation	N	22,489	4,719	8,708	4,588	13,627	54,131
		%	41.5	8.7	16.1	8.5	25.2	11.6
	Technical Occupation	N	6,930	4,405	640	1,614	3,495	17,084
		%	40.6	25.8	3.7	9.4	20.5	3.7
	Sales Occupation	N	12,066	11,785	3,646	4,013	4,728	36,238
		%	33.3	32.5	10.1	11.1	13.0	7.8
	Clerical Occupation	N	6,540	6,867	12,648	8,312	49,951	84,318
		%	7.8	8.1	15.0	9.9	59.2	18.1
	Service Occupation	N	18,421	1,082	6,136	536	15,123	41,298
		%	44.6	2.6	14.9	1.3	36.6	8.9
	Farm, Forestry, or Fishing Occupation	N	4,686	5	210	0	32	4,933
		%	95.0	0.1	4.3	0.0	0.6	1.1
	Craft Occupation	N	67,872	1,638	827	55	814	71,206
		%	95.3	2.3	1.2	0.1	1.1	15.3
	Operatives and Labor Occupation	N	50,128	15,436	16,086	5,205	3,921	90,776
		%	55.2	17.0	17.7	5.7	4.3	19.5
	Total 1980	N	197,124	94,218	57,702	24,438	91,732	465,214
		%	42.4	20.3	12.4	5.3	19.7	100.0

Table 8.3. Occupational Status Classification by Occupational Sex Segregation: 1980 and 1990 (continued)

Year	Occupational Status Classification		Percent of Persons in Status Classification in Segregation Category					Percent of Workers in Status Level
			Heavily Male	Moderately Male	Mixed Occupation	Moderately Female	Heavily Female	
1990	Management Occupation	N	777	50,488	38,785	2,186	2,368	94,604
		%	0.8	53.4	41.0	2.3	2.5	15.8
	Professional Occupation	N	23,652	10,269	14,184	7,953	22,230	78,288
		%	30.2	13.1	18.1	10.2	28.4	13.1
	Technical Occupation	N	7,546	9,732	390	2,806	6,365	26,839
		%	28.1	36.3	1.5	10.5	23.7	4.5
	Sales Occuaption	N	13,052	27,709	4,258	5,825	6,077	56,921
		%	22.9	48.7	7.5	10.2	10.7	9.5
	Clerical Occupation	N	866	11,449	6,638	24,867	56,158	99,978
		%	0.9	11.5	6.6	24.9	56.2	16.7
	Service Occupation	N	13,841	11,857	9,362	1,015	19,784	55,859
		%	24.8	21.2	16.8	1.8	35.4	9.3
	Farm, Forestry, or Fishing Occupation	N	7,065	74	119	405	0	7,663
		%	92.2	1.0	1.6	5.3	0.0	1:3
	Craft Occupation	N	75,215	874	1,432	2,213	250	79,984
		%	94.0	1.1	1.8	2.8	0.3	13.3
	Operatives and Labor Occupation	N	55,565	16,480	18,122	5,037	4,236	99,440
		%	55.9	16.6	18.2	5.1	4.3	16.6
	Total 1990	N	197,579	138,932	93,290	52,307	117,468	599,576
		%	33.0	23.2	15.6	8.7	19.6	100.0

Table 8.4. Earnings by Gender and Occupation Status Classification: 1980 and 1990

Occupational Classification	Gender Category	1980			1990		
		Number	Mean Income	Median Income	Number	Mean Income	Median Income
Administrative	Men	47,447	$25,926	$22,784	55,729	$48,576	$39,936
	Women	17,783	$14,339	$12,800	38,875	$28,001	$24,832
	Ratio	27.3	55.3	56.2	41.1	57.6	62.2
Professional	Men	34,358	$23,266	$21,504	43,115	$43,737	$37,888
	Women	19,773	$14,655	$13,824	35,173	$29,032	$27,136
	Ratio	36.5	63.0	64.3	44.9	66.4	71.6
Technical	Men	10,906	$20,037	$18,688	15,672	$34,568	$31,488
	Women	6,178	$12,340	$11,776	11,167	$23,897	$21,760
	Ratio	36.2	61.6	63.0	41.6	69.1	69.1
Sales	Men	24,556	$21,027	$18,176	35,574	$38,754	$29,952
	Women	11,682	$10,564	$8,960	21,347	$21,654	$17,920
	Ratio	32.2	50.2	49.3	37.5	55.9	59.8
Administrative Support	Men	24,028	$17,693	$17,664	24,875	$28,926	$27,392
	Women	60,290	$10,957	$9,984	75,103	$19,453	$17,920
	Ratio	71.5	61.9	56.5	75.1	67.3	65.4
Service	Men	22,641	$14,073	$12,800	29,339	$23,941	$20,992
	Women	18,657	$7,956	$7,168	26,520	$14,489	$12,288
	Ratio	45.2	56.5	56.0	47.5	60.5	58.5
Farming, Etc.	Men	4,431	$11,329	$9,984	6,756	$18,668	$15,616
	Women	502	$8,012	$6,912	907	$14,487	$11,776
	Ratio	10.2	70.7	69.2	11.8	77.6	75.4
Precision Production	Men	66,217	$18,654	$17,920	72,721	$29,518	$27,904
	Women	4,989	$11,408	$10,240	7,263	$20,529	$17,920
	Ratio	7.0	61.2	57.1	9.1	69.5	64.2

Table 8.4. Earnings by Gender and Occupation Status Classification: 1980 and 1990 (continued)

Occupational Classification	Gender Category	1980			1990		
		Number	Mean Income	Median Income	Number	Mean Income	Median Income
Operators and Laborers	Men	67,944	$16,111	$15,872	73,898	$24,914	$22,784
	Women	22,832	$9,477	$8,704	25,542	$16,072	$14,336
	Ratio	25.2	58.8	54.8	25.7	64.5	62.9
All Occupations	Men	302,528	$19,463	$17,920	357,679	$33,686	$28,928
	Women	162,686	$11,253	$9,984	241,897	$21,731	$18,944
	Ratio	35.0	57.8	55.7	40.3	64.5	65.5

We have considered only raw earnings up to this point but we now wish to examine some determinants of earnings. Table 8.5 presents the findings from a regression analysis of the determinants of the log of earnings in 1980 and 1990 for all persons combined and separately by gender. It is not surprising to find a strong positive association between earnings and number of hours worked. Nor is it surprising to find a strong positive association between education and earnings. Managerial, professional, and technical occupations had significantly higher earnings than craft occupations while service, farm, operative, and labor occupations had significantly lower earnings. In 1990 clerical workers also earned more than craftworkers although this was not the case for men in 1980. In 1990 the earnings of workers in sales occupations were significantly lower than those in craft occupations but in 1980 the earnings of men and all workers combined had been significantly higher. Persons who entered the United States prior to 1970 had significantly higher incomes than native-born Americans while persons entering during the five years prior to the census had significantly lower earnings. In 1980 the level of earnings of those persons having lived in the United States for an intermediate length of time (those entering between 1970 and 1974 in the 1980 population and between 1970 and 1984 for the 1990 population) did not significantly differ from those of native-born Americans, but they were significantly higher in 1990. American citizenship, age, speaking only English in the home (males and all workers combined only), and good spoken English are positively associated with earnings. Region, as a proxy for access to job markets, is related to earnings. Earnings tend to be higher in the Northeast than in most other areas. We simply note without further comment the fact that earnings also vary by race/ethnicity, with the exact pattern of variation differing by year and gender.

In 1980 women earned 37.8 percent less than men with all other variables including the sex composition of occupations controlled. By 1990 this gender earnings penalty had been reduced to 30.9 percent. With sex, race/ethnicity, human capital, occupational status, and location controlled, a significant earnings advantage accrues to workers in heavily male or moderately male as opposed to mixed sex occupations, while a significant disadvantage exists for workers in moderately female or heavily female occupations. And, a greater advantage accrues to workers in heavily male than in moderately male occupations and a greater disadvantage exists for workers in heavily female than in moderately female occupations. It is also important to note that in 1990 the advantage of being in heavily male occupations was greater for women than was the disadvantage of being in heavily female occupations while the reverse is the case for men. In 1980 both genders experienced a greater disadvantage for being in heavily female occupations than the advantage for being in heavily male occupations.

Table 8.5. Determinants of Earned Income by Gender: 1980 and 1990

Variable	1980 All Workers Estimate	1980 Male Workers Estimate	1980 Female Workers Estimate	1990 All Workers Estimate	1990 Male Workers Estimate	1990 Female Workers Estimate
Intercept	8.8467**	8.7453**	8.6701**	9.2332**	9.1262**	9.1156**
Hours Worked in 1979 (1989)	1.11E-04**	1.13E-04**	8.01E-05**	0.0002**	0.0002**	0.0002**
Sex	-0.3779**			-0.3086**		
Heavily Male Occupation	0.1021**	0.1030**	0.0906**	0.1332**	0.1242**	0.1879**
Moderately Male Occupation	0.0712**	0.0774**	0.0514**	0.0759**	0.0792**	0.0484**
Mixed Occupation (Comparative Referent)						
Moderately Female Occupation	-0.0931**	-0.1009**	-0.0986**	-0.0543**	-0.0412**	-0.0729**
Heavily Female Occupation	-0.0980**	-0.1422**	-0.1176**	-0.1021**	-0.1397**	-0.1180**
Management Occupation	0.1461**	0.1557**	0.1461**	0.3166**	0.3463**	0.2888**
Professional Occupation	0.0839**	0.0389**	0.2180**	0.3145**	0.2731**	0.3869**
Technical Occupation	0.0498**	0.0257**	0.1406**	0.1742**	0.1397**	0.2514**
Sales Occupation	-0.0427**	-0.0098*	-0.0667**	0.0647**	0.1069**	0.0197**
Clerical Occupation	0.0304**	0.0052	0.1014**	0.0923**	0.0610**	0.1374**
Service Occupation	-.02690**	-0.2545**	-0.2402**	-0.1962**	-0.1834**	-0.1822**
Farm, Forestry, or Fishing Occupation	-0.5127**	-0.5040**	-0.4716**	-0.4578**	-0.4582**	-0.3859**
Craft Occupation (Comparative Referent)						
Operatives and Labor Occupation	-0.0846**	-0.0754**	-0.0654**	-0.1125**	-0.1112**	-0.0958**
Euro-American (Comparative Referent)						
African-American	-0.1247**	-0.2042**	-0.0269**	-0.0708**	-0.1441**	0.0020

Table 8.5. Determinants of Earned Income by Gender: 1980 and 1990 (continued)

Variable	1980 All Workers Estimate	1980 Male Workers Estimate	1980 Female Workers Estimate	1990 All Workers Estimate	1990 Male Workers Estimate	1990 Female Workers Estimate
Native American	-0.1224**	-0.1476**	-0.0817**	-0.1247**	-0.1646**	-0.0723**
Mexican-American	-0.0877**	-0.0923**	-0.0736**	-0.0878**	-0.1047**	-0.0617**
Puerto Rican	-0.1062**	-0.1208**	-0.0581**	-0.0679**	-0.1051**	-0.0186
Cuban-American	-0.0720**	-0.0882**	-0.0586**	-0.0643**	-0.1081**	-0.0176
Chinese-American	-0.0620**	-0.1063**	0.0144	-0.0145	-0.0612**	0.0368**
Filipino-American	-0.0632**	-0.1650**	0.0058	-0.0778**	-0.1708**	-0.0033
Japanese-American	-0.0190	-0.0170	-0.0093	0.0414**	0.0557**	0.0328*
Asian Indian-American	0.0225	0.0118	0.0774*	0.0405**	0.0278	0.0474**
Korean-American	0.0326	-0.0253	0.0750*	-0.0557**	-0.1344**	0.0187
Other-American	-0.0778**	-0.1011**	-0.0446**	-0.0830**	-0.1235**	-0.0274**
Born in the U.S. (Comparative Referent)						
Came Before 1970	0.0525**	0.0629**	0.0443**	0.0763**	0.0913**	0.0627**
Came Between 1970 and 1984 (1970–1974)	0.0006	-0.0111	0.0247	0.0363**	0.0421**	0.0372**
Came Between 1985 and 1990 (1975–1980)	-0.1011**	-0.112**	-0.0623**	-0.0935**	-0.0732**	-0.1159**
American Citizen	0.0263**	0.0178*	0.0378**	0.0457**	0.0417**	0.0410**
Age	0.0070**	0.0091**	0.0034**	0.0088**	0.0117**	0.0044**
Spoke Only English	0.0476**	0.0673**	0.0094	0.0269**	0.0413**	0.0066
Speaks Good English	0.1482**	0.1614**	0.1304**	0.1488**	0.1597**	0.1347**
Did Not Graduate from High School	-0.1762**	-0.1965**	-0.1327**	-0.2161**	-0.2373**	-0.1798**

Table 8.5. Determinants of Earned Income by Gender: 1980 and 1990 (continued)

Variable	1980			1990		
	All Workers Estimate	Male Workers Estimate	Female Workers Estimate	All Workers Estimate	Male Workers Estimate	Female Workers Estimate
High School Graduate (Comparative Referent)						
Some Advanced Education	0.0818**	0.0742**	0.0811**	0.0354**	0.0134**	0.0559**
Bachelor's Degree	0.2429**	0.2426**	0.2194**	0.1766**	0.1462**	0.1953**
New England (Comparative Referent)						
Middle Atlantic	0.0543**	0.0487**	0.0608**	-0.0159**	-0.0123**	-0.0230**
East North Central	0.0916**	0.1050**	0.0626**	-0.0974**	-0.0689**	-0.1436**
West North Central	-0.0606**	-0.0517**	-0.0760**	-0.2305**	-0.2189**	-0.2484**
South Atlantic	-0.0527**	-0.0597**	-0.0379**	-0.1496**	-0.1445**	-0.1570**
East South Central	-0.1201**	-0.1174**	-0.1196**	-0.2464**	-0.2236**	-0.2789**
West South Central	-0.0297**	-0.0138**	-0.0566**	-0.1965**	-0.1761**	-0.2236**
Mountain	-0.0149**	-0.0058	-0.0289**	-0.1789**	-0.1682**	-0.1906**
Pacific	0.0885**	0.0892**	0.0920**	-0.0020	0.0038	-0.0055
Number=	465,214	302,528	162,686	599,576	357,679	241,897
F Value=	4,578.99**	1,745.60**	830.59**	7,495.46**	3,397.23**	2,300.12**
R-Square=	.30	.20	.18	.35	.29	.29
Adjusted R-Square=	.30	.20	.18	.35	.29	.29

* = $p < 0.05$
** = $p < 0.01$

Table 8.6. Gender Earnings Penalty by Occupational Sex Segregatation: 1990

Year	Heavily Male	Moderately Male	Mixed Occupation	Moderately Female	Heavily Female
1980	−37.7%	−42.4%	−36.8%	−34.8%	−31.1%
1990	−23.5%	−36.3%	−32.2%	−31.4%	−24.2%
Proportional Reduction	37.7%	14.4%	12.5%	9.8%	22.2%

The data presented in Table 8.5 reveal one important and unexpected finding. The introduction of controls for human capital, occupational status, and location reveal a linear relation between earnings and proportion of males in an occupation. Not only was there a significant earnings advantage to having an occupation that was heavily male, the magnitude of that advantage increased between 1980 and 1990 with the increase for women (from a 9.1 percent earnings advantage to 18.8 percent) being more than 4.5 times as great as it was for men (from 10.3 percent to 12.4 percent). The return of the linear relation between earnings and occupational sex segregation with the use of regression techniques was not accompanied by a linear relation between earnings inequality and the sex composition of occupations.

Next, a series of regressions were run to ascertain the determinants of earnings within each category of sex-segregated occupations for 1980 and 1990. Hours worked, human capital, occupational status, regional location, and sex were controlled. Table 8.6 presents the proportion by which women's earnings were reduced relative to men's earnings in each sex-segregated category of occupations for each of the two years. In 1980, gender earnings inequality was least in heavily female occupations but in 1990 there was even less gender inequality in heavily male occupations, although heavily female occupations followed close behind. In both years, the degree of gender earnings inequality generally increased with movement from heavily female occupations through moderately female and mixed occupations before peaking in moderately male occupations and then decreasing in heavily male occupations. In 1980 the degree of earnings inequality in heavily male occupations was between that found in the moderately male and the mixed occupations although closer to the latter. The most striking finding is the substantially less earnings inequality in 1990 than in 1980 within each grouping of occupations. The greatest movement toward gender equality was found in heavily male occupations and the second greatest movement was in heavily female occupations. The shift in each of the other three groupings, while substantial, fell short of that for all occupations combined (18.3 percent).

Table 8.7. Gender Earnings Penalty by Occupational Status Level: 1980 and 1990

Occupation Classification	1980	1990	Amount of Reduction	Proportional Reduction
Managment Occupation	−43.4%	−38.1%	−5.3%	12.2%
Professional Occupation	−23.7%	−18.8%	−4.9%	20.7%
Technical Occupation	−31.1%	−21.9%	−9.2%	29.6%
Sales Occupation	−45.8%	−35.1%	−10.7%	23.4%
Clerical Occupation	−34.0%	−28.3%	−5.7%	16.8%
Service Occupation	−32.8%	−25.8%	−7.0%	21.3%
Farm, Forestry, or Fishing Occupation	−41.8%	−27.1%	−14.7%	35.2%
Craft Occupation	−38.8%	−26.3%	−12.5%	32.2%
Operatives and Labor Occupation	−40.8%	−33.4%	−7.4%	18.1%

Table 8.7 reports the results of regressions run separately within each occupational status category for 1980 and 1990 to determine the size of the gender earnings difference with hours worked, human capital, location, and occupational sex segregation controlled. The 1980 rank order of occupational statuses ranked from largest to smallest gender penalty was sales, management, farm, labor, craft, clerical, service, technical, and professional. Still, a shift toward greater gender equality occurred in each of the occupational status categories during the decade. In 1990 management occupations exhibited the largest gender earnings penalty followed by sales, operative and labor, clerical, farm, craft, service, technical, and professional occupations. The proportional reduction in the gender penalty during the decade exceeded that for all workers (20.8 percent) in five of the occupational status categories and the difference was negligible in the case of a sixth (professional). Only management, clerical, and operatives and labor occupations displayed a smaller movement toward gender earnings equality.

A series of regressions were run for 1980 and 1990 in which variables were sequentially added to the equation in order to isolate the proportion of gender earnings inequality that could be attributed to occupational sex segregation and the proportion that could be attributed to each of the other factors. We then reran this series of regressions separately for each of four age categories (25 to 34, 35 to 44, 45 to 54, and 55 to 64). This gave us three ways of assessing change over time—the comparison of the gross results from the regressions on persons aged twenty-five to sixty-four in 1980 and 1990, the comparison of age cohorts within each census year, and the comparison of differences in patterns with regard to the age cohorts in the two census years. Table 8.8 presents a summary of these findings. Women earned 37.8 percent less than men in 1980 and 30.9 percent less in 1990 with hours worked, race/ethnicity, human capital, location, occupational status, and occupational sex segregation controlled. There has been significant movement toward gender earnings equality during the decade but a high degree of gender inequality remains.

An examination of the data by age cohort reveals a sharp reduction in gender inequality between the 25 to 34 and the 35 to 44 age cohorts in both 1980 and 1990 along with a similar sharp reduction between the 35 to 44 and the 45 to 54 age cohorts only in 1990. This suggests that societal and workplace conditions associated with the reduction in gender earnings inequality were present during the 1970s and continued, possibly even intensified, during the 1980s.

Let us now examine decade changes in the sources of the gender earnings penalty. The two major contributors to gender earnings inequality are sex and occupational sex segregation. The proportion of the gender penalty accounted for by occupational sex segregation increased during the decade from 14.7 percent to 17.7 percent and the residual unexplained proportion attributed to sex also increased (from 72.7 percent to 76.9 percent). Differences in number of hours worked increased in importance, accounting for 3.7 percent of the gender earnings penalty in 1980 and 8.2 percent in 1990. This occurred despite the fact that the gap in hours worked between men and women working full-time did not increase (women worked 93.0 percent as many hours as comparable men in 1980 and 93.1 percent as much in 1990). The proportional impact of hours worked increased because the absolute size of the gender earnings penalty had decreased.

Human capital accounted for 3.1 percent of the gender earnings penalty in 1980 but controlling for human capital slightly increased the size of the gender earnings penalty in 1990, suggesting that women received a smaller return on their human capital than men. A closer examination of the data broken down by age and census year demonstrates the declining significance of human capital in rather dramatic fashion by 1990 except among persons aged twenty-five to thirty-four, suggesting that, for this age cohort, return on human capital was substantially less for women. The contribution made by the interaction between race/ethnicity and gender to the gender earnings penalty was slightly reduced during the decade (from 2.1 percent to 1.5 percent). It is important to note that this analysis is structured to reveal only the impact of race/ethnicity upon the size of the gender earnings penalty and it does not reveal any of the direct impact that race/ethnicity has upon earnings.

These data enable us to compute the proportion by which women's earnings are reduced relative to men's earnings in association with each of the factors taken separately (see the bottom row in each section of the table). In 1990, differences in number of hours worked were associated with a 2.5 percent

Table 8.8. Women's Income Compared to Men's Income by Age and Controls

Year	Age	Gender Penalty with full Controls	Proportion of Gender Penalty Due to Hours Worked	Proportion of Gender Penalty Due to Human Capital	Proportion of Gender Penalty Due to Occ. Sex Segregation	Proportion of Gender Penalty Due to Ethnicity	Proportion of Gender Penalty Due to Sex
1980	25–34	−25.6%	5.4%	2.3%	18.8%	2.6%	66.0%
	35–44	−42.8%	3.5%	5.9%	12.7%	2.5%	71.6%
	45–54	−45.9%	3.1%	4.4%	11.8%	1.8%	74.2%
	55–64	−43.9%	2.3%	2.3%	11.5%	0.2%	78.8%
	Total	−37.8%	3.7%	3.1%	14.6%	2.1%	72.7%
Impact on Women's Earning			−1.9%	−1.6%	−7.5%	−1.1%	−37.8%
1990	25–34	−18.9%	12.8%	−8.6%	26.8%	1.6%	73.5%
	35–44	−31.7%	8.5%	0.7%	17.5%	1.9%	75.1%
	45–54	−43.0%	6.1%	0.0%	12.6%	1.1%	79.8%
	55–64	−41.3%	4.2%	0.8%	11.7%	1.0%	79.3%
	Total	−30.9%	8.2%	−1.5%	17.7%	1.5%	76.9%
Impact on Women's Earnings			−2.5%	0.5%	−5.5%	−0.5%	−23.8%

reduction in women's earnings relative to comparable men's. Corresponding figures for the other factors are 0.5 percent associated with the interaction between race/ethnicity and gender, 5.5 percent associated with occupational sex segregation, and 23.8 percent associated with sex net of the impact of all other factors. Controls for human capital are associated with a 0.5 percent increase in the gender earnings penalty. It should be noted that our measure of human capital does not include work experience; census data do not provide such information. However, O'Neill and Polacheck (1993) found that the gender difference in years of work experience has narrowed substantially in recent years, especially among younger workers. They conclude that the increase in women's work experience relative to men accounts for 25 percent of the closing of the gender wage gap since 1976 and the relative rise in return to women's work experience accounts for another 35 percent to 40 percent of the convergence (O'Neill and Polacheck 1993:207).

Similarly the impact of sex segregation at the level of the firm or the job cannot be measured using census data. Nevertheless, we found a very large gender earnings penalty associated with sex independent of all other variables and another large penalty associated with occupational sex segregation. One might call the former direct gender job-earnings discrimination as opposed to the latter, which could be seen as indirect discrimination channeled through socialization, gender tracking in schools, employer preferences, and other factors that contribute to women being channeled into "women's jobs."

DISCUSSION AND CONCLUSIONS

It is now time to make sense out of the detailed findings presented above. Braverman (1974:377–402) described a process in which capital and labor were becoming globalized as the United States experienced deindustrialization. There has been a shrinkage in the proportion of jobs that have traditionally been defined as "men's work" and an expansion in the proportion of service and other jobs traditionally defined as "women's work." Concomitantly, the labor force participation rate is declining among male workers and rising among female workers. Braverman's analysis is borne out by events during the past two decades and is reflected in our findings (also see Amott 1993 for an excellent summary).

Our data reveal that between 1980 and 1990 females twenty-five to sixty-four increased their representation from 45.0 percent to 48.1 percent among full-time workers, while keeping their representation relatively stable among persons working less than full-time for the full year (64.5 percent in 1980 and 64.1 percent in 1990). Women also closed the gap relative to men in terms of mean total hours worked during the year. They increased their average total hours of work from 1,548 to 1,663 among all workers, from 2,103 to 2,158 among those working full-time for the full year, and from 960 to 1,016 among those working less. Corresponding increases for men were smaller (from 2,034 to 2,069 among all workers, 2,260 to 2,318 among full-time workers, and from 1,228 to 1,211 among those working less than full-time for the full year). This closing of the gap in hours worked during the year helps to explain some of the closing of the gender gap in terms of mean annual earnings but it does not explain everything. Our data reveal that mean hourly wages for women in this age group increased from 63.1 percent to 69.8 percent of those of men among all workers and from 62.4 to 69.3 percent among those employed full-time for the full year. This should be viewed in conjunction with the fact that our regression analysis demonstrated that the annual earnings gap diminished even with hours worked and other variables controlled.

Clearly, the interrelations among gender, race, ethnicity, and earnings inequality are complex, and it is much too simplistic to attribute all earnings inequality to the capitalist organization of the labor process. At the same time, it would be shortsighted if we did not acknowledge the extent to which this organization helps to produce gender earnings inequality. However, the relation is not as straightforward as the simple working out of the capitalist drive toward fragmentation, deskilling, and degradation of work. At the very least, we have to recognize the role that class and related community struggles play.

First, let us consider what we might learn from the relations between occupational sex segregation and both earnings and gender earnings inequality in the context of the observed trends toward diminished occupational sex segregation and decreased gender earnings inequality. The decade between 1980 and 1990 produced a significant decrease in the level of occupational sex segregation, with males becoming less concentrated in heavily male occupations and females becoming less concentrated in heavily female occupations. An examination of occupations by status level revealed that the most heavily male occupations in 1980 experienced the least movement toward desegregation by 1990. The relation between occupational segregation and earnings was not linear in either year although higher earnings tended to be associated with a higher proportion of male workers from heavily female occupations through moderately male occupations. After that point, an increased proportion of male workers was accompanied by a decline in earnings. Nevertheless, the decade between 1980 and 1990 was characterized by a trend toward greater equalization of earnings of men and women. This was not solely the result of a declining level of occupational sex-segregation, since the trend toward earnings equality was observed within each of the categories of sex-segregated occupations as well as for all occupations combined. In 1990, the greatest degree of equality was found in heavily male occupations followed closely by heavily female occupations and the greatest degree of inequality was found in moderately male occupations. An examination of occupations by occupational status classifications revealed that every single occupational status category exhibited movement toward gender earnings equality during the decade. The movement was quite substantial in most cases except among clerical workers, where it was quite small.

Regression analysis revealed a trend toward greater gender earnings equality even with hours worked, human capital, location, and occupational sex segregation controlled. The gender difference in earnings decreased by more than one-fourth during the decade. A linear relation between earnings and sex composition of occupations returned when all other factors were controlled. The reward in terms of increased earnings for being in a more male occupation was substantially greater than was the penalty in terms of decreased earnings for being in a more female occupation. The magnitude of the earnings "reward" associated with heavily male occupations increased during the decade but this was especially evident for women workers. The trend toward greater gender earnings equality was evident at every occupational status level and in each category of sex-segregated occupations. The greatest reduction in inequality was observed in heavily male occupations followed by heavily female occupations. By 1990, women's earnings were more nearly equal to men's earnings in the heavily male occupations than in any other category of sex-segregated occupations. It appears that by 1990 women, especially younger women, had made great advances relative to men in their human capital and that, consequently, human capital differences ceased to explain much of the observed differences in earnings. When all other factors were controlled, sex, in and of itself, was the largest single contributor to the gender earnings gap and occupational sex segregation was the second largest.

A reasonable conclusion seems to be that women in the labor force are disadvantaged in the workplace in ways that cannot be attributed solely to capitalist fragmentation, deskilling, and degradation of work. The linear relation expected between occupational sex segregation and either earnings or earnings inequality failed to hold. Too, the trend toward occupational desegregation and reduced gender earnings inequality seems inconsistent with the notion that women are being brought into the workplace as less skilled workers replacing more highly skilled men at a time during which work is being fragmented, deskilled, and degraded. This is especially true in light of O'Neill and Polacheck's (1993) finding of substantial relative improvements in both women's education and the economic return to women's education.

Further, we must consider the results of our regression analyses of earnings. We recognize that skill is a slippery concept and that it is socially constructed in a manner to convey justification for inequalities created by differential amounts of power and privilege. Nevertheless, our regression equations controlled for the existing status classifications of occupations, occupational sex segregation, human capital factors, and location as a proxy for access to labor markets, and we still found that women paid a sizable price in terms of reduced earnings. This must be a result of the carryover into the workplace of aspects of the position that women occupy in the larger society—the social division of labor clearly impinges upon the technical division of labor.

However, we must not go overboard and conclude that the technical division of labor is irrelevant. Our regression analysis did find a significant portion of the gender gap in earnings to be directly attributable to occupational sex segregation and we did find a relation between earnings and the occupational status classification of occupations, even if their relation to gender earnings inequality was minimal.

THEORETICAL IMPLICATIONS

We believe that the best way to explain these results is to integrate the capitalist labor process and an expanded notion of class struggle into a single theoretical framework. We can begin with the assumptions made by Braverman (1974), integrate them with Bonacich's (1972; 1976) analysis of the split labor market, add the perspective on gender presented by Geschwender (1992), and then blend in the perspective on race and ethnicity provided by Geschwender and colleagues (see, for example, Geschwender 1978; 1987; and Geschwender and Levine, 1994). Capitalists are clearly interested in two things: maximizing control over labor and maximizing profits. Braverman's greatest strength lies in his analysis of the capitalist organization of the labor process which, he correctly argued, is precisely designed to accomplish both of these objectives. His analysis stimulated considerable criticism because he did not explicitly address class struggle. This led many critics to conclude that Braverman assumed that capitalists were free to reorganize production in a virtually unopposed manner or that resistance and opposition came only after the fact. He may have chosen not to address class struggle in order to keep his presentation simple and focused on capital's role but, by so doing, he opened the door for much unneeded opposition.

Braverman left the impression that women and minority workers were primarily less skilled, cheaper labor that could compete for what remained of the tasks formerly performed by more skilled, more highly paid, Euro-American men, after their work had been fragmented, deskilled, and degraded. Bonacich (1972; 1976) questioned why it was that capital did not completely eliminate higher-priced majority male workers and replace them with cheaper minority workers. She found her answer by examining the activities of majority male workers within a class struggle perspective—in other words, she attributed agency to the working class acting collectively in their own interests. She stated that Euro-American male workers recognized that capital was using minority workers to drive down their wages and to weaken their bargaining position. They also feared that they might, in time, be entirely replaced. Consequently, they organized themselves, fought with all their resources, and attempted to either exclude minorities from the workplace or to circumscribe and control them within it. This contributed to the emergence of jobs defined in terms of racial/ethnic identity and a variable pay scale for workers of different ancestries. These workers concluded that their best defense against capital's determination to use minority workers as a weapon was to remove that weapon by eliminating minority workers as potential competitors. In brief, Bonacich argued that majority male workers became racist in pursuit of the class struggle and, in so doing, helped to create the circumstances under which that segment of the working class comprised of racial and ethnic minorities could be more intensely exploited. It seems clear that, as a result, they helped to intensify their own exploitation.

Geschwender (1992) borrowed from that analysis and suggested that the inferior position occupied by women in the labor force could be explained in a similar manner. Male workers recognized that capital had in the past displayed a willingness to hire women when they were needed to undermine the growing strength of male workers or to reduce wages. Male workers sought to remove this weapon (women) from the hands of capital and they called upon the sacred institution of the family in order to do so. They argued that allowing women to work for wages outside the home created problems for women and their families. Women were exploited and damaged at work and their children and husbands suffered by their absence from the home. Male workers organized around the demand for the family wage—a wage that would allow a working man to support himself and a family; a wage that would allow wives to remain in the home where children could be fed, cared for, and properly socialized and where the physical and psychological needs of the husband could be met. Their rhetoric enabled them to attract the invaluable support of middle-class reformers (largely women) and, with their aid, gain the passage of state legislation that furthered their cause.

The ideology of the family wage carried with it some less obvious corollaries. It made it possible for capital to act as if every woman had a man caring for her—first a father and later a husband. Since her basic needs were being met through the earnings of a man, it logically followed that any earnings she generated through her own employment had a more frivolous purpose. In essence, she worked for pin money and frills—never for necessities. Thus, there was no reason to pay women workers at the same level as men. Ironically, the family wage that comprised the heart and soul of the fight to protect the working class as a whole became the very vehicle that stimulated the development of occupational sex segregation and a lower pay scale for women. The male attempt to increase working-class strength vis-à-vis capital took on a patriarchal tinge and helped created the context within which the female portion of the working class could be more intensely exploited, leading to conditions where male workers could be more intensely exploited as well.

Thus, Braverman's analysis may be strengthened by incorporating an explicit consideration of class struggle (defined as struggle over relations of production). We argue herein that it would be further strengthened if it incorporated a number of other forms of struggle that grow out of the social division of labor and that this would aid in developing an understanding of recent and ongoing changes. The Civil Rights Movement of the 1950s and 1960s brought about passage of the 1964 Civil Rights Bill, which included Title VII that addressed equal employment opportunities. Folklore has it that sex was initially added to the list of prohibited bases for discrimination as a joke that was designed to undermine support for the bill, but women congresspersons and feminist groups across the nation immediately threw their support behind the inclusion of sex in Title VII and behind the passage of the entire bill (McCann 1994:35–48). This led to a strengthening of the struggle over both equal access and pay equity.

The pursuit of equal access eventuated in the creation of federal, state, local, and private employers' affirmative action programs, guidelines published, and rulings enforced with varying degrees of enthusiasm. This provided the leverage needed by women and racial/ethnic minorities to open doors that had remained closed for generations. Neither capital nor majority male labor could completely resist their demands although both tried.

The pursuit for pay equity had begun to bear fruit even before Title VII but it was greatly strengthened by its passage. McCann (1994) documents the fact that women's groups and unions exerted continual pressure in pursuit of this objective. A number of bills were introduced to Congress and defeated between 1945 and 1962. But then in 1963 feminists were able to win support from the Kennedy administration and gain passage of the Equal Pay Act, which prohibited payment of unequal wages to men and women performing equal work (which was defined in terms of equal skill, effort, responsibility, and working conditions). This was an advance but a rather limited one. Pressure continued and Title VII was soon followed by Executive Orders 11246 in 1965 and 11375 in 1968 strengthening the prohibition against gender discrimination when federal contracts were involved. Perhaps the most valuable aspect of this was that proof of adverse impact was sufficient even in the absence of proof of discriminatory intent.

There is considerable debate over exactly how much of a mass movement was involved in the pay equity struggle and just how much progress has been made in this direction. McCann (1994) concludes that the past few decades have seen unions, women workers, and middle-class feminists organizing in the pursuit of pay equity and other feminist interests (see also Acker 1989; Bell 1985; Blum 1991; Gelb and Palley 1982) and that there has been a substantial reduction in discrimination against women in the labor market (pp. 207–8). There may not have been a mass movement but sufficient strength was developed to conduct battles at the level of public opinion, at the level of the state, and on the shopfloor. Some victories were won and many defeats were experienced. Among the victories for women was increased access to education, increased occupational opportunities, and laws which, at least in principle, barred discrimination in employment. At least some portion of the occupational desegregation and movement toward gender earnings equality observed during the 1980s must be attributed to the actions of women and their allies.

However, the growing agency of women is not the only factor responsible for these changes. Capital has moved many jobs out of the United States in recent years, thereby undermining the strength of organized labor and resulting in declining labor force participation rates for men relative to increased labor force participation rates for women. Undoubtedly, some of the movement toward a reduction in occupational sex segregation has been brought about by a decrease in the number of what were previously heavily male occupations. Consequently, a substantial portion of the movement toward gender earnings equality has resulted from a decrease in men's earnings.

Simultaneously, women won greater access to the more attractive occupations in terms of earnings potential, though they were not able to hold on to all of the earnings previously accorded to male workers. In both 1980 and 1990, management occupations had the highest mean annual earnings for men, women, and all workers combined. Women comprised 31.5 percent of the full-time managerial workers at the beginning of the decade and 44.8 percent at the end—an increase of 13.3 percent. Of the 26 occupations in the category, 15 became more female during the decade while 11 maintained the same general sex distribution. Professional occupations had the second highest mean annual earnings in all categories of workers for both years. Women increased their representation in these occupations by 5.1 percent during the decade—from 52.6 percent to 57.7 percent. Thirty-four of 107 professional occupations became more female in composition during the decade while 72 remained the same. The increase in proportion of women in all other occupational classifications was less than 5 percent and, in fact, slight decreases in the proportion of women occurred in three occupational classifications (service, farm, and labor). The fact that women had their largest increased representation in the two most desirable occupations and relatively small ones in manufacturing jobs suggests that it is the combination of improved qualifications and doors being opened by affirmative action that is most relevant here and not the relocation of male jobs outside the United States. At least some portion of those improved qualifications also reflect the impact of affirmative action in opening doors for training and schooling.

Thus, we would argue that a complete explanation of the changes that took place between 1980 and 1990 requires that we integrate a consideration of changes in the economic climate, changes in the technical division of labor, class struggle, and the growing agency of women and their allies. This has to be linked to our argument presented above that understanding the origin of occupational sex segregation, the gender earnings penalty, and racial/ethnic discrimination in the workplace requires us to add a class struggle perspective to the analysis of the capitalist organization of the labor process. We are not suggesting that we abandon the marvelous insights of Braverman; rather, we must build upon them and recognize that struggles over both the technical and social divisions of labor have a central role to play in any emerging theoretical synthesis.

APPENDIX

Heavily Male Occupations (0 percent to 24.99 percent female)

A. Executive, Administrative, and Managerial Occupations. Funeral directors; purchasing agents and buyers, farm products; and construction inspectors

B. Professional Specialty Occupations. Architects; aerospace engineers; metallurgical & materials engineers; mining engineers; petroleum engineers; chemical engineers; nuclear engineers; civil engineers; agricultural engineers; electrical & electronic engineers; industrial engineers; mechanical engineers; marine and naval architects; engineers, n.e.c.; surveyors & mapping scientists; physicists and astronomers; atmospheric and space scientists; geologists and geodesists; forestry and conservation scientists; physicians; dentists; optometrists; podiatrists; physics teachers; economics teachers; engineering teachers; theology teachers; clergy; lawyers; judges; and announcers.

C. Technicians and Related Support Occupations. Electrical & electronic technicians; industrial engineering technicians; mechanical engineering technicians; drafting occupations; surveying and mapping technicians; chemical technicians; airplane pilots and navigators; air traffic controllers; broadcast equipment operators; and tool programmers, numerical control.

D. Sales Occupations. Sales engineers; sales representatives, mining, manufacturing, and wholesale; sales workers, motor vehicles and boats; sales workers, hardware and building supplies; sales workers, parts; and auctioneers.

E. Administrative Support Occupations, Including Clerical. Messengers; and meter readers

F. Service Occupations. Supervisors, firefighting and fire prevention occupations; supervisors, police and detectives; supervisors, guards; fire inspection and fire prevention occupations; firefighting occupations; police and detectives, public service; sheriffs, bailiffs, and other law enforcement officers; correctional institution officers; guards and police, except public service; elevator operators, pest control occupations; barbers; and baggage porters and bellhops.

G. Farming, Forestry, and Fishing Occupations. Farmers, except horticultural; horticultural specialty farmers; managers, farms, except horticultural; supervisors, farm workers; farm workers; supervisors, related agricultural occupations; groundskeepers and gardeners, except farm; supervisors, forestry and logging workers; forestry workers, except logging; timber cutting and logging occupations; captains and other officers, fishing vessels; fishers; hunters and trappers.

H. Precision Production, Craft, and Repair Occupations. Supervisors, mechanics & repairers; automobile mechanics; automobile mechanic apprentices; bus, truck, and stationary engine mechanics; aircraft engine mechanics; small engine repairers; automobile body and related repairers, aircraft mechanics, except engine; heavy equipment mechanics; farm equipment mechanics; industrial machinery repairers; machinery maintenance occupations; electronic repairers, communications and industrial equipment; data processing equipment repairers; household appliance and power tool repairers; telephone line installers and repairers; telephone installers and repairers; miscellaneous electrical and electronic equipment repairers; heating, air conditioning, and refrigeration mechanics; camera, watch, and musical instrument repairers; locksmiths and safe repairers; office machine repairers; mechanical controls and value repairers; elevator installers and repairers; millwrights; specified mechanics and repairers, n.e.c.; not specified mechanics and repairers; supervisors, brickmasons, stonemasons, and tile setters; supervisors, carpenters and related workers; supervisors, electricians and power transmission installers; supervisors, painters, paperhangers, and plasterers; supervisors, plumbers, pipefitters, and steamfitters; supervisors, construction, n.e.c.; brickmasons and stonemasons, brickmason and stonemason apprentices; tile setters, hard and soft; carpet installers; carpenters; carpenter apprentices; drywall installers; electricians; electrician apprentices; electrical power installers and repairers; painters, construction and maintenance, plasterers; plumbers, pipefitters, and steamfitters; plumber, pipefitter, and steamfitter apprentices; concrete and terrazzo finishers; glaziers; insulation workers; paving, surfacing, and tamping equipment operators; roofers; sheetmetal duct installers; structural metal workers; drillers, earth; construction trades, n.e.c.; supervisors, extractive occupations; drillers, oil well; explosives workers; mining machine operators; mining occupations, n.e.c.; supervisors, production occupations; tool and die makers; tool and die maker apprentices; precision assemblers, metal; machinists; machinist apprentices; boilermakers; precision grinders, filers, and tool sharpeners; patternmakers and model makers, metal; lay-out workers; sheet metal workers; sheet metal worker apprentices; miscellaneous precision metal workers; patternmakers and model makers, wood; cabinet makers and bench carpenters; miscellaneous precision woodworkers; upholsterers; hand molders and shapers, except jewelers; patternmakers, lay-out workers, and cutters; miscellaneous precision workers, n.e.c.; butchers and meat cutters; inspectors, testers, and graders; water and sewage treatment plant operators; power plant operators; stationary engineers; and miscellaneous plant and system operators.

I. **Operators, Fabricators, and Laborers.** Lathe and turning machine set-up operators; lathe and turning machine operators; milling and planing machine operators; rolling machine operators; drilling and boring machine operators; grinding, abrading, buffing, and polishing machine operators; forging machine operators; numerical control machine operators; miscellaneous metal, plastic, stone and glass working machine operators; molding and casting machine operators; metal plating machine operators; heat treating equipment operators; miscellaneous metal and plastic processing machine operators; wood lathe, routing, and planing machine operators; sawing machine operators; miscellaneous woodworking machine operators; printing press operators; extruding and forming machine operators; mixing and blending machine operators; separating, filtering, and clarifying machine operators; compressing and compacting machine operators; painting and paint spraying machine operators; roasting and baking machine operators, food; furnace, kiln, and oven operators, except food; crushing and grinding machine operators; motion picture projectionists; welders and cutters; supervisors, motor vehicle operators; truck drivers; driver-sales workers; taxicab drivers and chauffeurs; parking lot attendants; motor transportation occupations, n.e.c.; railroad conductors and yardmasters; locomotive operating occupations; railroad brake, signal, and switch operators; rail vehicle operators, n.e.c.; ship captains and mates, except fishing boats; sailors and deckhands; marine engineers; bridge, lock, and lighthouse tenders; supervisors, material moving equipment operators; operating engineers; longshore equipment operators; hoist and winch operators; crane and tower operators; excavating and loading machine operators; grader, dozer, and scraper operators; industrial truck and tractor equipment operators; miscellaneous material moving equipment operators; supervisors, handlers, equipment cleaners, and laborers, n.e.c.; helpers, mechanics, and repairers; helpers, construction trades; helpers, surveyor;

helpers, extractive occupations; construction laborers; production helpers; garbage collectors; stevedores; freight, stock and material handlers, n.e.c.; garage and service station related occupations; vehicle washers and equipment cleaners; and laborers, except construction.

Moderately Male Occupations (25 percent to 39.99 percent female)

A. Executive, Administrative, and Managerial Occupations. Chief executives and general administrators, public administration; administrators, protective services; purchasing managers; managers, marketing, advertising, and public relations; managers and administrators, n.e.c.; management analysts; and inspectors and compliance officers, except construction.

B. Professional Specialty Occupations. Computer systems analysts and scientists; actuaries; mathematical scientists, n.e.c.; chemists, except biochemists; physical scientists, n.e.c.; agricultural and food scientists; veterinarians; health diagnosing practitioners, n.e.c.; pharmacists; earth, environmental, and marine science teachers; biological science teachers; chemistry teachers; history teachers; political science teachers; sociology teachers; social science teachers, n.e.c.; mathematical science teachers; computer science teachers; medical science teachers; agriculture and forestry teachers; law teachers; teachers, postsecondary, n.e.c.; postsecondary teachers, subject not specified; urban planners; musicians and composers; actors and directors; photographers; and athletes.

C. Technicians and Related Support Occupations. Engineering technicians, n.e.c.; science technicians, n.e.c.; computer programmers; and technicians, n.e.c.

D. Sales Occupations. Supervisors and proprietors, sales occupations; insurance sales occupations; securities and financial services sales occupations; sales occupations, other business services; sales workers, radio, TV, hi-fi, and appliances; and news vendors.

E. Administrative Support Occupations, Including Clerical. Supervisors, computer equipment operators; supervisors, distribution, scheduling, and adjusting clerks; mail carriers, postal service; traffic, shipping, and receiving clerks; and stock and inventory clerks.

F. Service Occupations. Supervisors, cleaning and building service workers; janitors and cleaners; attendants, amusement and recreation facilities; and ushers.

G. Farming, Forestry, and Fishing Occupations. Managers, horticultural specialty farms; and marine life cultivation workers.

H. Precision Production, Craft, and Repair Occupations. Paperhangers; precious stones and metals workers (jewelers); engravers, metal; furniture and wood finishers; shoe repairers; dental laboratory and medical appliance technicians; and adjusters and calibrators.

I. Operators, Fabricators, and Laborers. Punching and stamping press machine operators; fabricating machine operators, n.e.c.; shaping and joining machine operators; nailing and tacking machine operators; photoengravers and lithographers; cementing and gluing machine operators; washing, cleaning, and pickling machine operators; slicing and cutting machine operators; miscellaneous machine operators, n.e.c.; machine operators, not specified; hand cutting and trimming occupations; hand molding, casting, and forming occupations; hand painting, coating, and decorating occupations; miscellaneous hand working occupations; and production testers; stock handlers and baggers; machine feeders and offbearers.

Mixed Sex Occupations (40 percent to 59.99 percent female)

A. Executive, Administrative, and Managerial Occupations. Legislators; administrators and officials, public administration; financial managers; personnel and labor relations managers; administrators, education and related fields; postmasters and mail superintendents; managers, food serving and lodging establishments; managers, properties and real estate; managers, service organizations, n.e.c.; accountants and auditors; other financial officers; personnel, training, and labor relations specialists; buyers, wholesale and retail trade except farm products; purchasing agents and buyers, n.e.c.; and business and promotion agents.

B. Professional Specialty Occupations. Operations and systems researchers and analysts; statisticians; biological and life scientists; medical scientists; physicians' assistants; psychology teachers; business, commerce, and marketing teachers; art, drama, and music teachers; physical education teachers; education teachers; English teachers; trade and industrial teachers; teachers, secondary school; archivists and curators; economists; psychologists; sociologists; social scientists, n.e.c.; religious workers, n.e.c.; authors; technical writers; designers; painters, sculptors, craft-artists, and artist printmakers; artists, performers, and related workers, n.e.c.; editors and reporters; and public relations specialists.

C. Technicians and Related Support Occupations. Biological technicians.

D. Sales Occupations. Real estate sales occupations; advertising and related sales occupations; sales workers, furniture and home furnishings; and sales support occupations, n.e.c.

E. Administrative Support Occupations, Including Clerical. Peripheral equipment operators; duplicating machine operators; mail preparing and paper handling machine operators; postal clerks, except mail carriers; mail clerks, except postal service; dispatchers; production coordinators; and weighers, measurers, checkers, and samplers.

F. Service Occupations. Protective service occupations, n.e.c.; supervisors, food preparation and service occupations; bartenders; cooks; waiters'/waitresses' assistants; miscellaneous food preparation occupations; and guides.

G. Farming, Forestry, and Fishing Occupations. Nursery workers; and inspectors, agricultural products.

H. Precision Production, Craft, and Repair Occupations. Tailors; optical goods workers; bookbinders; and bakers.

I. Operators, Fabricators, and Laborers. Miscellaneous printing machine operators; textile cutting machine operators; miscellaneous textile machine operators; packaging and filling machine operators; photographic process machine operators; assemblers; hand engraving and printing occupations; production inspectors, checkers, and examiners; production samplers and weighers; graders and sorters, except agricultural; and bus drivers.

Moderately Female Occupations (60 percent to 74.99 percent female)

A. Executive, Administrative, and Managerial Occupations. Managers, medicine and health; and underwriters.

B. Professional Specialty Occupations. Respiratory therapists; therapists, n.e.c.; foreign language teachers; social work teachers; teachers, n.e.c.; counselors, educational and vocational; social workers; and recreation workers.

C. Technicians and Related Support Occupations. Radiologic technicians; and health technologists and technicians, n.e.c.

D. Sales Occupations. Sales workers, shoes; sales workers, other commodities; sales counter clerks; street and door-to-door sales workers.

E. Administrative Support Occupations, Including Clerical. Supervisors, general office, supervisors, financial records processing; chief communications operators; computer operators; hotel clerks; transportation ticket and reservation agents; order clerks; cost and rate clerks; office machine operators, n.e.c.; communications equipment operators, n.e.c.; expediters; material recording, scheduling, and distributing clerks, n.e.c.; insurance adjusters, examiners, and investigators; investigators and adjusters, except insurance; bill and account collectors; statistical clerks; and administrative support occupations, n.e.c.

F. Service Occupations. Crossing guards; food counter, fountain and related occupations; supervisors, personal service occupations; and personal service occupations, n.e.c.

G. Farming, Forestry, and Fishing Occupations. Animal caretakers, except farm; and graders and sorters, agricultural products.

H. Precision Production, Craft, and Repair Occupations. Miscellaneous precision apparel and fabric workers; electrical and electronic equipment assemblers; and food batchmakers.

I. Operators, Fabricators, and Laborers. Typesetters and compositors; winding and twisting machine operators; knitting, looping, taping, and weaving machine operators; shoe machine operators; pressing machine operators; laundering and dry cleaning machine operators; folding machine operators; solderers and brazers; and hand packers and packagers.

Heavily Female Occupations (75 percent or more female)

A. Executive, Administrative, and Managerial Occupations. Management related occupations, n.e.c.

B. Professional Specialty Occupations. Registered nurses; dietitians; occupational therapists; physical therapists; speech therapists; health specialties teachers; home economics teachers; postsecondary teachers, subject not specified; teachers, prekindergarten and kindergarten; teachers, elementary school; teachers, special education; librarians; and dancers.

C. Technicians and Related Support Occupations. Clinical laboratory technologists and technicians; dental hygienists; health record technologists and technicians; licensed practical nurses; and legal assistants.

D. Sales Occupations. Sales workers, apparel; cashiers; and demonstrators, promoters and models, sales.

E. Administrative Support Occupations, Including Clerical. Secretaries; stenographers; typists; interviewers; receptionists; information clerks, n.e.c.; classified-ad clerks; correspondence clerks; personnel clerks, except payroll and timekeeping; library clerks; file clerks; records clerks; bookkeepers, accounting, and auditing clerks; payroll and timekeeping clerks; billing clerks; billing, posting, and calculating machine operators; telephone operators; eligibility clerks, social welfare; bill and account collectors; general office clerks; bank tellers; proofreaders; data entry keyers; and teachers' aides.

F. Service Occupations. Launderers and ironers; cooks, private household; housekeepers and butlers; child care workers, private household; private household cleaners and servants; waiters and waitresses; kitchen workers, food preparation; dental assistants; health aides, except nursing; nursing aides, orderlies, and attendants; maids and housemen; hairdressers and cosmetologists; public transportation attendants; welfare service aides; family child care providers; early childhood teacher's assistants; and child care workers, n.e.c.

G. Farming, Forestry, and Fishing Occupations. None.

H. Precision Production, Craft, and Repair Occupations. Dressmakers.

I. Operators, Fabricators, and Laborers. Textile sewing machine operators.

NOTE

This chapter is part of a larger collaborative project begun several years ago by James A. and Laura E. Geschwender. Co-authored papers were presented at the 1994 annual meetings of the Society for the Study of Social Problems and the American Sociological Association. A third co-authored manuscript grew out of discussions that arose at the sessions in which these papers were presented. Material from these three manuscripts is incorporated into the sections of this chapter entitled "Occupational and Gender Earnings Inequality," "Findings," and "Methodology." The material in the sections entitled "The Labor Process and Gender Earnings Inequality," "Discussion and Conclusions," and "Theoretical Implications" represents the thinking of James, who is solely responsible for their content.

1. We recognize gender and sex are not interchangeable terms and will use the term "sex" when referring to any notion suggestive of an empirical referent of gender since sex is the proxy measure for gender in this analysis.

9

Forms of the Labor Process and Labor's Share of Value

THOMAS L. STEIGER

The publication of *Labor and Monopoly Capital* stood in stark contrast to the generally optimistic views of the postindustrialists, especially that of Daniel Bell in *The Coming of Post-Industrial Society* (1973). Although Braverman was not alone in asking the question whether the increasing application of science and technology in the workplace, loosely labeled "automation," was positive for workers (see Bright 1958; Horowitz and Herrenstadt 1966), he linked them to inherent tensions found in the capitalist employment relationship. Since Braverman, development of labor process theory with rare exception has taken one of the following forms: the shopfloor studies of the transformation of the labor process (cf. Burawoy, 1979; Zimbalist 1979; Shaiken 1994); or studies placing the labor process in a historical political economy (cf. R. Edwards 1979; Clawson 1980; Gordon, Reich, and Edwards 1982).

Critics, too, have developed and refined labor process theory. Braverman's concept of skill was critiqued (Beechey 1982; Littler 1982; Cockburn 1983; Hochschild 1983; Spenner 1983; Leidner 1993) as was, eventually, his idea that work was degraded or deskilled (Kusterer 1978; Hirschorn 1984; Zuboff 1988, Penn 1984), as well as his placing of Taylorism at the heart of capitalism (A. Friedman 1977; Stark 1980; Piore and Sabel 1984; V. Smith 1990). (See Meiksins [1994:46–52] for a full review of Braverman's critics.) But few scholars who have taken Braverman as a point of departure kept his greatest theoretical contribution in full view: the linking of the capitalist employment relationship to change in the workplace.

I contend that a problem with current studies of the workplace and labor process is that, while focusing on the crucial issue of control, questions about why a struggle occurs over workplace control are being ignored (for an exception, see Kraft, this volume). It should not be forgotten that "the theoretical context of Braverman's *Labor and Monopoly Capital* is a classical Marxist analysis of the specifically capitalist labor process" (Cohen 1987:36). What defines the capitalist labor process is "a unity of the process of production and the process of valorization" (Cohen 1987:36).

Valorization is the process of producing an object (or service) with use-value, exchange value, and surplus value. Use-value refers to the particular use a commodity can be put or to the human need it fulfills. Exchange value refers to the value a particular commodity has in relation to other commodities and in a cash economy to the monetary value of that commodity. Surplus value is created through the reduction of the socially necessary labor time to produce a particular commodity (object to be sold). In other words, workers must produce commodities or services whose total exchange value surpasses the value of their wages, the salaries of their managers, and other production costs. In short, workers must be exploited. Following Cohen (1987:35), restoring "a Marxist understanding of *valorization* and *exploitation* as central to the operation of the capitalist labor process" (italics in original) might clear a path through the current theoretical doldrums plaguing labor process theory.

THE CONCEPT OF LABOR'S SHARE

The concept of labor's share finds its roots in the classical political economists' assumptions regarding the laws that govern the distribution of the fruits of production among the classes that produce them (Kalleberg, Wallace, and Raffalovich 1984:386). In essence, labor's share must be part of any answer to the question of how the fruits of production are divided among the classes. Importantly, labor's share does not directly correspond to labor's effort, yet labor's share and that of other employees and stakeholders is created in the labor process. Rather than focus on the market as the source of value creation, for labor process theory it is the point of production, the workplace, where value is created and appropriated. Adding a measure of the amount of appropriation should be important to labor process research.

Nevertheless, few sociologists have employed this useful concept (for exceptions, see Kalleberg, Wallace, and Raffalovich 1984 and Raffalovich, Wallace, and Leicht 1992). Rather, most sociologists, even self-identified Marxist sociologists, have analyzed class differences in economic rewards using data on individuals (Wright 1985). Labor economists, meanwhile, use the concept to gauge long-term changes in the distribution of income (rewards) to different groups, but rarely do they relate these changes to the labor process or features of the workplace. Seldom do labor economists relate the value of the product or services rendered to the producers' share of income.

Most of the literature on labor's share is highly technical, focusing on one of two questions. One question is related to Marx's idea of the tendency for the rate of profit to fall; the other question accounts for labor's share, focusing for the most part on macroeconomic factors responsible for shifts in the division of the economic pie. Some observers raise questions about relative shares of value produced and issues of exploitation (see Shakow, Graham, and Gibson 1992), an issue that has relevance to labor process theory.

Kalleberg et al. (1984) represent possibly the only effort to incorporate labor's share into labor process research. Their multivariate time series analysis of the printing and publishing industry included three variables related to the labor process, referred to as indicators of worker power. Using strike frequency, percent unionized, and an interaction term of percent unionized and time, they found that percent unionized was positively related to labor's share as measured by an income–profits ratio. The union–time interaction term was negatively related, indicating the diminishing strength of unions over the time period covered, while the impact of strike frequency was positive.

I use the concept of labor's share to explore decennial data (1950 to 1990) on nineteen manufacturing industry groups for evidence of increasing exploitation of labor and decreasing shares of labor's income. Central to this investigation will be evidence of changes in socially necessary labor time, the time workers spend producing products or services equivalent to their wages. Using eight proxy measures of the labor process, I also explore four trends in the labor process and relate them to changes in labor's share and socially necessary labor time.

VARIABLES AND DATA

Decennial data from 1950 to 1990 on nineteen manufacturing industries allows for systematic cross-industry comparisons over a long period of time. Long-term trends are likely to suggest structural changes as opposed to shorter, more cyclic, or possibly more superficial changes. (All measures of labor's share, necessary labor time, and the labor process, as well as the data sources, can be found in the Appendix.)

The primary source of data is the *Annual Survey of Manufactures* for 1950, 1960, 1970, 1980, and 1990. The industries examined are the nineteen two-digit Standard Industry Code groups. They are: Food and kindred products (FOOD); Tobacco products (TOBC); Textile mill products (TEXT); Apparel and other textile products (APRL); Paper and allied products (PAPR);

Printing and publishing (PRTG); Chemicals and allied products (CHEM); Petroleum and coal products (PETC); Rubber and miscellaneous plastics products (RUBR); Leather and leather products (LEAT); Lumber and wood products (LUMB); Furniture and fixtures (FURN); Stone, clay, and glass products (STON); Primary metal industries (PRIM); Fabricated metal products (FABM); Industrial machinery and equipment (MACH); Electronic and other electric equipment (ELCM); Transportation equipment (TRAN); and Instruments and related products (INST).

I use two measures of labor's share. The first is a wages-surplus value ratio (LSV), analogous to the rate of surplus value (Moseley 1991:49). This provides a measure of exploitation. In this case, if the ratio decreases over time, it means that labor is producing increasingly more than the value of the wages received for doing so. The other labor's share measure is labor's share of income (LSI). Together, these measures represent the monetary rewards of production distributed to productive labor. I also construct measures of capital's share of income (CSI) and unproductive labor's share of income (ULSI). These measures represent the proportions of the total combined incomes (total after tax profits and total payroll) divided among the principal groups responsible for production.

A word should be said about the important distinction made between productive and unproductive labor. Theoretically this is a crucial distinction if the categories used are to reflect differences in types of labor processes and levels of authority surrounding the points of production. Moseley (1991:34) made this point, for example:

> Marx's concepts of constant capital and variable capital refer only to capital invested in *production activities*, where "production" is defined fairly broadly to include such activities as transportation and storage. However the definition of "production" specifically does not include the following two types of activities within capitalist enterprises:
> 1. *Circulation activities* related to the exchange of commodities and money. . . .
> 2. *Supervisory activities* related to the control and surveillance of the labor of production workers, including such functions as the transmission of orders, the direct supervision of production workers, the supervision of supervisors, etc. up to top management, the creation and processing of production and payroll records for individuals and groups of employees, etc. (emphasis in original)

A closely related variable to labor's share is socially necessary labor time (SNLT). SNLT is the amount of time it takes a worker to produce products with the value equivalent of his or her wages, while the remaining time is spent producing products which generate value used to support nonproductive activities. Assuming the standard of an eight-hour day, SNLT is estimated by dividing production wages by value added by manufacture and multiplying by eight.

Other than measures of skill, few "conventional" quantitative measures of the labor process exist and few attempts have been made to quantify the labor process. One exception is Bowles, Gordon, and Weisskopf (1983). They estimated employer control over workers using four variables: (1) cost of job loss: the average number of weeks pay lost due to layoffs; (2) degree of supervision: the ratio of nonproduction workers to production workers; (3) index of earnings inequality: the ratio of white male earnings to female and black male earnings; (4) the inverse of strength of unions: the percentage of the labor force that are union members. Moseley (1986:211–12) identified a fifth variable, "workers' motivation" to work estimated by the industrial accident rate. Workers' motivation is assumed to be predicated on the quality of working conditions, and if the conditions are poor, resulting in what workers perceive as unnecessary accidents, their motivation levels will be low. Of the above, I found industry-specific data for three of these labor process proxy measures: the rate of supervision (RPUW); the proportion of the labor force that are union members (UNIO); and the accident rate (INJR).

I added five additional proxy measures of the labor process: the percent skilled production workers (SKLD); the percent female production workers (FEML); two measures of work stoppages (STP1, STP2); and the average length (in hours) of the work week (WRKW). The percent skilled is perhaps the only "conventional" quantitative measure of the labor process. Assuming that highly paid, highly skilled work typically has been reserved for males, the percent female taps a different dimension related to control. Increases in the proportion of females could indicate a loss of control over portions of the labor process (Cockburn 1985). Aside from the issue of control, the entrance of females into an occupation has been accompanied by a devaluation of labor (Reskin and Roos 1990; see also Geschwender, this volume).

Insofar as work stoppages must be organized, this variable taps another source of control. Two measures are used, one being the total number of strikes over the year in the industry and the other being the total number of man-days idle. Ideally I would have used a measure of "strike volume" (Wallace 1979), which would include a third measure, strike duration, but it was not available for all the industries.

FINDINGS

Because of the volume and cumbersome nature of the data,[1] I determined for each industry whether the variables were either increasing or decreasing over time. In most cases this was easily done via visual inspection of the data. However, in some cases the pattern was curvilinear, increasing (or decreasing) for a few decades then reversing direction. In some cases, to help determine the most general trend, I calculated two-year moving averages, using the adjoining decennial figures (i.e., the average of 1950 and 1960, the average of 1960 and 1970, etc). For the variables STP1, STP2, and WRKW I used two-year moving averages for each industry (these averages are not shown). I have indicated with an asterisk the variables and industries for which I used this method to determine the general trend.

Obviously focusing just on the trend ignores some important differences among these industries, namely, the amount of change. But for now I am interested only in seeing, at a very aggregate level, whether identifiable forms of the labor process can be observed and whether different forms might produce different outcomes. Also, 1950 and 1990 become more important data points than the other years because I do not permit any other conclusion than increasing or decreasing. Thus, if the indices for 1990 were less than 1950, generally the trend will be decreasing and if the 1990 indices are greater than 1950, generally the trend will be increasing.

Table 9.1 shows the general trends found in labor's share of value (LSV), socially necessary labor time (SNLT), and the income share measures (LSI, CSI, and ULSI). The column labeled LSV shows the trends for labor's share of value. Eighteen of nineteen industries show evidence of declining LSV. STON is the only exception and this is only because 1990 labor's share is the highest of the years examined, but labor's share declined in each prior decade beginning in 1950. In every industry SNLT decreased. The trends for LSV and SNLT leave no other conclusion than the exploitation of labor is increasing among these manufacturing industries.

A more common way of measuring labor's value, however, relies simply on shares of income (cf. Raffalovich, 1992). It stands to reason that we should examine labor's share of income, since the income workers receive is one way they gauge their value in the employment relationship. Also, doing so will permit us to see if there is an obvious relationship between income and value as well as whether shares of income vary with changes in the labor process. Looking at the column labeled LSI, the results suggest a possible correlation with LSV and SNLT. Of the eighteen industries that show declining trends in both LSV and SNLT, fourteen industries show declining trends of LSI (ELCM, FURN, LEAT, PAPR, CHEM, INST, MACH, PETC, LUMB, TOBC, APRL, PRTG, FABM, and FOOD). STON shows an increasing trend for LSV, a decreasing trend for SNLT, and an increasing trend for LSI. Nevertheless, since LSI has decreased in fourteen of the nineteen industries, the income measure of labor's value correlates with the LSV

Table 9.1. Summary of General Trends for Labor's Share of Value, Socially Necessary Labor Time, and Income Shares, 1950–90

	LSV	SNLT	LSI	CSI	ULSI
STON	I*	D	I	D	I
ELCM	D	D	D	D	I
RUBR	D*	D	I*	D	I
FURN	D	D	D	D*	I
LEAT	D	D	D*	I	I
PAPR	D	D	D*	D	I
CHEM	D	D	D*	D	I
INST	D	D	D	D	I
MACH	D	D	D	D*	I
TEXT	D	D	I	D	D*
PRIM	D	D	I*	D	I
PETC	D	D	D	I	I
LUMB	D	D	D*	D	I
TOBC	D	D	D	I	I
APRL	D	D	D	I	I
PRTG	D	D	D	I	I
FABM	D	D	D*	I	D*
TRAN	D	D	I	D	D
FOOD	D	D	D*	I*	D*

FOOD—Food and kindred products
TOBC—Tobacco products
TEXT—Textile mill products
APRL—Apparel and other textile products
PAPR—Paper and allied products
PRTG—Printing and publishing
CHEM—Chemicals and allied products
PETC—Petroleum and coal products
RUBR—Rubber and miscellaneous plastics products
LEAT—Leather and leather products

LUMB—Lumber and wood products
FURN—Furniture and fixtures
STON—Stone, clay, and glass products
PRIM—Primary metal industries
FABM—Fabricated metal products
MACH—Industrial machinery and equipment
ELCM—Electronic and other electric equipment
TRAN—Transportation equipment
INST—Instruments and related equipment

LSV—Labor's share of value
SNLT—Socially necessary labor time
LSI—Labor's share of income
CIS—Capital's share of income
ULSI—Unproductive labor's share of income

* Two-year (decennial data) moving averages used to determine trend.

and SNLT measures in suggesting a declining value of labor over time and across industries.

The results for CSI, capital's share of income, suggests that capital is losing shares of income in more industries than it is gaining. In twelve industries, the trend is toward a declining share of income for capital (STON, ELCM, RUBR, FURN, PAPR, CHEM, INST, MACH, PRIM, LUMB, and TRAN). These findings lend themselves to the idea of a "profit squeeze," suggesting why capital has sought to reduce costs and gain efficiency through reorganizing labor processes. In seven industries, ELCM, FURN, PAPR, CHEM, INST, MACH, and LUMB, both LSI and CSI are declining. This suggests a more complex relationship between capital and labor than simply one gains at the expense of the other.

While labor or capital is losing shares in most industries, unproductive labor is gaining income share in fifteen of the nineteen industries. As Moseley (1991) stressed, the intensification of labor increases the rate of surplus value and reduces socially necessary labor time on the one hand, but it simultaneously contributes to massive bureaucratic structures needed to supervise the labor process on the other. Similar to the trust put in foremen who profited greatly from the inside contracting system (Clawson 1980), middle managers may have gained because of the drive to intensify the productive labor process.

The results shown in Table 9.1 suggest that from 1950 to 1990 the exploitation of labor increased. Although in a handful of industries labor appears to have made gains relative to capital in terms of income shares, the larger picture suggests that unproductive labor (middle management and their administrative workers) have fared better than either labor or capital. Perhaps this provides some insight into the increased layoffs among this group of workers since the mid to late 1980s.

Table 9.2 summarizes the findings for the proxy measures of the labor process. One purpose for examining data across industries was to see if different forms of the labor process were evident. Using the eight proxy measures of the labor process and the general direction of the trend in those variables over the forty-year period, six industry groups emerge suggestive of different forms of the labor process.

One group consisting of STON, ELCM, FURN, and LEAT, match on six variables. Each industry shows increasing SKLD, FEML, and INJR. They match on decreasing RPUW, UNIO, and WRKW. STON, ELCM, and RUBR also share increasing STP1 and STP2. Another group of industries (PAPR, CHEM, INST, and MACH) shows increasing SKLD and FEML and decreasing RPUW, INJR, UNIO, and WRKW. PAPR and CHEM also show increasing STP1 and STP2. This group really only differs from the first group on injury rates (INJR). Otherwise, they are very similar. Another group (TEXT, PRIM, PETC, LUMB) shows increasing SKLD, FEML, and

Table 9.2. Summary of General Trends for Selected Proxy Measures of the Labor Process, 1950–90

	SKLD	FEML	RPUW	INJR	UNIO	STP1*	STP2*	WRKW*
STON	I	I	D	I	D	I	I	D
ELCM	I	I	D	I	D	I	I	D
RUBR	I	I	D	I	D	I	I	D
FURN	I	I	D	I	D	D	I	D
LEAT	I	I	D	I	D	D	D	D
PAPR	I	I*	D	D	D	I	I	D
CHEM	I	I	D	D	D	I	I	D
INST	I	I	D	D	D	D	I	D
MACH	I	I	D	D	D	I	D	D
TEXT	I	I	D	I	D	D	D	I
PRIM	I	I	D	I	D	D	I	I
PETC	I	I	D	D	I	I	I	I
LUMB	I	I	D	D	D	D	D	I
TOBC	I	D	D	I	D	D	D	I
APRL	I	D*	D	I	D	D	D	I
PRTG	D	I	D	I	D	I	I	D
FABM	D	I	D	I	D	I	I	D
TRAN	D	I	D	I	D	D	I	D
FOOD	I	I	I	I	D	D	I	D

FOOD—Food and kindred products
TOBC—Tobacco products
TEXT—Textile mill products
APRL—Apparel and other textile products
PAPR—Paper and allied products
PRTG—Printing and publishing
CHEM—Chemicals and allied products
PETC—Petroleum and coal products
RUBR—Rubber and miscellaneous plastics products
LEAT—Leather and leather products

LUMB—Lumber and wood products
FURN—Furniture and fixtures
STON—Stone, clay, and glass products
PRIM—Primary metal industries
FABM—Fabricated metal products
MACH—Industrial machinery and equipment
ELCM—Electronic and other electric equipment
TRAN—Transportation equipment
INST—Instruments and related equipment

SKLD—Percent skilled production workers
FEML—Percent female production workers
STP1—Work stoppages, number
STP2—Work stoppages, man days idle
INJR—Injury frequency rate

RPUW—Ratio of productive to unproductive workers
UNIO—Percent of workforce covered by collective bargaining agreement
WRKW—Average hours per week worked, production workers

* Two-year (decennial data) moving averages used to determine trend.

WRKW and decreasing RPUW. TEXT and PRIM both show increasing injury rates (INJR) while PETC and LUMB show decreasing injury rates. This group differs from the first two groups mainly in the increasing average work week. These three industrial groups have in common increasing skill and the feminization of production workers, and a decline in productive workers relative to supervisory and other unproductive workers.

TOBC and APRL suggest a different form of the labor process. Both show increasing SKLD, INJR, and WRKW but decreasing FEML, RPUW, UNIO, STP1, and STP2. PRTG, FABM, and TRAN form another group showing increasing FEML, INJR, and STP2 and decreasing SKLD, RPUW, UNIO, and WRKW. Finally FOOD is exceptional because it is the only industry to show an increasing ratio of productive to unproductive workers (RPUW).

The most common trends across industries are the decreasing ratios of productive to unproductive workers (RPUW) (18 of 19 industries), decreasing UNIO (18 of 19 industries, though the data are only for 1980 to 1990), increasing proportion of female production workers (FEML) (17 of 19 industries), and increasing proportions of skilled production workers (SKLD) (16 of 19 industries).

Undoubtedly some may be surprised at the number of industries with increasing proportions of skilled production workers. These findings would appear to contradict one of Braverman's (1974) central notions regarding capitalist labor processes. However, when coupled with the increasing proportions of female production workers, and based on case studies of bakers (Steiger and Reskin 1990) and printers (Roos 1990) and the research of Steiger and Wardell (1992), it seems reasonable that some portion of those women entered the ranks of the skilled. Based on the case studies of bakers and printers, despite skilled occupations retaining their skilled status, enough happened socially and technologically to those occupations that they lost economically over time. Thus, although the evidence does not support a "deskilling" hypothesis, the question of labor's value is quite another matter.

Only one industry, STON, shows evidence for increasing LSV. Yet it shows identical patterns on all labor process variables as ELCM and RUBR, who show declining LSV. Every industry, regardless of measures of the labor process shows declining SNLT. Indeed, in 1950 twelve industries showed socially necessary labor time of three hours or greater; by 1990 only nine industries showed socially necessary labor time of two hours or more. Furthermore, decreasing shares of income for labor seem to be associated with increasing SKLD, increasing FEML, decreasing RPUW, decreasing UNIO, and decreasing WRKW. Of the nine industries that share that pattern (STON, ELCM, RUBR, FURN, LEAT, PAPR, CHEM, INST, and MACH), seven show decreasing labor's share of income. Of the six industries that show increasing labor's share of income, those industries have increasing INJR rates in common. But TOBC and APRL also show increasing INJR with decreasing LSI.

Considering these seeming anomalies, STON, ELCM, and RUBR are identical in terms of the direction of the trends among the eight labor process variables, yet STON is the only industry to show evidence for increasing LSV (but still a decreasing socially necessary labor time). And, consider that TOBC, APRL, PRTG, and FABM are about as different in terms of their labor processes as can be found here. They match on only three of eight labor process measures. Yet, all four show declining LSV, declining SNLT, declining LSI, and increasing CSI and three of the industries show increasing ULSI. The data taken as a whole suggest a general trend toward greater exploitation of labor regardless of the form taken by the capitalist labor process.

DISCUSSION AND CONCLUSION

One major finding of this research suggests that "reskilling" (Penn 1984) has been more common than deskilling, at least when measured at the aggregate level. Perhaps this is indicative of the spread of "flexible specialization" (Piore and Sabel 1984). Yet, how can reskilling and the greater presence of skilled workers, usually associated with higher levels of wages and workers' control, be reconciled with the other major finding, namely, increasing exploitation? Cohen (1987:48) wrote: "labor process writers have never considered the labor process from the point of view of value; the issue simply has not been on their theoretical agenda." By examining the labor process from the perspective of value, a different conceptualization of this phenomenon can be proposed that incorporates expanded skills, changes in the degree of control, and changes in the gender and race composition of the labor force. Instead of focusing on deskilling or loss of workers' control, as was common in the early days of labor process research, conceptualizing transformations of the workplace as part of a larger process, in which expanded skills might not result in augmented value of labor, should permit all of these factors to be explained. "Devaluation" is not just a matter of cheapening labor costs at the point of production through deskilling or breaking craft traditions. It could take a variety of forms, including deskilling, reskilling, or reallocating who does specific work.

Additionally, patriarchy and racism fit well with the requirements of a capitalist political economy and produce whole groups of devalued labor—women, racial minorities, children, and increasingly the aged (see Geschwender, this volume). The work typically assigned to these groups is considered of less skill, not necessarily because the work is less skilled in an objective sense, but because valued or privileged people can avoid it or push it off on devalued people to do. Consequently, it has been easier for women and racial minorities to raise the value of their labor by gaining access to the exclusive white males' work environment than it has been to raise the value of the work traditionally done by women and minorities. Viewed in this way, should it be surprising that the industries which have had the most spectacular stories of deskilling and breaking of craft organizations were mostly industries with white male craftsmen? In the nineteen manufacturing industries examined here, the vast majority experienced significant incorporations of women into production jobs, once the province of men (were complete data available, an increase in the proportion of racial minorities in production jobs would likely be observed as well).

Finally, one intriguing aspect of the findings reported here is that perhaps variations in labor processes are largely inconsequential for labor's share. If true, the emphasis traditionally placed on deskilling in the labor process literature must now be reassessed, as skill and the value of labor might well be independent of each other. Consider, for example, that the introduction of computers into the office has enhanced the skills of secretaries, but secretarial work has not generally been thought to have increased in value (see Greenbaum as well as Rogers, this volume). Moreover, since the three industries that show evidence of deskilling are printing and publishing, fabricated metal products, and transportation equipment (including autos) (see Gartman, this volume), and given how many labor process studies have been conducted in these industries, it might be wise to branch out to other industries. Perhaps conclusions about deskilling reached by labor process researchers in the 1970s and 1980s reflect their research site or the historical context. Shopfloor studies in the stone, clay, and glass industries might prove very enlightening considering that is it the only industry group to show increases in labor's share of value, though only because of the tremendous increase from 1980 to 1990. Studies of the food industry, with its increasing SKLD, might prove valuable in furthering our understanding of capitalist labor processes, especially since it is alone in showing evidence of an increasing ratio of productive to nonproductive workers. Additional research of this kind, joined with a "value perspective," would undoubtedly yield more theoretical insights about the connections among variations in the labor processes, work-related changes (e.g., contingent work), and workers' agency (see Isaac and Christiansen, this volume).

Still, the forms of capitalist labor processes, however varied, do not take away from the common result of this research. The transformations, whatever they are, generally seem to be successful at increasing the exploitation of labor, as measured by labor's share of value, necessary labor time, and labor's income. Indeed, what does it mean if reskilling or upgrading occurs without a correlational increase in the value of labor? The evidence presented here suggests such an occurrence is not unusual. Perhaps the future holds a more complex and vexing experience for workers, a future that combines continuous reskilling and more mental than manual work with decreases in the value of that labor.

APPENDIX

Data Sources and Estimation of Variables

1. *Wages–surplus value ratio.* Data were taken from the 1950, 1960, 1970, 1980, and 1990 "Annual Survey of Manufactures." Using columns "Value-added by manufacture" and "Production workers—wages," subtract "wages" from "value-added," then divide this remainder by "wages."

   (value added − wages) / wages

2. *Socially necessary labor time.* Data were taken from the 1950, 1960, 1970, 1980, and 1990 "Annual Survey of Manufactures." Using columns "Value-added by manufacture" and "Production workers—wages," I divided "wages" by "valued-added" and multiplied by 8.

   (wages / value added) $\times$ 8

3. *Wages–profit ratio.* Data were taken from the 1950, 1960, 1970, 1980, and 1990 "Annual Survey of Manufactures" and volumes 1 and 2 of the "National Income and Product Accounts" (1950 through 1980) and the "Survey of Current Business" (August 1993). Using data from column "After-tax profits" from Table 6.19B (1950 to 1980) and Table 6.19C for 1990, and data from the "Annual Survey of Manufactures" in column "Production workers—wages," divide "wages" by "after-tax profits."

   wages / profits

4. *Labor's share of income.* Data were taken from the 1950, 1960, 1970, 1980, and 1990 "Annual Survey of Manufactures" and volumes 1 and 2 of the "National Income and Product Accounts" (1950 through 1980) and the "Survey of Current Business" (August 1993). Using data from column "After-tax profits" from Table 6.19B (1950 to 1980) and Table 6.19C for 1990, and data from the "Annual Survey of Manufactures" in column "Production workers—wages" and "All employees—payroll." Divide "production workers—wages" by the total of "payroll" and "after-tax profits."

   wages/(payroll + profits)

5. *Capital's share of income.* Data were taken from the 1950, 1960, 1970, 1980, and 1990 "Annual Survey of Manufactures" and volumes 1 and 2 of the "National Income and Product Accounts" (1950 through 1980) and the "Survey of Current Business" (August 1993). Using data from column "After-tax profits" from Table 6.19B (1950 to 1980) and Table 6.19C for 1990, and data from the "Annual Survey of Manufactures" in column "Production workers—wages" and "All employees—payroll," I divided "after-tax profits" by the total of "payroll" and "after-tax profits."

profits / (payroll + profits)

6. *Unproductive labor's share of income.* Data were taken from the 1950, 1960, 1970, 1980, and 1990 "Annual Survey of Manufactures" and volumes 1 and 2 of the "National Income and Product Accounts" (1950 through 1980) and the "Survey of Current Business" (August 1993). Using data from column "After-tax profits" from Table 6.19B (1950 to 1980) and Table 6.19C for 1990, and data from the "Annual Survey of Manufactures" in column "Production workers—wages" and "All employees—payroll," I subtracted "wages" from "payroll," then divided this remainder by the total of "payroll" and "after-tax profits."

(payroll − wages) / (payroll + profits)

7. *Percent skilled production workers* (SKLD). For 1950, 1960, 1970, and 1980 these data were taken from the special subject reports, "Occupation by Industry," from the decennial census that provides breakdowns by both detailed occupation and detailed industry. The estimate of "skilled production workers" was taken by first estimating the total number of production workers (technicians, craftsmen and kindred workers, operatives, and laborers) then dividing this total by the sum of technicians and craftsmen and kindred workers). The 1990 data were taken from "Occupation by Industry," a CD-ROM from the Department of Commerce that contains data broken down by detailed occupation and detailed industry and using the same procedure as indicated above.

8. *Percent female production workers* (FEML). For 1950, 1960, 1970, and 1980 these data were taken from the special subject reports, "Occupation by Industry," from the decennial census, which provides breakdowns by both detailed occupation and detailed industry by sex. The estimate of "percent female production workers" was taken by first estimating the total number of production workers (technicians, craftsmen and kindred workers, operatives, and laborers), then dividing this total by the sum of

female production workers. The 1990 data were taken from a special tabulation of data obtained from the Bureau of Labor Statistics for 1990 that contained breakdowns by detailed occupation and detailed industry by sex. The same procedure was used as in previous years to derive the estimate.

9. *Work stoppages, number* (STP1). Data were taken directly from the "Statistical Abstract of the United States," 74th edition, 84th edition, 93rd edition, and 103rd edition. Data are not available for industry groups after 1980.

10. *Work stoppages, man days idle* (STP2). Data were taken directly from the "Statistical Abstract of the United States," 74th edition, 84th edition, 93rd edition, and 103rd edition. Data are not available for industry groups after 1980.

11. *Injury frequency rate* (INJR). Data were taken directly from the "Statistical Abstract of the United States," 74th edition, 84th edition, 93rd edition, 103 edition, and 113th edition. Data reported by the Department of Commerce from 1950 to 1970 is calculated thus: average number of disabling work injuries per million employee hours worked. For 1980 and 1990, the official calculation of this statistic changed. For these years the calculation is: any occupation injury or illness, the number of incidents or lost workdays, multiplied by 200,000 as base for one hundred full-time equivalent workers divided by total hours worked for all employees.

12. *Ratio of productive to unproductive workers* (RPUW). Using data from the 1950, 1960, 1970, 1980, and 1990 "Annual Survey of Manufactures," subtracting totals under "Production workers—number" from total found under "All employees," then dividing "Production workers—number," for each industry, by the remainder of above.

production workers / (all employees − production workers)

13. *Percent of workforce covered by collective bargaining agreement* (UNIO). Data are not available for this estimate prior to 1983. Data were taken from Hirsch and Macpherson (1994), Table 12b, %Cov. Data were not available for either 1980 or 1990, thus I used data from 1983 for 1980 and for 1988 for 1990.

14. *Average hours per week worked, production workers* (WRKW). Data were taken from the 1950, 1960, 1970, 1980, and 1990 "Annual Survey of Manufactures." Using columns "Production workers—number" and "Production workers—hours," I divided hours by production workers (converted to millions) and divided again by 52.

(production hours / production workers) / 52

NOTE

An earlier version of this essay, "Trends in Labor's Share of Value, 1950–1990," was presented at the annual meetings of the Society for the Study of Social Problems, Los Angeles, California, August 1991. Special thanks to Paul Burkett and Scott Camp for discussions on the share debate, the labor process, and for comments on earlier drafts of this essay. Thanks also to my co-editors, Mark and Peter, for their comments on an earlier draft, their support, and impromptu discussions regarding this research. Special thanks to Mark for his editorial suggestions, which greatly improved the chapter. Any mistakes or misinterpretations are entirely my own. Funding to purchase the CD-ROM, *Occupation by Industry*, SSTF14 from the U.S. Bureau of the Census and for the special tabulation of 1990 data from the Bureau of Labor Statistics, came from the generous support of the Department of Sociology, Indiana State University, Terre Haute, IN 47809.

1. Because of space limitations, a lengthy appendix containing a detailed discussion of the findings including six tables was omitted. Interested parties may contact the author at Department of Sociology, Indiana State University, Terre Haute, IN 47802.

10

Reevaluating the Labor
Process Debate

CHRIS SMITH AND PAUL THOMPSON

A question on a recent U.K. university exam paper read, "To what extent is labor process theory (LPT) appropriate to the contemporary study of work organization?" This testifies both to the continuing centrality of LPT to mainstream academic debate, but also to the increasing questioning of its practical and theoretical relevance. A growing number of commentators claim that LPT has either been bypassed by real changes in production and work organization, or has marginalized itself by the particular directions the analysis has taken.

With respect to the first, this chapter critically evaluates the claims made by the advocates of various "new paradigms" that the contemporary division of labor in the workplace has developed in substantially different directions than envisaged by Braverman and labor process theorists. It will argue that those claims are largely unjustified, but that real changes are nevertheless taking place. As for the latter, we examine the diverse paths taken within labor process analysis in order to extend the original framework, notably the attempts to provide an account of subjectivity, and to reconnect the analysis to class theory. Our view is that these are flawed enterprises and that there are more fruitful ways to open out labor process theory, in particular, to situate workplace relations between capital and labor within the context of new patterns of global competition. Of course this kind of argument partly reflects the particular form the debate has taken in Britain and it is part of our purpose to reflect those issues. But the general issues are also of wider concern and help to answer the question of whether LPT has a future as well as a past.

THE CONTEMPORARY DIVISION OF
LABOR IN THE WORKPLACE

LPT became associated, in many ways misleadingly, with a deskilling thesis. For a decade after the publication of *Labor and Monopoly Capital* argument raged over the extent and character of changes in workplace divisions of labor, but the *trend* toward fragmentation of traditional skills and limits to new ones seemed clear. The 1980s, however, brought with it the rise of "new paradigms"—flexible specialization, regulation theory, post-Fordism, and lean production. Though distinctive in their concepts and claims, supporters of new paradigms were all optimistic about the link between advanced manufacturing systems and the utilization of skilled labor. In most cases this did not rely on an argument that Braverman and LPT were wrong, merely that they were outdated. Each of the new paradigms relied on a polarity between mass production and some form of flexibility that breaks with Fordism and Taylorism. Nor was this debate confined to manufacturing and the shopfloor. For example, Baran (1988) conceded that the first wave of office automation largely conformed to Braverman's picture, but argued that a second wave is ushering in a reintegrated labor process and multi-activity jobs.

Some perspectives appear to go backwards from Braverman and emphasize new forms of craft labor. This is particularly the case with flexible specialization theories (Piore and Sabel 1984) that argue a division of labor based on fragmented skills and repetitive work is incompatible with the new technological, market conditions. These require intellectual participation from workers with upgraded skills and greater autonomy. Similar themes emerge in the influential work of Kern and Schumann (1984) on "new production concepts." They talk of reprofessionalization based on reintegration of mental and manual labor and an extensive degree of autonomy in the work environment. In contrast to craft labor, the new "professionals" combine a variety of different skills. More recently partisans of "lean production" have pursued the twin themes of "smarter" and more autonomous workers, but with the emphasis shifting to the value of team-based operations, within which multiskilled workers use highly flexible, automated machines to produce the necessary variety of products (Womack, Roos, and Jones 1990:13–14). Even postmodernists have been getting in on the act, with an emphasis on de-differentiation in the division of labor: "Post-modernism points to a more organic, less differentiated enclave of organization than those dominated by the bureaucratic designs of modernity" (Clegg 1990:181).

The optimistic outcomes of all these processes are summarized by Mathews (1993:7): "In place of command and control structures designed to enforce rigidity and compliance, the new production systems call for management that offers facilitation, guidance, and co-ordination between self-managing groups of employees who are capable of looking after the details of production themselves." Other managerial initiatives, notably Total Quality Management (see Kraft, this volume), are held to offer a more interdependent workplace, with flatter structures and reduced hierarchy. The human resource measures are aimed at replacing control with high commitment (Wood and Albanese 1995).

If these greater practical and ideological interdependencies are created and sustained, the logical outcome would be decisive changes in relations between the major actors in the workplace. The differences between capital (and its managerial agents) and labor would be blurred and alliances of self-interest developed. Tony Smith summarizes the argument: "In flexible production systems the rational self-interest of those who own and control capital leads them to transform work relations in a way that is in the interests of labor" (1994:42). Not only is labor utilized in a manner that mobilizes its intelligence, skills, and involvement, but policy measures in the employment sphere, such as profit-sharing and greater job security, reinforce a system of mutual obligation.

There are some well known and highly effective general critiques of the idea of a fundamental break in capitalist production and markets (Williams et al. 1987; Pollert 1991; Hyman 1991). Researchers, particularly those influenced by LPT, have also mounted a sustained critique of the claims of new paradigms with respect to the two traditional labor process spheres of skill and control.

Skill and the Division of Labor

It is recognized that skill variety is necessary to exploit arrangements such as just-in-time and modular production. But variations or new responsibilities such as self-maintenance may be small and it is more accurate to speak of an enlarged number of interchangeable tasks carried out by substitutable labor, or a broader scope of skills not higher ones (Elger 1991; Pollert 1991; Delbridge et al. 1992; Altmann 1995). As for "new" skills such as being a good team member, Nissen and Seybold (1994:42), following Braverman's perspective, have argued that "This is not genuine skill being sought, but rather worker attitudes and personal characteristics most useful for company profitability." Teamworking certainly creates opportunities for restructuring the labor process in ways that undermine traditional skill hierarchies. In the commercial vehicle sector in the United Kingdom, management now exclusively recruits semiskilled workers (Thompson et al. 1995). Teamworking provides a focus for the break with craft traditions and their associated demarcation problems. In many factories inside and outside the sector, it is not unusual to see ex-craft, semiskilled, and "raw" labor deployed in the same team. The same restructuring also affects supervisors, who are either eliminated, are moved sideways, or have to compete with others for new positions such as team leader, echoing some of Braverman's themes of proletarianization.

Importantly, new developments also build on the old patterns rather than replace them:

> Much of the restructuring of work activity takes place in jobs that have been designed to re-integrate or knit tasks back together, shifting the pattern of the division of labor. Yet the newer division of labor, often incorporating 'head' and 'hand' tasks, is built on the early base of divided work. (Greenbaum 1994:64)

This emphasis on continuity with the past is given partial endorsement by more realistic management writers such as Peter Wickens, ex- Nissan United Kingdom Personnel Director, and Paul Adler in the United States. Wickens admitted that "lean production retains many Taylorist elements" (1993:84), and noted that the work of line operators is still 95 percent prescription and 5 percent discretion. Adler (1993) described the system in operation at NUMMI and other advanced manufacturing plants as a "learning bureaucracy," but that learning is based on an obsession with standardized work procedures based on a more sophisticated application of Taylorist techniques. Other new management initiatives such as Total Quality Management (TQM) are underpinned by benchmarking systems that require a concern for standardized procedures and uniform, dependable practices (Wilkinson and Willmott 1994; Tuckman 1994).

It is also possible to extend one of Braverman's themes of the spread of the logic of capitalist rationalization into the service sector. While Ritzer's (1993) "McDonaldization of society" thesis derives from a Weberian analysis rather than a Marxist one, it tells substantially the same story of the spread of calculable, predictable, quantified processes to an increased range of retail, leisure, and media services. Nor is this an isolated study. Drawing more explicitly on LPT, Gabriel's (1988) study of catering shows how an industry has shifted from reliance on the social and technical skills of the workforce to an industrial model that rests on standardized organization of tasks and technologically determined work pace. In the contemporary retail outlet maintenance of a competitive edge is linked to the reproduction of a standardized service encounter, often monitored through new control systems such as report card surveys on employee attitudes and behavior through real and company-employed "shoppers" (Fuller and Smith 1991). Radical critics of current managerial initiatives also draw on research such as Hochschild (1983) on flight attendants, where "feelings rules" rely on standardized displays through smiles, forced niceness, and other forms of verbal interplay and body posture.

The "working smarter rather than harder" argument is also challenged by emphasizing the costs of labor process restructuring in terms of work intensification (Turnbull 1988; Parker and Slaughter 1988; Elger 1991; Garrahan and Stewart 1992; McArdle et al. 1994). A number of studies of the Japanese/lean production model argue that it leads to hyperintensive work (see T. Smith 1994:54). Certainly, intensification has been a major characteristic of advanced work arrangements such as JIT, which rely on continual and controlled pressure (Turnbull 1988). TQM is also partly geared toward eliminating slack and waste in the system. Whether it be the "flexibility" of adding extra duties, eliminating breaks, or shouldering the increased workloads of "delayered" organizations, mainstream business opinion now regards work intensification as the inevitable price of contemporary competitiveness. Such competition has increasingly been introduced into the public service sector, particularly in the United Kingdom. Internal markets, new forms of managerialism, and funding cuts that increase the staff–client ratio also lead to increased workloads and degradation of labor (Willmott 1993b; Dent 1993).

Control

One of the most remarkable and naive features of many of the new paradigm arguments is the view that organizations are moving from models of control to ones of commitment. Given that LPT has spent much of its time outlining alternative modes of control, this is a clear challenge. As with earlier research on job enrichment or quality circles, commentators are highly skeptical about the extent and character of organizational change (cf. Ramsay 1991 for an overview). More specifically, studies of "self-managed" teamworking stress the relatively limited nature of delegation of authority (Boreham 1992), while studies about the amount of decision-making autonomy in teams show the empowerment rhetoric is often empty and the managerial prerogative largely intact, with, for example, only a small minority of teams electing their team leader (Murakami 1994). Though there are a few high-profile examples of higher levels of autonomy such as those sites investigated by Cutcher-Gershenfeld et al. (1994), most case studies confirm a much more pessimistic conclusion about the extent to which control practices have been altered significantly. With respect to TQM, recent evidence shows that while workers do respond positively to attempts to draw on their expertise and reductions in close supervision, existing hierarchies still constrain attempts to delegate power and expand involvement for employees (Dawson and Webb 1989; McArdle et al. 1994; Kerfoot and Knights 1994) and even managers (Munro 1994). Even among professionals, self-regulation is increasingly giving way to regulation through external audits and assessment (Smith et al. 1996).

Radical critics of new management practices have not necessarily been content to provide empirical justification for a skeptical outlook. There is also an emphasis on new forms of labor subordination, particularly from those researchers in the United Kingdom who combine LPT with Foucauldian influences concerning the rise of a distinctively modern form of disciplinary power (Foucault 1977). While TQM, teamworking, and other aspects of new production systems devolve some responsibilities to teams and operators, tasks are, if anything, more closely monitored and stringently controlled. To add to the managerial armory of external surveillance, the additional twist is often extensive peer surveillance of behavioral norms and outcomes such as attendance and productivity (Delbridge et al. 1992; Sewell and Wilkinson 1992a; Barker 1993). Self-management becomes self-policing, aided by electronic technologies (or panopticons, to use Foucauldian terminology) that allow management to have an omnipresent eye on the shop or office floor. Panopticons are less likely to be buildings, but electronic or informational devices focused on technical and social supports to JIT and TQM systems.[1] While, as we mention below, this writing has an overdeterministic view of technology and leaves out worker resistance and management incompetence, it nevertheless signifies the centrality of control to management thought and practice.

Evaluation

The maintenance of a critical account of the "dark side" of new production systems is a substantial achievement of research informed by labor process theory. But sometimes a tension has existed between skepticism about the extent and nature in workplace divisions of labor and a no-change perspective. Little is gained by simple refutation or seeking to replace one overarching label with another, albeit negative one. Good research is increasingly sensitive to national, company, and sector variations in change processes (Sandberg 1995). We return to this question later, but we can extract some general conclusions about the issues raised.

We would argue that real, though uneven, changes have been taking place and that it is wrong to dismiss new production arrangements as a form of super-Taylorism. For example, the fact that workers are controlling and monitoring themselves clearly matters. Though workers' knowledge continues to be appropriated by management, the move away from narrow specialization and devolved responsibilities, however limited, marks a significant break from those parts of Taylorism based on a clear separation of conception and execution. The other big change is in the conception of skill. While some commentators have always maintained that Braverman's notion of skill was too individually based (e.g., Elger 1982), our understanding of the labor process needs to be rethought in circumstances where the relation between a person and a machine is being replaced by the relation between a team and an increasingly integrated production system.

Recent research by one of the authors (Thompson et al. 1995) into changes in the commercial vehicle industry illustrates the point. Many of the individual tasks continue to be further deskilled under the impact of standardized procedures and uses of new technology. But, the *collective* labor of the group involves expanded cognitive abilities and extrafunctional skills, for example, in the form of greater need for problem-solving and decision-making powers, or qualities such as communication and cooperation. These skills are different, but in contrast to the views of critics mentioned earlier, in principle they are no less significant for the technical division of labor, nor for any conceivable socially useful system of production. How advantageous such changes are for workers in terms of job satisfaction or job controls is contingent on the relative strengths of labor and capital in given circumstances. But LPT is not dependent on deskilling or Taylorism as the characteristic form of the capitalist labor process. Its core theory merely recognizes that competitive relations compel capital to constantly revolutionize the labor process and that within that framework, capital and labor will contest the character and consequences of such transformations.

Indeed, the process of contestation has been in danger of being neglected in many recent accounts of new forms of control. It is true, as we have already observed, that labor market conditions have led to employees accepting much heavier workloads inside lean organizations. We also accept that while some controls have been lightened, new normative ones have often been introduced whereby management asks for and rewards conformity to behavioral rules, for example, those governing attitudes and action inside the team. But we are in real danger of returning to the accusation leveled at Braverman—what happened to worker resistance?—at least in the sense that no actual accounts of resistance can normally be found in such studies. In many of the new Foucauldian-influenced studies resistance has been squeezed out by the success of new management practices. For example, Delbridge et al. (1992:105) have said that "worker counter-control (in the sense described by Roy and many others) is effectively eliminated." Barker (1993:435–36) claimed that workers "have harnessed themselves into a rational apparatus out of which they truly cannot squirm."

The idea that the modern worker is inside a prison of all-powerful electronic, social, or self-surveillance confuses the formal characteristics of systems such as JIT, TQM, or teamworking and the intent of some managements, with the real outcomes, which remain influenced by uneven and incompetent management implementation, plus continued resistance and informal workforce controls (Graham 1994; McKinlay and Taylor 1996; Stephenson 1996). It is unfortunate, therefore, that radical skepticism has been focused on questioning the *nature* rather than *effectiveness* of new management practices. Supplanting the concept of control with that of surveillance is particularly unfortunate in that it leads to a one-sided and top-down approach. Labor therefore disappears from the process partly because of the tendency to believe management monopolizes knowledge and marginalizes other representations and identities (Deetz 1992). McKinlay and Taylor (1996:282) pinpoint the general problem:

> So seductive is Foucault's panopticon metaphor, however, that if simply transposed onto the labor process perspective it can seriously overestimate the scope and depth of management control. . . . The image in these accounts [Sewell and Wilkinson 1992a; Garrahan and Stewart 1992] is a form of self-subordination so complete, so seamless that it stifles any dissent, however innocuous. . . . To paraphrase Foucault, in team-based work regimes every 'prisoner' becomes a 'warden' and every 'warden' a 'prisoner.'

There is, of course, a national and global context to such pessimism. In the United Kingdom, trade unionism has been consistently bruised by legal, economic, and political constraints, such that strikes and other expressions of workers' overt confidence have declined dramatically. Manufacturing industry now employs half (4 million) the numbers it did in the 1970s; self-employment has doubled, and part-time employment covers 7 million workers. In fact employment growth has been among contingent workers on nontenured contracts in smaller workplaces, and in regimes where nonunionism is increasingly common and managerial power increasingly unchecked (cf. Ackers et al. 1996 for a review). High levels of structural unemployment and low wages also have contributed to a loss of confidence in labor as a source of opposition. These conditions have contributed to more pessimistic and management-dominated views of the world. They have also led to a decentering of class and labor, and increased attention to other "identities" and "subjectivities" that influence work organization.

In this context, the earlier emphasis in the labor process debate in the United Kingdom on identifying patterns of control and resistance has been increasingly challenged by what one of its younger advocates bluntly describes as "the importation of critical social-psychology concerned with the management of identity and security, and the subjugation and constitution of individuals through panopticism and cultural managerial discourse" (O'Doherty 1994:2). The next section examines whether we have gotten any further by linking a concern with subjectivity to labor process theory.

SUBJECTIVITY—A MISSING LINK
IN LABOR PROCESS THEORY?

Though few cared to admit it, Braverman's decision to exclude consideration of employees' subjective responses to the transformation of work came as a relief after seemingly interminable discussion of class consciousness and alienation. But, it was unsustainable and soon rectified by Friedman, Burawoy, and others. During this second wave of LPT the *subject* was (re)inserted in three main ways. First, as a source of opposition to capital; hence the creation of the famed "control–resistance paradigm." Second, as a source of creativity, without which capital could not successfully transform labor power into profitable labor. Third, as a source of consent, notably through labor's participation in capitalist exploitation through workplace games and routines.

This emphasis on the means to explain both antagonism and accommodation may seem contradictory, but as Cressey and MacInnes (1980) put it, that contradictoriness is at the heart of the twofold relationship between capital and labor. What had been added in this phase was labor as an active agency. In one sense it can be seen as a classic case of bending the stick back in the dialectic between action and structure, though clearly within the specific parameters of the wage-effort bargain and employment relationship. For two of the leading lights of the U.K. labor process debate, putting action back was not enough. Knights, Willmott, and their associates have for a decade conducted a relentless campaign to insert what they call "subjectivity" into LPT. Their objections to existing approaches that link individual consciousness to the labor process were twofold. First, despite some useful corrective features and lively ethnography, no one had adequately *theorized* subjectivity, and second, all contributors manifested some version of the deadly sin of *dualism*, thinking through labor–capital relations in terms of paired oppositions, control and resistance, structure and action, subject and object, and the like.

There are two central facets to Knights and Willmott's own alternative to existing LPT (see 1989 for the clearest summary). At its core is a notion of *identity work* carried out by individuals. In modern society identity becomes a major preoccupation because the modern "subject" is constituted as both "autonomous" and divided from others. Therefore, a tension exists between the attempt to secure a stable identity and the particular conditions of modern life.[2] This attempt to create a sense of the ambiguity of human agency appears, and to an extent is, a timeless, existential problem. But the workplace is a key terrain for identity work and this eternal struggle to realize self-identity helps to explain the interdependent relationships between capital and labor and employee identification with the goals of the enterprise.

Additionally, a further layer of explanation is added that draws on Foucault, for whom power and subjectivity are understood as a condition and consequence of one another (Knights and Willmott 1989:566–67). In other words, an individual's subjectivity arises from power relations, which in turn generate conceptions of identity. This mutually reinforcing feature of power and identity is supposedly the escape hatch from dualism, but in practice, it leads, as mentioned below, to a view of power as all-pervasive, with "no identifiable source in society" and hence no base to direct resistance (McNally 1995:17). Moreover, following discourse analysis Knights and Willmott (1989:567) see power as "constituted by language, [and] our inability to break through the barriers constructed by language means that power is ultimately irresistible." Power relations in modern society are seen as focusing on a plurality of disciplinary mechanisms, techniques of surveillance, and power-knowledge discourses. Despite the pervasive imagery of the panopticon, such mechanisms are not simply top-down, but are self-disciplinary, working in part through tying individual identity to the positive attraction of participation in practices that provide a sense of belonging. In turn, this renders them vulnerable to the expectations and demands of power.

Though not working self-consciously in a labor process tradition, the most comprehensive application of Foucauldian perspectives comes from N. Rose (1990). The twentieth century has seen the progressive infiltration of subjectivity by power discourses. Organizations in the workplace and society have, with the help of psychologists and other experts, increasingly produced the employee and citizen as a knowable person whose subjectivity is publicly constructed, observed, and recorded, then internalized as self-discipline. The 1980s are seen as marking a qualitative leap forward in revamping the "psycho-technology of the workplace" and fashioning the "optimized autonomous subjectivity of the worker" (Rose 1990: 103, 105).

Such themes, as we saw earlier, have been taken up and turned into a critique of contemporary management control methods by a number of writers in a labor process tradition. We are presented with the familiar themes of panopticons, peer pressure, internalized surveillance, and TQM as *total management control*. What is produced technically by the electronic panopticon can also be produced socially from within the team in a process that "operates directly on the subjectivity of individual members" (Sewell and Wilkinson 1992b:108). This judgment of the disciplinary potential of new management practices is partially shared by the Knights and Willmott camp (cf. McCabe and Knights 1995). But there is more opportunity for exploring issues of identity in the rise of corporate culture given that such theory and practice often have a more explicit concern with "engineering the soul" and acting directly on employees' subjectivity and emotions. Willmott (1993a) made a powerful critique of such programs as nascently totalitarian monocultures in which alternative values and sources of resistance are marginalized or squeezed out. He endorsed Deetz's judgment that "The disciplined member of the corporation wants on his or her own what the corporation wants" (Deetz 1992:42).

Unfortunately, in the search for subjectivity *labor* as a subject is missing. As we have already observed, management has become the central actor, the author of new initiatives and disciplinary practices that labor is subject *to*, or subjects *itself* to. There is, in other words, far too much emphasis on discourses that operate on the subjectivity of labor, without labor as an alternative voice, with its own distinctive themes, accents, and meanings being centered (McNally 1995:18). Too often the language of Foucauldian-influenced researchers is of the good or docile worker who adjusts to the techniques propounded by those who would engineer our souls (cf. Rose 1990:11). More often, the voice of labor is not accessed, but constituted within managerial discourse. Discourse analysis is antithetical to historical analysis, which leads to grand theory without context, a point we develop below in our discussion of LPT in a more internationalized capitalism.

A particular problem in the failure to see labor as a continually resistive subject is a loss of distinction between intention and effect in managerial action. Referring to an earlier phase of psychological doctrine, Rose (1990:115) said that "The point here is not whether this research is valid or invalid, accurate or inaccurate portrayal of the top companies. Nor is it whether such practices do, indeed, produce results. Rather, what is important is the forging of a new image of work, based on a new image of the worker, and a new role for psychology within this complex." Everything therefore becomes discourse in which the subject of action is lost (Newton 1994). No matter what the employee does at work as individual or collectivity, labor remains trapped in a seemingly self-defeating struggle against normalizing disciplines or searching for the holy grail of ontological security (cf. Willmott 1995:22–23). These problems are part of the explanation for the absence of any substantial recognition of resistance in applications of Foucauldian ideas to the labor process. Despite its formal place in the understanding of power relations, the role of resistance is undertheorized and seems to exist mainly as a reaction to and stimulation of power (Smart 1985; Dews 1986).[3]

Labor is also marginalized in a second, significant way. Employee action is used as an illustrative example of the eternal struggle for and against self, and as subjects of modernity engaging with constraints and opportunities offered by disciplinary power. But any distinctive features of the relations between capital and labor in the workplace or wider political economy are largely set aside. Surveillance replaces control as the central concept, the former reflecting the view of the workplace as just one site of disciplinary power. The indeterminacy of identity replaces the indeterminacy of labor within which relations of control and exploitation are seen as embedded by LPT.

The debate about subjectivity has divided U.K. labor process debates in an increasingly sterile way. Given the particular analytical basis of the core of LPT (P. Thompson 1990), it is more important to recover the missing self-active, historically constituted subject than to develop a full account of subjectivity or identity. Nevertheless, these processes are important, but the issue is *how* we should understand the processes involved. Our starting point is that both capital and labor draw on *symbolic resources* in their relations of contestation and cooperation in the workplace. They do so within power struggles in order to assert their own identities or shape others, and to legitimate their own actions or delegitimate others; or as a means of surviving and mastering particular conditions of work and employment. The task is not so much to insert an understanding of the missing subject into labor process *theory*, but to develop an account of such relations that is located within the specific contest of the capitalist labor process and political economy.

Building more structural connections between the labor process and social structure was clearly part of LPT. Class and skill structures went together in Braverman's analysis. In the 1980s, debates on changes to the class structure and the labor process tended to drift apart. By the mid-1990s, some British writers had tried to recover this link (Carter 1994), but as we discuss below, in ways that had not progressed beyond the fixations with social classification and functional class determination of the 1970s.

THE LABOR PROCESS AND CLASS

Making Classes in the Labor Process: From Ownership to Control

Ownership and nonownership of property is the principal basis for making classes in Marx's writings. To be a worker in capitalism is to be a wage laborer, selling one's labor power through the labor market. With the expansion of waged labor in the post–World War II boom, *ownership-based* definitions of class appeared to be too indiscriminate as a tool of social analysis, as the category of waged worker embraced everyone from the senior executive to the cleaner, as the *wage form* became the general contract of engagement in employment in advanced capitalism, and therefore a necessary but not sufficient basis for distinguishing what those working within these categories actually did.

Part of Braverman's intention in *Labor and Monopoly Capital* was to theoretically expand the numbers within the working class by reclassifying those in clerical, technical, service, and retail employment from white-collar middle-class labor, to white-collar workers. He did this partly through a discussion about the labor process of these jobs, showing that Taylorism had colonized the office as much as the shopfloor, and partly through an argument about the growth in product and labor *markets*. Mass services, mass retailing, and mass clerical services demanded a mass labor market, not one with employment privileges pertinent to when these activities operated as luxury or handicraft services. For Braverman, capital expanded into all areas of productive activity, and commodified labor, degraded work, as well as enforced sharper polarizations between those with and without education, qualifications, skills, and power. His thesis was that skill levels in these nonmanual areas had declined, that routine work was the norm, that the same pattern of polarization between a skilled minority and an unskilled majority had affected the working life of a clerk, and "objectively" the class position of millions of white-collar waged workers.

Following Braverman, other writers also attempted to look inside the labor process, at relations of authority and command, at productive and unproductive labor, at relations between those who have technical knowledge and those who have routine skills, to make refinements to the category of waged labor and construct classes from *within* production relations. Weberian writing has always used authority, prestige, and the *content* of waged labor as well as its *form*, as central to class determination. Marxists tended to see prestige, status, and skill differences as epiphenomena of the fundamental split between owners and nonowners of property. For Marx (1976:1044) the link between work and class was not through the actual activity or occupation of an agent, but the *form* in which work was conducted. Hence the same activity could be performed as petty commodity production, as merchant capital, and as labor of a laborer working for capital (see Wardell, this volume).

Braverman, while "objectivist" in laying out the broad trends in the expansion of different kinds of waged labor, tended to stress processual rather than rigid structural implications of these trends for the nonowners. In the 1970s and early 1980s, more rigorous and functional links between the organization of the labor process and "structural class places" were suggested, especially by structural Marxists, such as Poulantzas (1975) and Carchedi (1977), and their followers. Whereas Braverman was principally engaged with arguing from the consequences of the widespread expansion of the working class and types of waged labor, writers in the late 1970s and early 1980s shifted attention to the middle layers or "new middle class," which appeared to be outstripping manual, clerical, and routine white-collar labor. The middle class and not the working class was the new force in capitalism. While a longstanding preoccupation of revisionist socialist thought, constructing this middle class appeared to take on a more systematic, formalistic, and functional quality during this period as "the technical division of labor [became] the central site of the origins of social classes" (C. Smith 1987:58).

For Carchedi this involved reducing class to an economic category, and for Poulantzas politicizing authority relations and skill structures within the

workplace. Both writers, following wider trends, continued to ignore the consequences of real *ownership* relations, and focused instead on *control* relations
between types of workers and managers in the production process. Carchedi
saw the performance of labor as being collectivized and made more complex
with the greater application of science, engineering, and technical knowledge
to labor, which fragmented labor into manual, technical, and other categories,
some engaged directly, others indirectly in production, but all contributing in
a collective fashion to the production of surplus labor and surplus value.
Similarly, the role of capitalists had been collectivized, with owners withdrawing or expanding the functions of capital by employing specialist managers to
directly oversee the coordination and control of production. In addition, the
category of owners was made more problematical, as the collectivization and
institutionalization of ownership of capital displaced a simple class of family
capitalists who had a direct link between their property and the operation of
the capitalist labor process. Rather, owners recruited people to manage in
their place, to function as capital for them. Hence what became known as the
separation of ownership from control both discharged the operational duties
of capitalists to a new class of managers and paid technical advisors, and
removed the correspondence between a class of owners who *simultaneously*
own and expand their capital. Braverman's work on class and the labor process
seeks to move beyond an ownership-based definition of class in these two
respects: within the monopoly corporation, managers not owners rule; and
within the class of nonowners of capital, qualities of labor other than wage
labor status define who is in and out of the working class.

The Thus Carchedi argued that labor and capital had been collectivized into
the "collective laborer" and the "global capitalist." More important, these polar
functions were combined for some waged workers, such as managers and
supervisors, who formed a *new* middle class by virtue of performing both functions. Marx also distinguished between types of waged labor within the labor
process, hence those responsible for exercising supervision over others.
Overseers were a special category of waged labor, who functioned as capital—
managing the control of the labor process which required coercion because the
ends of the labor process were not shared. But they were also paid as waged
labor, and therefore subject to the labor market pressures of other workers, to
cost pressures from capital concerned to reduce indirect labor costs. Moreover,
to function as capital is not to own capital. Possession may be confused with
ownership, but in a period of intense international competition and recurrent
crises, it is the owners and not their employees who hold strategic power.

The dominant trend within capitalism appeared to be a continued integration of these dual functions, such that the new middle class was the rising
class of the system. Thus the senior manager and the lowly supervisor, leading
hand, or teamleader, shared the position of being in the same new middle class
by virtue of their involvement in controlling workers in the interests of capi-

tal. How capital decided its interests, and the implied homogeneity of interest between managers and owners of capital was not discussed (see Cutler et al. 1977:311 for a critique). Carter (1994:59) has even suggested that team-based production systems, which use peer pressure and not separate supervision to pace the line, means that "workers accept the performance of the function of capital via surveillance of other workers" and must logically transform themselves into a new middle class. The adoption of team-based systems production effects a mutation in the class structure, changing workers into a new middle class. Piece rate systems, which involve workers pacing their own productivity, effect a similar class transformation, exposing the absurdity of a definition of class that is not informed by changes in economic ownership of property, but shifts in payment systems and the technical organization of production (C. Smith 1987; Smith and Willmott 1996). This goes against Marx's definition of class in terms of form and ownership.

Poulantzas shares with Carchedi and Carter an aversion to empirical work and a tendency to create classes alfresco, not through the process of constructing social relations within particular capitalist workplaces and societies. Poulantzas manufactured his "new petty bourgeois" by a tight definition of productive labor, and a class separation of manual labor and supervision based on its ideological and political subordination of direct, manual, and supervised workers under their forces.

In general, the very sterile functionalist project of manufacturing classes out of the technical division of labor within waged labor in a pure and abstracted capitalist system expired in the mid-1980s. Class came to be more closely connected with the ownership and nonownership of capital, and ceased to be the *control* category it was for 1970s writers. Ownership became increasingly important in the 1980s as entrepreneurial ideology and opportunity, and renewed competition between national forms of capital, meant a separate class of real owners exerted more direct control over the lives of those they employed (including their managers). Concomitantly, the national formation of ownership of capital appeared to affect significantly the way work was organized. Class also seemed a more discursive category, or at least, a historically and comparatively varied and socially constructed grouping, rather than a thing functionally determined by universal "capitalism" or tightly coupled to uniform "relations of production."

Owners and Managers

Classes in capitalism, as Braverman insisted, remain divided between capitalists and workers, buyers and sellers of waged labor. How these two classes relate in the labor process involves different sets of problems today. First, there has been a material change in the relationship between owners and managers.

Managerial views of capitalism, where owners have left the production area and devolved control and coordination to managers, meant managers and not owners received central theoretical attention. Owners appeared to leave the production area, as management specialists appeared to routinize this problematic sphere of capital accumulation. However, in the conjunctural crisis of corporate capitalism from the mid-1970s, entrepreneurial capitalism was renewed ideologically, and real owners came to see management itself as problematical and an increasing target for rationalization. So in the 1980s and 1990s owners of capital reintervened in the management of the corporation, and we have witnessed repositioning between ownership and control, as stockholders have made direct intervention in corporate management by forced mergers and acquisitions, rationalization of layers of management and intermediate technical labor, management buyouts of capital, and delayering of command hierarchies in the interest of simplifying and cheapening the costs of managing the firm (Useem 1990). The high rates of mergers and acquisitions from the mid-1980s could have been interpreted as replacing one set of passive owners with another. But, as Useem (1990:690) shows, the new owners have had organizational consequences, "perhaps most notably in moving direct control of the corporation more firmly back into the hands of owners."

As a result, stable bureaucratic centers of the corporation—Braverman's status hierarchy for the middle layers of employment within the firm—have been experiencing levels of employment insecurity previously reserved for manual waged labor. Whereas for Braverman the creation of these middle layers acted as a buffer and potential career ladder between capitalists and workers within the firm, today's corporation has subjected these middle layers to continuous rationalization and cost–benefit analysis, and pushed down responsibilities to lower levels of the corporate hierarchy, while centralizing budgetary controls to the higher echelons (Marginson et al. 1988).

Prechel's (1994) detailed historical examination of restructuring managerial labor within a large U.S. steel corporation, for example, indicates that the catalyst for standardizing and rationalizing the middle layers and subjecting them to tight central budgetary controls was triggered by a crisis in accumulation and dip in profits in the early 1980s. Increasing availability of information technology acted as the mechanism, and new accounting techniques the instrument, for tighter controls by corporate staff over operational management:

> These formal controls were based on the principles of scientific management: measurement, quantification, and the separation of conception from execution. . . . The way the centralization of control affected the managerial process resembles the way the transfer of information from labor to management in the early twentieth century affected the labor process. (Prechel 1994:741–42)

Waged Labor in Crisis

We have seen a growth in self-employment and decline in waged labor within advanced economies—thereby making sharper the distinctions between working for a wage within a contract to an employer and selling one's labor through market mechanisms in the form of a price for a job that may contain a profit element. The growth of petty bourgeois or merchant labor increased involuntarily, as firms increasingly contracted activities outside the formal structure of employment, put out work to subcontractors, undermined the shelters for waged labor established within internal labor markets, and began to use the pressure of the external labor market to undermine conditions and wages of remaining workers. In Britain self-employment doubled in the 1980s, and this trend also characterized other countries. In addition, getting into waged labor had become harder in the early 1990s, hence widening the distinction between employed and unemployed in Britain.

We could say that ownership relations have reasserted their power since the 1980s, both ownership of capital and ownership of jobs. This reflects capitalism in crisis, when capital finds it harder to valorize itself and workers find it harder to get work. Braverman was dealing more with conditions of easier access to profits for capital and work for workers, when it appeared that attempts to construct class-based differentiations within the category of waged labor gave a more rigorous or critical insight into class relations, than differences derived from ownership and nonownership of property.

We would reassert, therefore, the importance of ownership in class determination, without ignoring the issue of control. First, capitalists have to employ managers to function in their place, but managers are not equivalent to owners, neither are they the *real* owners, as implied by control-based rather than ownership-based definitions of class, and semantic debates about ownership and possession. In crisis owners manage more directly, while not necessarily stepping into the labor process of production, which management has effectively routinized. Owners of capital from the 1980s on intervened more forcefully in capital accumulation to arrest a crisis in profitability and in so doing struggled with managers, pushing many out of the corporation and a few into the ranks of real capitalists. Second, workers have to sell their labor power to capital to live, and the uncertainty of getting into the labor process grew dramatically in the 1980s, as contracting with capital became more unsettled and the category of wage labor more problematical. Long-term unemployment grew, and the length of job tenure shortened, while insecure, contract, temporary, part-time, franchised, and other forms of contingent ways of selling one's labor power blossomed. Initially this was confined to more market-based forms of capitalism, the United Kingdom and United States especially, but there has been a general movement toward contingent labor in Europe. In Japan, the security of core workers was always at the expense of the insecure periphery, but today even the core workforce is under attack (Berggren 1995). Being a worker has generally fragmented into a more disparate experience, as the conventional male breadwinner definition of the worker imploded with the growth of female labor and contingent work. This has contributed to the more discursive experience of class, fragmenting and separating capital–labor bargains into more individualistic forms that reinforce the power of owners and the vulnerability of workers. At the center of uncertainty for capital and labor has been the growth of the global market and the international division of labor, which have exposed the labor process to patterns of rationalization and standardization no longer informed by a national economy.

NATIONAL AND GLOBAL DIMENSIONS AND THE LABOR PROCESS

Putting the National in the Labor Process

In contrast to Braverman's focus on capitalism as a *system*, post-Braverman debates have sought to introduce the idea of national variants in capitalist formation, of competition between capitalist forms of labor process organization, and a much more conservative agenda of change *within* rather than *beyond* capitalist social relations. *Labor and Monopoly Capital* appeared when the United States was the preeminent world capitalist power, when U.S. institutions, such as the multidivisional firm, and labor–management practices, such as Scientific Management and Human Relations, were considered the most "modern" available. There is one (historical) reference to Japan in the book (Braverman 1974:284); discussion of newly industrializing countries is only in terms of their subordination to developed countries; continental European capitalism, especially that of Germany, is only mentioned in relation to its historical development, and not as a rival to the United States. The idea that there could be competing forms of organizing the labor process *within* capitalism does not fit Braverman's project. Yet, today it is hard to speak of the *capitalist* labor process as a single experience, as though U.S. capital–labor relations were equivalent to those in Japan, France, or Sweden. The *political* has become critically important in the post-Braverman debates on the labor process (Sabel 1982; Burawoy 1985; Thompson 1989).

Conversely, at the same time that the nation has been written into labor process debate, the power of the global marketplace and what some see as the hollowing out of the national economy, became incomparably more developed than when Braverman was writing. Production has become transnational; foreign direct investment by companies increased four times faster than world output, and three times faster than trade between 1983 and 1990 (Beneria 1995:45). The growth of transnational companies has extended the production of commodities, sucking millions into waged labor and integrating their contribution to commodity production in disaggregated and spatially distinct ways. Moreover, trade liberalization schemes and the regionalization of economic activity into distinct blocs are accelerating globalization and eroding the autonomy of national economic actors. Therefore, the national is becoming more vulnerable as a viable boundary of economic activity and consequently as a seriously autonomous space for instituting distinct forms of labor process organization.

To understand the labor process today, therefore requires that we decenter the United States as capitalist exemplar par excellence, and introduce political considerations, such as the influence of national institutional settlements on employment relations, the role of regional economic forces, such as the European Union, and local forces, such as in the idea of "industrial districts," where cooperative and corporate agencies aim to construct factory regimes of particular sorts within distinct geographical areas. Antithetically, the spatial disintegration of the firm, the reemergence of subcontracting, the growing international division of labor, and the powerful place of transnational companies within capitalism mean the nation-state is not the only force operating on labor inputs and labor process organization. Benchmarking, best practices, and extensive and accelerating borrowing of methods of organizing work between companies and countries, especially those regarded as pace setters or models, mean labor is socialized and labor processes are exposed, simultaneously to national (local) and international (universal/global) pressures. Where Braverman spoke through the experience of U.S. capitalism and treated this as both a modern and *universal* functional capitalism, today we need to retain a clear sense of the *global* and the *national* when studying particular labor processes.

European writers can be said to have been influential in rediscovering the national. Europeans had to deal with the rise of U.S. economic hegemony, which produced defenders of national ways of doing things, typical of British defense of craft organization enthusiasts for U.S. methods. Within a universalist labor process analysis, the United States was identified as the most advanced, and therefore the most modern, one best way of organizing work. European writers who emphasized the continued role of national diversity and difference, could be labeled reactionary in the face of U.S. technology and methods of production. There is still strong tendency within U.S. writing to regard deviation or critical engagement with modern (U.S. or U.S.-created) production methods as reactionary.[4] But when the deviants proved neither aberrant nor unsuccessful, but rather presented competitive advantages in the international marketplace, writers were increasingly compelled to take seriously and acknowledge other ways of doing things. U.S. writers who acknowledge the place of the national, have tended to do research in or engage with European societies (Sabel [1982]—Italy; Burawoy [1985]—Hungary) or other powerful states, such as Japan (Kenney and Florida 1993). Theoretically, though, some of the most sophisticated attempts in comparative labor process analysis have been by European writers.

The "societal effects" school, or Aix Group (M. Rose 1985), emerged within organizational sociology in the 1970s, and produced ideas that have advanced across industrial sociology, industrial relations, and the labor process debate.

> By means of cross-national comparisons of organizational units which were fairly identical with regard to acknowledged contingencies, this Group has identified quite a large cross-national variety of organizational forms and practices which though unrelated to task context or performance difference, is very closely bound to institutionalized human resources (education, training, work careers), social stratification and industrial relations. (Sorge 1991:162)

British writers using their methodology (Lane 1989) have critiqued the universalism of Braverman's "deskilling thesis" by bringing into focus different patterns of training and skill formation between capitalist societies, suggesting that social "institutions" mold capitalist social relations in distinctly "national" ways, so that there is no generalized tendency for capitalism to deskill or for the labor process to express the same antagonistic relationships between labor and capital as seen in the United Kingdom or United States. Workers' and managers' expectations of and perceptions of each other are partially cultural, informed by historical experience, and the training, education, and qualifications learned through different social institutions. In extreme form, this school discounts the idea of the *capitalist labor process*; all that exists are national variants of ways of working, a menu of social relations prepared by national histories and not economic or functional structures of a supranational capitalist system.

The problems with this approach are many. Nations do not circumscribe capital, as transnational firms, cross-border economic integration, and regional trading and political blocs increasingly constrain the nation-state. Ideas such as "globalization" even suggest the demise of the nation-state as an economic actor and arena for workers' struggle, but there are many problems with such a view.[5] Moreover, dominant countries have always evolved ways of organizing work that are emulated by other firms in other states. In addition, the idea that different national ingredients produce totally different national cakes overstates the range of diversity within the capitalist market system, where structural essentials, such as waged labor, unemployment, and wage-effort bargaining and conflict inscribe a limited repertoire of roles and parts for those on this particular stage. Finally, supply-side assumptions of a common societal patterning to work ignore subnational and supranational structures, such as international industrial sectors, common technological imperatives, and the very specific histories of particular factories in local labor markets and regions (Turner and Auer 1994; Mueller 1994; Thompson et al. 1995). Societal or institutional approaches are close to functional sociology; firm action is overdetermined within this framework, and action by managers and workers removed from the firm to the institutional competencies of particular training, industrial relation, and education systems. For these reasons, a strict societal effects model of the labor process is inadequate. It must be synthesized with wider structures and forces of capitalism and rival state models of how to organize work, and it must retain the autonomy for social action within the firm, rather than reducing such action to an epiphenomena of institutional capabilities.

National-Systemic Thinking and the Labor Process

However, even for strict followers of the societal effects school there is a tendency to see some national institutional arrangements as more effective in handling new technologies or more leading-edge practices than others (C. Smith and Meiksins 1995). Not all states evolve levels of efficiency in the workplace that are functionally equivalent and equally effective. Those who have tried to develop more synthetic comparative analysis (Child 1981; Lane 1989), or those who have attempted to construct post-Taylorist or alternative modern versions of work organization, have sought to transform certain national patterns into systemic or general models. Certain societies are identified as evolving or representing *paradigmatic* exemplars of labor process and business organization. It is then assumed that these more advanced or modern forms will diffuse to other societies as best practice models through the imperatives of market competition and efficiency superiority. The tension between the nation as a distinct historical arena and the general model is therefore set up, but rarely critically dissected.

Labor process writing post-Braverman has advocated postmanagerial, post-Taylorist models of capitalism, and looked to different national examples, especially German and Japanese experiences, as sources of *new model* capitalism. Common to such models is a stress on *cooperative* relations among firms, workers, and managers, and between firms and the state. The idea of moving beyond market relations, beyond economic calculations based on price and the cash nexus, toward a concern for quality and reciprocity are also common themes. Traditional bases of action, such as the family, community, or clan have been retheorized as both persisting within rational-legal capitalism and being more effective at delivering higher productivity, as trust and shared values are deemed solvents of the complications and corrosive features of the narrow economic self-interest of naked or "pure" capitalism. Hence, premodern/pre-Fordist forms, such as family organization and subcontracting communities or industrial districts, have been rediscovered *within* monopoly capitalism, such as the high-technology cottage industry (Sabel 1982). And postmodern, post-Taylorist forms that stress cooperation or the partial socialization of the market, are discovered to be dominant in certain societies (Japan, Germany) that provide exemplars or new paradigms for organizing work more generally.

Cooperative capitalism can be produced through powerful legislative frameworks, cartel-like interfirm links, and powerful trade unions, typical of German inspired cooperative capitalism (Chandler 1990), or from the dominance of giant enterprises, extensive interfirm, long-term relational subcontracting networks, and the integration of labor into secure employment, typical of Japanese-inspired alliance (Gerlach 1992) or collective capitalism (Lazonick 1991:24). Kenney and Florida's (1993) concept of innovation-mediated production or Womack's et al. (1990) lean production borrow from Japanese large firm practices. However, they also abstract and disconnect these conceptions from their national context to create more neutral/universal paradigms. But in theories of new model capitalism there remains an unresolved tension between national-institutional or embedded conceptions of capitalism, tied to a particular society, and national-systemic conceptions, which posit looser relations between society and system. This raises the idea of decoupling national competitive advantages from national context, and their packaging and diffusion as techniques, models, and principles learnable in other societies. For example, Fruin (1994:318) berates managerialist efforts to learn from Japan by abstracting practices such as just-in-time, quality circles, and the like, and bolting these onto the Western firm as fundamentally misunderstanding the institutionally embedded nature of Japanese enterprise system. Managerialists (Vogel 1979; Pascale and Athos 1982; Ouchi 1981; Womack et al. 1990) have a tendency to take the paradigmatic case from the national, whereas business and economic historians (Chandler 1990; Fruin 1994; Lazonick 1991) either remain at the level of national historical specificity, or build more cautious national systemic models that lack generalizability.

The problems with national-systemic thinking is that it:

- freezes historical evolution of national models and thereby ignores continued development—witness the recent crisis in Japan at the time when the Japanese model is being diffused as a panacea of

Western capitalism (cf. Berggren 1995; Elger and Smith 1994; C. Smith and Meiksins 1995). Similarly, the German model has been changing, when those outside Germany identify it as a way forward for capitalism such as the British Labor Party (Lane 1994).

- reproduces universalistic thinking about the labor process—the idea of one best way when diversity is further increasing. In particular, ideas such as Confucian capitalism, which abstract from the experience of several Southeast Asian economies, or Eastern versus Western capitalism, squeeze the national out of the picture (cf. Wilkinson 1996).

- creates the possibility of as many models of capitalism as there are nation-states, which effectively means abandoning any notion of capitalism in favor of national economic systems as the theoretical platform from which to study labor processes.

Models of capitalism have their roots within particular national contexts and have always existed in writing about the labor process. Marx wrote through the British experience to speak of capitalism in general, when Britain was far from archetypal, simultaneously containing special and common features (cf. Lazonick 1991 for a discussion). Braverman, less self-consciously, used the United States as typical of monopoly capital in general. Given that pure capitalism cannot exist, historical accounts of labor process organization are always *particular* stories. Therefore, caution is required when attempting to abstract from history common or typical features of a system. We have to disentangle the various levels of influence offered by the international trends and forces of global capitalism, the distinct institutional patterning of work within a given country, the borrowing and diffusion of new best practices, and the specificities of workplace-level historical and local contingencies. In some instances the national speaks to the experience of labor process organization across industrial sectors and geographical exigencies; in others, the autonomy of the workplace, as well as local labor market conditions and patterns, override any national or international typicality of standards. Theoretically, we cannot a priori rank such influences. We can only suggest methodologies and research strategies that will capture the nuances of analyzing the labor process in today's more complex workplace.

Some recent European research projects have developed more dynamic, synthetic accounts of the evolving nature of labor process organization cross-nationally. Jurgens et al. (1993) in *Breaking from Taylorism* examined shifting competitive relations between global car companies, with particular attention to the labor process organization of new dominant players, such as the Japanese, and how labor process organization has been transferred from new rising models to other car firms through emulation. Their work, unlike others looking at the same sector, refuses to identify a single way of organizing the labor process, but rather identifies clashes among national methods, industrial relation traditions, and social settlements (C. Smith 1996b). Turner and Auer (1994), examining work organization in the U.S., Swedish, and German car industries, came to a similar conclusion on the persistence of national variants of labor process organization, rather than convergence to benign managerialist models (lean production) or maligned, Marxist ones (management by stress). Mueller (1994), again from car industry comparative research (this time of engine, not assembly plants), reiterated the importance of local contingencies within the life history of factories as local labor markets and capital–labor relations at workplace level provide diversity in labor process organization. Thompson et al. (1995), examining teamworking in the commercial vehicle industry in six European countries, focused on the meaning of skills and new labor process organizational initiatives, such as teamwork, within the plants of the companies and the wider national contexts. Their analysis agrees with what is emerging as the new orthodoxy of national specificities and embeddedness to labor process, at the same time as reinforcing the importance of the perceptions of labor use within the firm.

> The evidence in our cases . . . illustrates that the theorizations of change pitched at the institutional and universal levels are both flawed. Various elements of skill formation—the task structure, the degree of dependence on workers' knowledge, the extent of autonomy—do not necessarily form a consistent [national] 'package'. National differences remain important, but over a period of time transnationals are seeking to standardize practices within particular sectors. [But] despite the commonalties the result is not convergence given that particular companies bring their own approach to work organization. (Thompson et al. 1995:16)

These works emphasize the importance of examining country, company, and factory levels for interpreting changing patterns of labor process organization. Moreover, they advocate a more dynamic model of development than simple convergence to one capitalist norm, or infinite national variations in labor process arrangements. It is the dynamic tension between convergence and divergence pressures that comes out most fully.

CONCLUSION

This review of recent developments in labor process writing and theory has signaled the continued importance of the broad approach for understanding change in contemporary capitalist societies. The continuing need to look behind official claims for up-skilling or fundamental shifts in the quality of work, central to Braverman's agenda, remain relevant to getting behind the almost daily claims of paradigmatic changes to the nature of work within contemporary capitalism. What has changed over the past decade has been shifts in the pattern of managerial controls, with an extension of self-control systems typical of professional labor to manual labor, and the use of values and culture as more reliable and profitable methods of releasing labor power, as against more overt or crude coercion. But, concomitant with the sophistication of controls, we have witnessed, with the rise of unemployment and decline in trade unionism, a return of back street employment, sweated trades, homeworking, casual labor, and employer despotism (Ackers et al. 1996).

Technical controls have broadened with new technologies, and we have witnessed the rebirth and generalization of both external and internal contracting systems, as employment tenure has shortened in response to more global patterns of competition, together with changes to public sector employment under fiscal crises in Welfare States. Many workplaces have become connected to complex international commodity chains, as technology, trade, new communications, and more rationalized management systems permit ever greater geographical dispersal and integration of the design, manufacture, and assembly of commodities. New players, especially the Japanese, have intensified work in novel ways and imposed and bargained distinct contracts between labor and capital, which are now spreading outside Japan through transfer, borrowing, and transplantation by Japanese firms. These trends are dynamic and contradictory however, with on the one hand, new deals on employment tenure in some areas and increasing flexible and temporary patterns of employment on the other. We see no single, qualitative break from the core concerns of capital–labor dynamics in any of these trends, but neither are we dismissive of the substantive changes that are taking place and their effect on bargaining between capital and labor within the labor process. We have tried to stress that ownership of capital has been made more important as capital flows increase internationally through trade, but more important, through the globalization of production and therefore labor processes. In sum, then, LPT needs to combine sensitivity to the more individualized and employer-dominated forms of employment that seek to engage workers' subjectivity in realizing labor power, as well as contextualize the workplace within international structural relations. Micro and macro changes speak to each other, but it remains the duty of writers within a labor process tradition to develop methodologies that are capable of listening to both.

NOTES

1. The disciplinary gaze may also be present through power/knowledge discourses controlled by management. This is somewhat marginal to the concerns

of this chapter, but research focusing on the social technologies of contemporary specialists in human and organizational behavior develop techniques to observe and normalize performance and behavior (Townley 1993).

2. This concern for securing identity has reached somewhat extreme proportions in the recent work of David Knights. Criticizing so-called orthodox labor process theorists such as the authors of this chapter, he says that our efforts are motivated by "a (masculine) concern with ordering and controlling the world as part of a project to secure their author's own identity" (Knights 1995:17).

3. There is in fact a growing distance between the writings of David Knights and Hugh Willmott. Knights appears, from his 1995 paper at the Labour Process Conference, to be trapped within the limitations of discourse analysis, where language defines everything, and material practice and action are reduced to discourses. For a critique of this idealism, and an alternative perspective on language and class struggle, see McNally (1995). Willmott draws inspiration not only from French poststructuralism, but Eastern religion, particularly Buddhism. His attacks on humanism in his 1995 Labour Process Conference paper come directly from Buddhist philosophy and the construction of the self as a problem. In Buddhism security in the material world is an illusion. Self-identity based on material security is false. The core concern with securing the inner self and discarding all imposed, material identities is a strong theme in Willmott's writing and in Buddhist philosophy. The critique of what he calls the "compulsion to secure self in identity" (Willmott 1995:22) comes partly from Foucault and partly from Buddhist philosophy. Both treat consciousness in a highly formalistic manner and through transhistorical categories. While Willmott has offered some valuable criticisms of the totalitarian nature of management controls, such as corporate culture and business process reengineering, neither offers a socialist vision for another way of organizing work. In fact there remains a intellectual vacuum between these critiques of managerial paradigms and the actual labor process.

4. New production paradigms, such as lean production (Womack et al. 1990) and innovation mediated production (Kenney and Florida 1993:314–15) regard challenges as reactionary. This follows a strong tendency within U.S. thinking to regard their production arrangement for work as the best available, rather than one of many. It is typical of a dominant state to persist in practices that are perceived to have made them strong. Britain has been historically resistant to change, despite a need to change with the growth of continental European and later U.S. competition. Institutional inertia and vested interests in the old ways present obstacles to change. These forces are now apparent in the United States, and in Japan, in the light of growing competition from newly industrializing countries (NICs). There is also the problem,

however, of knowing how to change, in what direction, and under what authority. Becoming like another state is easier said than achieved.

5. Discussions around the idea of the globalization of the labor process suggest ever more limited space to local and national patterns and coloring to social relations within the workplace, as factories disintegrate vertically and spatially, the combined plant, secure pattern of employment, and bureaucratic career can appear a thing of the past. But again, trends are never unidirectional. Globalization overstates the amount of production taking place across borders, which is limited and concentrated in certain industrial sectors, while it presents a zero-sum relationship between the national and the global, when states both aid and inhibit internationalization. Moreover, trends are not one way toward the global market, as counterveiling political and economic pressures at national and regional levels inhibit such unidirectional change. For a wide-ranging debate on the impact of globalization on work and workers' rights, see Tilly (1995) and replies by Wallerstein, Zolberg, Hobsbawm, and Beneria.

References

Abernathy, William. 1978. *The Productivity Dilemma: Roadblock to Innovation in the Automobile Industry*. Baltimore, Maryland: Johns Hopkins University Press.

Abrahamson, Mark, and Lee Sigelman. 1987. "Occupational Sex Segregation in Metropolitan Areas." *American Sociological Review* 52:588–97.

Acker, Joan. 1992. "The Future of Women and Work: Ending the Twentieth Century." *Sociological Perspectives* 35:53–68.

———. 1990. "Hierarchies, Jobs, Bodies: A Theory of Gendered Organizations." *Gender & Society* 4:139–58.

———. 1989. *Doing Comparable Worth: Gender, Class, and Pay Equity*. Philadelphia, Pennsylvania: Temple University Press.

Ackers, Peter, Chris Smith, and Paul Smith. 1996. "Against All Odds? British Trade Unions in the New Workplace." In *The New Workplace and Trade Unionism*, edited by Peter Ackers, Chris Smith, and Paul Smith. London: Routledge.

Adler, Paul. 1993. "Time and Motion Regained." *Harvard Business Review* 71:1.

———. 1986. " New Technologies, New Skills." *California Management Review* 29:1.

Aglietta, Michel. 1979. *A Theory of Capitalist Regulation—The U.S. Experience*. London: New Left Books.

Albeda, Randy P. 1986. "Occupational Segregation by Race and Gender, 1958–1981." *Industrial and Labor Relations Review* 39:404–18.

Altmann, N. 1995. "Japanese Work Policy: Opportunity, Challenge or Threat?" In *Enriching Production*, edited by A. Sandberg. Aldershot: Avebury.

Altshuler, Alan, Martin Anderson, Daniel Jones, Daniel Roos, and James Womack. 1984. *The Future of the Automobile*. Cambridge, Massachusetts: MIT Press.

Aminzade, Ronald. 1992. "Historical Sociology and Time." *Sociological Methods & Research* 20:456–80.

Amott, Teresa. 1993. *Caught in the Crisis: Women the U.S. Economy Today*. New York: Monthly Review Press.

Amott, Teresa, and Julie Matthaei. 1991. *Race, Gender, and Work: A Multicultural Economic History of Women in the United States*. Boston, Massachusetts: South End Press.

Antonio, Robert. 1990. "The Decline of the Grand Narrative of Emancipatory Modernity: Crisis or Renewal in Neo-Marxian Theory?" In *Frontiers of Social Theory*, edited by George Ritzer. New York: Columbia University Press.

Applebaum, Eileen. 1992. "Structured Change and Growth of Part-time and Temporary Employment." In *New Policies for the Part-time and Contingent Workforce*, edited by Virginia duRivage. New York: M. E. Sharp.

Applebaum, Eileen, and Rosemary Batt. 1994. *The New American Workplace: Transforming Work Systems in the United States*. Ithaca, New York: ILR Press.

Arnold, Horace L., and Fay L. Faurote. [1915] 1972. *Ford Methods and the Ford Shops*. New York: Arno.

Aronowitz, Stanley. 1979. "The End of Political Economy." *Social Text* 2:3–52.

———. 1978. "Marx, Braverman, and the Logic of Capital." *Insurgent Sociologist* 8:126–46.

———. 1973. *False Promises: The Shaping of American Working Class Consciousness*. New York: McGraw-Hill.

Aronowitz, Stanley, and William DiFazio. 1994. *The Jobless Future: Sci-tech and the Dogma of Work*. Minneapolis, Minnesota: University of Minnesota Press.

Asher, Robert, and Ronald Edsforth. 1995. "A Half Century of Struggle: Auto Workers Fighting for Justice." In *Autowork*, edited by Robert Asher and Ronald Edsforth. Albany: SUNY Press.

Attewell, P. 1990. "What Is Skill?" *Work and Occupations* 17:422–48.

Baethge, Martin, and Harald Wolf. 1995. "Continuity and Change in the 'German Model' of Industrial Relations." In *Employment Relations in a Changing World Economy*, edited by Richard Locke, Thomas Kochan, and Michael Piore. Cambridge: The MIT Press.

Baran, Barbara. 1988. "Office Automation and Women's Work: The Technological Transformation of the Insurance Industry." In *On Work*, edited by R. E. Pahl. Oxford: Basil Blackwell.

———. 1987. "The Technological Transformation of White-Collar Work." In *Computer Chips and Paper Clips*, edited by Heidi Hartmann, vol. 2. Washington, D.C.: National Academy Press.

Barker, J. R. 1993. "Tightening the Iron Cage: Concertive Control in Self-Managing Teams." *Administrative Science Quarterly* 38:408–37.

Barley, Steven, and Gideon Kunda. 1992. "Design and Devotion: Surges of Rational and Normative Ideologies of Control in Managerial Discourse." *Administrative Science Quarterly* 37:363–99.

Baron, James N., and William T. Bielby. 1985. "Organizational Barriers to Gender Equality: Sex Segregation of Jobs and Opportunities." In *Gender and the Life Course*, edited by Alice S. Rossi. New York: Aldine.

Baron, James N., and Andrew E. Newman. 1990. "For What It's Worth: Organizations, Occupations and the Value of Work Done by Women and Non-Whites." *American Sociological Review* 55:155–75.

Baskerville, Richard, et al., eds. 1994. *Transforming Organizations with Information Technology*. Amsterdam: North-Holland.

Batt, Rosemary, and Eileen Applebaum. 1995. "Worker Participation in Diverse Settings: Does the Form Affect the Outcome, and If So, Who Benefits?" *British Journal of Industrial Relations* 33:355–78.

Baxandall, Rosalyn, Elizabeth Ewen, and Linda Gordon. 1976. "The Working Class Has Two Sexes." *Monthly Review* 28:1–9.

Baylis, Thomas A. 1974. *The Technical Intelligentsia and the East German Elite*. Berkeley, California: University of California Press.

Beechey, Veronica. 1982. "The Sexual Division of Labor and the Labor Process: A Critical Assessment of Braverman." In *The Degradation of Work? Skill, Deskilling, and the Labor Process*, edited by Stephen Wood. London: Hutchinson.

Bélanger, Jacques. 1994. "Job Control under Different Labor Relations Regimes: A Comparison of Canada and Great Britain." In *Workplace Industrial Relations and Global Challenge*, edited by Jacques Bélanger, P. K. Edwards, and Larry Haiven. Ithaca, New York: ILR Press.

Bell, Daniel. 1973. *The Coming of Post-Industrial Society*. New York: Basic Books.

Bell, Deborah E. 1985. "Unionized Women in State and Local Government." In *Women, Work, and Protest: A Century of U.S. Women's Labor History*, edited by Ruth Milkman. Boston, Massachusetts: Routledge & Kegan Paul.

Belous, Richard. 1989. *The Contingent Economy: The Growth of the Temporary, Part-time, and Subcontracted Workforce*. Washington, D.C.: National Planning Association.

Beneria, Lourdes. 1995. "Response: The Dynamics of Globalization." *International Labor and Working Class History* 47:45–52.

Berg, Peter. 1997. "The Effects of Workplace Practices on Job Satisfaction in the United States Steel Industry." Unpublished paper. Washington, D.C.: Economic Policy Institute.

Berg, Peter, Eileen Applebaum, Thomas Bailey, and Arne L. Kalleberg. 1996. "The Performance Effects of Modular Production in the Apparel Industry." *Industrial Relations* 35:356–73.

Berggren, Christian. 1995. "Japan as Number Two: Competitive Problems and the Future of Alliance Capitalism after the Burst of the Bubble Boom." *Work, Employment, and Society* 9:53–96.

———. 1992. *Alternatives to Lean Production: Work Organization in the Swedish Auto Industry*. Ithaca, New York: ILR Press.

Bernhardt, Annette, Martina Morris, and Mark S. Handcock. 1995. "Women's Gains or Men's Losses? A Closer Look at the Shrinking Gender Gap in Earnings." *American Journal of Sociology* 101:302–28.

Berry, Thomas H. 1991. *Managing the Total Quality Transformation*. New York: McGraw-Hill.

Bjørn-Andersen, Niels, and Jon A. Turner. 1994. "Creating the 21st Century Organization: The Metamorphosis of Oticon." In *Transforming Organizations with Information Technology*, edited by Richard Baskerville et al. Amsterdam: North-Holland.

Bluestone, Barry, and Irving Bluestone. 1992. *Negotiating the Future: A Labor Perspective on American Business*. New York: Basic Books.

Bluestone, Barry, and Bennett Harrison. 1982. *The Deindustrialization of America*. New York: Basic Books.

Blum, Linda M. 1991. *Between Feminism and Labor: The Significance of the Comparable Worth Movement*. Berkeley, California: University of California Press.

Boje, David M., and Robert D. Winsor. 1993. "The Resurrection of Taylorism: Total Quality Management's Hidden Agenda." *Journal of Organizational Change and Management* 4:57–70.

Bonacich, Edna. 1976. "Advanced Capitalism and Black/White Relations in the United States: A Split Labor Market Interpretation." *American Sociological Review* 41:34–51.

———. 1972. "A Theory of Ethnic Antagonism: The Split Labor Market." *American Sociological Review* 37:547–59.

Boreham, P. 1992. "The Myth of Post-Fordist Management: Work Organization and Employee Discretion in Seven Countries." *Employee Relations* 14:13–24.

Bosquet, Michel. 1977. *Capitalism in Crisis and Everyday Life*. Hassocks: Harvester.

Bowen, William. 1986. "The Puny Payoff from Office Computers." *Fortune* 26 May.

Bowles, Samuel, David M. Gordon, and Thomas E. Weisskopf. 1983. *Beyond the Waste Land: A Democratic Alternative to Economic Decline*. New York: Anchor Press/Doubleday.

Bradley, Harriet. 1986. "Technological Change, Management Strategies, and the Development of Gender-Based Job Segregation in the Labour Process." In *Gender and the Labour Process*, edited by David Knights and Hugh Wilmott. Brookfield, Vermont: Gower.

Braverman, Harry. 1976. "Two Comments." *Monthly Review* 28:119–24.

———. 1974. *Labor and Monopoly Capital: The Degradation of Work in the Twentieth Century*. New York: Monthly Review Press.

Bridges, William P., and Robert L. Nelson. 1989. "Markets in Hierarchies: Organizational and Market Influences on Gender Inequality in a State Pay System." *American Journal of Sociology* 95:616–59.

Bright, James R. 1958. "Does Automation Raise Skill Requirements?" *Harvard Business Review* 36:84–98.

Burawoy, Michael. 1991. "The Extended Case Method." In *Ethnography Unbound*, edited by Michael Burawoy et al. Berkeley, California: University of California Press.

———. 1985. *The Politics of Production*. London: Verso.

———. 1979. *Manufacturing Consent: Changes in the Labor Process under Monopoly Capitalism*. Chicago, Illinois: University of Chicago Press.

———. 1978. "Towards a Marxist Theory of the Labor Process: Braverman and Beyond." *Politics and Society* 8:247–312.

Burris, Beverly H. 1993. *Technocracy at Work*. Albany, New York: SUNY Press.

———. 1989a. "Technocratic Organization and Control." *Organization Studies* 10:1–22.

———. 1989b. "Technocracy and Gender in the Workplace." *Social Problems* 36:165–80.

———. 1983. *No Room at the Top: Underemployment and Alienation in the Corporation*. New York: Praeger.

Calem, Robert. 1993. "Working at Home, for Better or Worse." *New York Times* 18 April, Section 3, p. 1.

Callaghan, Polly, and Heidi Hartmann. 1991. *Contingent Work*. Washington, D.C.: Economic Policy Institute.

Cappelli, Peter. 1996. "Technology and Skill Requirements: Implications for Establishment of Wage Structures." *New England Economic Review* (Special Issue) May/June:139–53.

Carchedi, G. 1977. *On the Economic Identification of Social Classes*. London: Routledge & KeganPaul.

Carlson, Susan M. 1992. "Trends in Race/Sex Occupational Inequality: Conceptual and Measurement Issues." *Social Problems* 39:268–90.

Carre, F. , V. duRivage, and C .Tilly. 1994. "Representing the Part-time and Contingent Workforce: Challenges for Unions and Public Policy." In *Restoring the Promise of American Labor Law*, edited by Sheldon Friedman,

Richard W. Hurd, Rudolph A. Oswald, and Ronald L. Seeber. Ithaca, New York: ILR Press.

Carter, B. 1994. "A Growing Divide: Marxist Class Analysis and the Labour Process." *Capital and Class* 55:33–72.

Chandler, Alfred Dupont, Jr. 1990. *Scale and Scope: The Dynamics of Industrial Capitalism.* Cambridge, Massachusetts: Harvard University Press.

———. 1977. *Visible Hand: The Managerial Revolution in Management.* Cambridge, Massachusetts: Harvard University Press/Belknap Press Cambridge.

Child, John. 1981. "Culture, Contingency and Capitalism in the Cross-National Study of Organisations." In *Research in Organizational Behaviour,* edited by B. M. Staw and L. L. Cumings, 3:303–56. JAI Press.

Chrysler Corporation. 1963. *Story of the Airflow Cars, 1934–1937.* Detroit: Chrysler Corporation.

Clark, Kim, and Takahiro Fujimoto. 1991. *Product Development Performance: Strategy, Organization, and Management in the World Auto Industry.* Boston, Massachusetts: Harvard Business School Press.

Clawson, Dan. 1980. *Bureaucracy and the Labor Process: The Transformation of U.S. Industry, 1860–1920.* New York: Monthly Review Press.

Cleaver, Harry. 1979. *Reading 'Capital' Politically.* Austin, Texas: University of Texas Press.

Clegg, Stewart. 1990. *Modern Organizations: Organization Studies in the Postmodern World.* London: Sage Publications.

Cockburn, Cynthia. 1992. *In the Way of Women: Men's Resistance to Sex Equality in Organizations.* Ithaca, New York: ILR Press.

———. 1991. *In the Way of Women: Men's Resistance to Sex Equality in Organizations.* Ithaca, New York: ILR Press.

———. 1985. *Machinery of Dominance.* London: Pluto Press.

———. 1983. *Brothers: Male Dominance and Technological Change.* London: Pluto Press.

———. 1981. "Sex and Skill: Notes Towards a Feminist Economics." *Feminist Review* 6:79–88.

Cohen, Sheila. 1987. "A Labour Process to Nowhere?" *New Left Review* 165 (September/October):34–50.

Colclough, Glenna, and Charles M. Tolbert III. 1992. *Work in the Fast Lane: Flexibility, Divisions of Labor, and Inequality in High-Tech Industries.* Albany, New York: SUNY Press.

Cole, Robert E. 1979. *Work, Mobility, and Participation: A Comparative Study of American and Japanese Industry.* Berkeley, California: University of California Press.

Collins, Sharon. 1997. *Black Corporate Executives: The Making and Breaking of a Black Middle Class.* Philadelphia, Pennsylvania: Temple University Press.

Córdova, Efrén. 1986. "From Full-time Wage Employment to Atypical Employment: A Major Shift in the Evolution of Labour Relations?" *International Labour Review* 125:641–57.

Cotter, David A., JoAnn M. Difiore, Joan M. Hermsen, Brenda Marsteller Kowalewski, and Reeve Vanneman. 1994. "Occupational Gender Segregation and the Earnings Gap: Changes in the 1980s." Washington, D.C.: paper presented before the American Sociological Association.

Cressey, Paul, and John MacInnes. 1980. "Industrial Democracy and the Control of Labour." *Capital and Class* 11.

Crompton, Rosemary, and Gareth Jones. 1984. *White-collar Proletariat: Deskilling and Gender in Clerical Work*. Philadelphia, Pennsylvania: Temple University Press.

Cutcher-Gerschenfield, J., et al. 1994. "Japanese Team-based Work Systems in North America: Explaining the Diversity." *California Management Review* 37:42–63.

Cutler, Anthony, Barry Hindess, Paul Hirst, and Alan Hussain. 1977. *Marx's Capital and Capitalism Today*, Vol. 1. London: Routledge & Kegan Paul.

Davenport, Thomas H., and James E. Short. 1990. "The New Industrial Engineering: Information Technology and Business Process Redesign." *Sloan Management Review* 31:11–27.

Davis, Mike. 1986. *Prisoners of the American Dream*. London: Verso.

———. 1975. "The Stop Watch and the Wooden Shoe: Scientific Management and the Industrial Workers of the World." *Radical America* 9:69–95.

Dawson, Patrick, and Janette Webb. 1989. "New Production Arrangements: The Totally Flexible Cage?" *Work, Employment, and Society* 3:221–38.

Deetz, S. 1992. "Disciplinary Power in the Modern Corporation." In *Critical Management Studies*, edited by Matts Alvesson and Hugh Willmott. London: Sage Publications.

Delbridge, Rick, Peter Turnbull, and Barry Wilkinson. 1992. "Pushing Back the Frontiers: Management Control and Work Intensification under JIT/TQM Factory Regimes." *New Technology, Work, and Employment* 7:97–106.

Deming, Edwards W. 1984. *Out of the Crisis*. Cambridge, Massachusetts: MIT Press.

Dent, Mike. 1993. "Professionalism, Educated Labour, and the State: Hospital Medicine and the New Managerialism." *Sociological Review* 41:244–73.

Derber, Charles, ed. 1982. *Professionals as Workers*. Boston, Massachusetts: G. K. Hall.

Derber, Charles, William A. Schwartz, and Yale Magrass. 1990. *Power in the Highest Degree: Professionals and the Rise of a New Mandarin Order*. New York: Oxford University Press.

Dews, P. 1986. "The Nouvelle Philosophie and Foucault." In *Towards a Critique of Foucault*, edited by M. Gane. London: Routledge & Kegan Paul.

Doeringer, Peter B. 1991. "Workplace Turbulence and Workforce Preparedness." In *Turbulence in the American Workplace*, edited by Peter B. Doeringer et al. New York: Oxford University Press.

Donovan, Frank. 1965. *Wheels for a Nation*. New York: Thomas Crowell.

Drucker, Peter F. 1964. *Managing for Results: Economic Tasks and Risk-Taking Decisions*. New York: Harper & Row.

———. 1954. *The Practice of Management*. New York: Harper.

duRivage, Virginia, ed. 1992. *New Policies for the Part-time and Contingent Workforce*. New York: M. E. Sharp.

Dubofsky, Melvyn. 1995. "Labor Unrest in the United States, 1906–90." *Review* 18:125–35.

Edwards, P. K. 1994. "A Comparison of National Regimes of Labor Regulations and the Problem of the Workplace." In *Workplace Industrial Relations and the Global Challenge*, edited by Jacques Bélanger, P. K. Edwards, and Larry Haiven. Ithaca, New York: ILR Press.

———. 1990. "Understanding Conflict in the Labour Process: The Logic and Autonomy of Struggle." In *Labor Process Theory*, edited by David Knights and Hugh Willmott. London: Macmillan.

———. 1986. *Conflict at Work: A Materialist Analysis of Workplace Relations*. London: Basil Blackwell.

———. 1983. "The Political Economy of Industrial Conflict." *Economic and Industrial Democracy* 4:461–500.

Edwards, P. K., and Colin Whitston. 1991. "Workers Are Working Harder: Effort and Shop-floor Relations in the 1980s." *British Journal of Industrial Relations* 29:593–601.

Edwards, Richard. 1979. *Contested Terrain, The Transformation of the Workplace in the Twentieth Century*. New York: Basic Books.

Ehrenreich, Barbara. 1989. *Fear of Falling: The Inner Life of the Middle Class*. New York: HarperCollins.

Elger, Tony. 1991. "Task Flexibility and Intensification of Labour in UK Manufacturing in the 1980s." In *Farewell to Flexibility?*, edited by Anna Pollert. Oxford: Blackwell.

———. 1982. "Braverman, Capital Accumulation and Deskilling." In *The Degradation of Work: Skill, Deskilling, and the Labour Process*, edited by Stephen Wood. London: Hutchinson.

Elger, Tony, and Chris Smith, eds. 1994. *Global Japanization? The Transnational Transformation of the Labour Process*. London: Routledge.

England, Paula, George Farkas, Barbara Stanek Kilbourne, and Thomas Dou. 1988. "Explaining Occupational Sex Segregation and Wages:

Findings from a Model with Fixed Effects." *American Sociological Review* 53:544–58.

England, Paula, Melissa S. Herbert, Barbara Stanek Kilbourne, Lori L. Reid, and Lori McCreary Megdal. 1994. "The Gendered Valuation of Occupations and Skills: Earnings in the 1980 Census Occupations." *Social Forces* 73: 65–100.

Etzioni, Amitai. 1965. "Organizational Control Structure." In *Handbook of Organizations*, edited by James G. March. New York: Rand McNally.

Fanning, J., and R. Maniscalco. 1993. *Workstyles to Fit Your Lifestyle: Everyone's Guide to Temporary Employment.* Englewood Cliffs, New Jersey: Prentice-Hall.

Fantasia, Rick. 1988. *Cultures of Solidarity: Consciousness, Action, and Contemporary American Workers.* Berkeley, California: University of California Press.

Feigenbaum, Armand V. 1951. *Quality Control: Principles and Administration.* New York: McGraw-Hill.

Feldberg, Roslyn, and Evelyn Glenn. 1980. "Technology and Work Degradation: Re-examining the Impacts of Office Automation." Unpublished paper, Boston University.

Feldman, Elliot J., and Jerome Milch. 1982. *Technocracy versus Democracy: The Comparative Politics of International Airports.* Boston, Massachusetts: Auburn House.

Fierman, Jaclyn. 1994. "The Contingency Work Force." *Fortune* 24 January: 30–36.

Fischer, Frank. 1990. *Technocracy and the Politics of Expertise.* Newbury Park, California: Sage Publications.

———. 1984. "Ideology and Organization Theory." In *Critical Studies in Organization and Bureaucracy*, edited by Frank Fischer and Carmen Sirianni. Philadelphia, Pennsylvania: Temple University Press

Flink, James J. 1988. *The Automobile Age.* Cambridge, Massachusetts: MIT Press.

Foucault, Michel. 1977. *Discipline and Punish: The Birth of the Prison.* Harmondsworth: Penguin.

Fox, Richard W. 1983. "Epitaph for Middletown: Robert S. Lynd and the Analysis of Consumer Culture." In *Culture of Consumption*, edited by Richard W. Fox and T. J. Jackson Lears. New York: Pantheon.

Frank, Dana. 1994. *Purchasing Power: Consumer Organizing, Gender, and the Seattle Labor Movement, 1919–1929.* New York: Cambridge University Press.

Friedman, Andrew. 1990. "Managerial Strategies, Activities, Techniques and Technology: Towards a Complex Theory of the Labour Process. In *Labour Process Theory*, edited by David Knights and Hugh Willmott, 177–208. London: Macmillan.

———. 1977. *Industry and Labour: Class Struggle at Work and Monopoly Capitalism*. London: Macmillan.

Friedman, David. 1983. "Beyond the Age of Ford: The Strategic Basis of the Japanese Success in Automobiles." In *American Industry in International Competition*, edited by John Zysman and Laura Tyson. Ithaca, New York: Cornell University Press.

Fruin, Mark. 1994. *The Japanese Enterprise System*. Oxford: Clarendon Press.

Fuller, Linda, and Vicki Smith. 1991. "Consumers' Reports: Management by Customers in a Changing Economy." *Work, Employment, and Society* 5:1–16.

Gabriel, Yiannis. 1988. *Working Lives in Catering*. London: Routledge.

Game, Ann, and Rosemary Pringle. 1983. *Gender at Work*. Sydney: George Allen & Unwin.

Garrahan, P,. and P. Stewart. 1992. *The Nissan Enigma*. London: Mansell.

Garson, Barbara. 1988. *The Electronic Sweatshop*. New York: Penguin Books.

———. 1984. "Lordstown: Work in an American Auto Factory." In *Work in Market and Industrial Societies*, edited by Herbert Applebaum. Albany, New York: SUNY Press.

———. 1975. *All the Livelong Day: The Meaning and Demeaning of Routine Work*. Harmondsworth: Doubleday.

Gartman, David. 1993. "The Historical Roots of the Division of Labor in the U.S. Auto Industry." In *The Labor Process and Control of Labor*, edited by Berch Berberoglu. Westport, Connecticut: Praeger.

———. 1986. *Auto Slavery: The Labor Process in the American Automobile Industry: 1897–1950*. New Brunswick, New Jersey: Rutgers University Press.

———.1982. "Basic and Surplus Control in Capitalist Machinery: The Case of the Auto Industry." *Research in Political Economy* 6:23–57.

———. 1979. "Origins of the Assembly Line and Capitalist Control of Work at Ford." In *Case Studies on the Labor Process*, edited by Andrew Zimbalist. New York: Monthly Review Press.

Gelb, Joyce, and Marian Lief Palley. 1982. *Women and Public Policies*. Princeton, New Jersey: Princeton University Press.

Genovese, Eugene D. 1976. *Roll, Jordon, Roll: The World the Slaves Made*. New York: Vintage.

Gerlach, Michael. 1992. *Alliance Capitalism: The Social Organization of Japanese Business*. Berkeley, California: University of California Press.

Geschwender, James A. 1992. "Ethgender, Women's Waged Labor, and Economic Mobility." *Social Problems* 39:1–16.

———. 1987. "Race, Ethnicity, and Class." In *Recapturing Marxism: An Appraisal of Recent Trends in Sociological Theory*, edited by Rhonda F. Levine and Jerry Lembcke. New York: Praeger.

―――. 1978. *Racial Stratification in America.* Dubuque, Iowa: William C. Brown.

―――. 1977. *Class, Race, and Worker Insurgency: The League of Revolutionary Black Workers.* New York: Cambridge University Press.

Geschwender, James A., and Laura E. Geschwender. 1994. "Ethnicity, Married Women's Waged Labor, and The American Stratification Order: Causes and Consequences of Class and Ethnic Differentials in Married Women's Participation in the Waged Labor Force." Paper presented at the Annual Meetings of the American Sociological Association, Los Angeles, California, August.

Geschwender, James A., and Rhonda F. Levine. 1994. "Classical and Recent Theoretical Developments in the Marxist Analysis of Race and Ethnicity." In *From the Left Bank to the Mainstream: Historical Debates and Contemporary Research in Marxist Sociology,* edited by Patrick McGuire and Donald McQuari. New York: General Hall.

Glenn, Evelyn N., and Charles M. Tolbert III. 1992. "From Servitude to Service Work: Historical Continuities in the Racial Division of Paid Reproductive Labor." *Signs* 18:1–43.

―――. 1987. "Technology and Emerging Patterns of Stratification for Women of Color: Race and Gender Segregation in Computer Occupations." In *Women, Work, and Technology: Transformations,* edited by Barbara Wright et al. Ann Arbor, Michigan: University of Michigan Press.

Golden, Lonnie, and Eileen Applebaum. 1992. "What Was Driving the 1982–88 Boom in Temporary Employment: Preferences of Workers or Decisions and Power of Employers?" *Journal of Economics and Society* 51:473–94.

Goldman, Robert, and John Wilson. 1977. "The Rationalization of Leisure." *Politics and Society* 7:157–87.

Goldratt, Eliyahu M. 1986. *The Goal: A Process of Ongoing Improvement.* New York: North River Press.

Gordon, David, Michael Reich, and Richard Edwards. 1982. *Segmented Work, Divided Workers: The Historical Transformation of Labor in the United States.* New York: Cambridge University Press.

Gottfried, Heidi. 1992. "In the Margins: Flexibility as a Mode of Regulation in the Temporary Help Service Industry." *Work, Employment, and Society* 6:443–60.

―――. 1991. "Mechanisms of Control in the Temporary Help Service Industry." *Sociological Forum* 6:699–713.

Gouldner, Alvin. 1954. *Patterns of Industrial Bureaucracy.* Glencoe, Illinois: Free Press.

Graham, Laurie. 1994. "How Does the Japanese Model Transfer to the United States? A View from the Line." In *Global Japanization? The*

Transnational Transformation of the Labour Process, edited by Tony Elger and Chris Smith. London: Routledge.

Gramsci, Antonio. 1971. "Americanism and Fordism." In *Selections from the [1930] Prison Notebooks*, edited by Quintin Hoare and Geoffrey Nowell Smith. New York: International Publishers.

Greenbaum, Joan. 1995. *Windows on the Workplace: Computers, Jobs and the Organization of Office Work in the Late Twentieth Century*. New York: Cornerstone Books.

———. 1994. "The Forest and the Trees." *Monthly Review* 46:60–70.

———. 1979. *In the Name of Efficiency*. Philadelphia, Pennsylvania: Temple University Press.

Gregory, Judith. 1983. "The Next Move: Organizing Women in the Office." In *The Technological Woman*, edited by Jan Zimmerman. New York: Praeger.

Griffin, Larry J. 1992. "Temporality, Events, and Explanation in Historical Sociology." *Sociological Methods & Research* 20:403–27.

Gutek, Barbara. 1983. "Women's Work in the Office of the Future." In *The Technological Woman*, edited by Jan Zimmerman. New York: Praeger.

Hacker, Sally. 1990. *Doing It the Hard Way*. Boston, Massachusetts: Unwin & Hyman.

———. 1989. *Pleasure, Power, and Technology*. Boston, Massachusetts: Unwin & Hyman.

Hammer, Michael. 1990. "Reengineering Work: Don't Automate, Obliterate." *Harvard Business Review* 69:104–12.

Hammer, Michael, and James Champy. 1992. *Reengineering the Corporation: A Manifesto for Business Revolution*. New York: Warner Books.

Harvey, David. 1990. *The Condition of Postmodernity: An Enquiry into the Origins of Cultural Change*. Cambridge, Massachusetts: Blackwell.

———. 1982. *The Limits of Capital*. Chicago, Illinois: University of Chicago Press.

Haug, Marie. 1977. "Computer Technology and the Obsolescence of the Concept of Profession." In *Work and Technology*, edited by Marie Haug and Jacques Dofny. Beverly Hills, California: Sage Publications.

Head, Simon. 1996. "The New, Ruthless Economy." *New York Review of Books* 29 February.

Henson, Kevin. 1996. *Just a Temp: The Disenfranchized Worker*. Philadelphia, Pennsylvania: Temple University Press.

Herman, Peter. 1975. "In the Heart of the Heart of the Country: The Strike at Lordstown." In *The Rise of the Workers' Movements*, edited by Root & Branch Collective. Greenwich, Connecticut: Fawcett.

Herzenberg, Stephen, John Alic, and Howard Wial. Forthcoming. *Better Jobs for More People: A New Deal for the Service Economy*. Washington, D.C.: Twentieth Century Fund.

Heydebrand, Wolf. 1983. "Technocratic Corporatism: Toward a Theory of Occupational and Organizational Transformation." In *Organizational Theory and Public Policy*, edited by Richard Hall and Robert Quinn. Beverly Hills, California: Sage Publications.

———. 1979. "The Technocratic Administration of Justice." *Research in Law and Society* 2:29–64.

Hill, Stephen. 1991. "Why Quality Circles Failed but Total Quality Management Might Succeed." *British Journal of Industrial Relations* 29:541–68.

Hirsch, Barry, and David Macpherson. 1994. *Union Membership and Earnings Data Book 1993: Compilations from the Current Population Survey*. Washington, D.C.: The Bureau of National Affairs, Inc.

Hirschhorn, Larry. 1984. *Beyond Mechanization: Work and Technology in a Postindustrial Age*. Cambridge, Massachusetts: MIT Press.

Hochschild, Arlie. 1983. *The Managed Heart*. Berkeley, California: University of California Press.

Hodson, Randy. 1988. "Good Jobs and Bad Management: How New Problems Evoke Old Solutions in High-Tech Settings." In *Sociological and Economic Approaches to Labor Markets*, edited by Paula England and George Farkas. New York: Plenum Press.

Holliday, Barbara. 1969. "Harley Earl, the Original Car Stylist." *Detroit Free Press, Detroit Magazine* 25 May:8–16.

Horowitz, Morris, and Irwin Herrenstadt. 1966. "Changes in Skill Requirements of Occupations in Selected Industries." In *National Commission on Technology, Automation, and Economic Progress, The Employment Impact of Technological Change, Appendix*, Vol. II to *Technology and the American Economy*. Washington, D.C.: U.S. Government Printing Office.

Houseman, Susan N. 1995. "Job Growth and the Quality of Jobs in the U.S. Economy." *Labour* (Special Issue):S93–S124.

Hyman, Richard. 1996. "Institutional Transfer: Industrial Relations in Eastern Germany." *Work, Employment & Society* 10:601–39.

———. 1991. "Plus ça change? The Theory of Production and the Production of Theory." In *Farewell to Flexibility*, edited by Anna Pollert. Oxford: Blackwell.

Ichniowski, Casey. 1992. "Human Resource Practices and Productive Labor–Management Relations." In *Research Frontiers in Industrial Relations and Human Resources*, edited by David Lewin, Olivia S. Mitchell, and Peter D. Sherer. Madison: Industrial Relations Research Association.

Institute for Women's Policy Research. 1993. "The Wage Gap: Women's and Men's Earnings." Research-in-Brief. Washington, D.C.: Institute for Women's Policy Research.

In These Times Editorial Board. 1988. "Brave New Office?" *In These Times* 27:5.

Isaac, Larry, Susan Carlson, and Mary Mathis. 1994. "Quality of Quantity in Comparative/Historical Analysis: Temporally Changing Wage Labor Regimes in the United States and Sweden." In *The Comparative Political Economy of the Welfare State*, edited by Thomas Janoski and Alexander Hicks. New York: Cambridge University Press.

Isaac, Larry, and Larry Griffin. 1989. "A Historicism in Time-Series Analyses of Historical Process: Critique, Redirection, and Illustrations from U.S. Labor History." *American Sociological Review* 54:873–90.

Ishikawa, Kaoru. 1985. *What Is Total Quality Control? The Japanese Way.* Englewood Cliffs, New Jersey: Prentice-Hall.

Jackall, Robert. 1988. *Moral Mazes: The World of Corporate Managers.* New York: Macmillan.

Jacobs, Jerry A. 1989. "Long-Term Trends in Occupational Segregation by Sex." *American Journal of Sociology* 95:160–73.

Jacobs, Jerry A., and Ronnie J. Steinberg. 1990. "Compensating Differentials and the Male–Female Wage Gap: Evidence from the New York State Comparable Worth Study." *Social Forces* 69:439–68.

Jacoby, Sanford. 1985. *Employing Bureaucracy.* New York: Columbia University Press.

Jermier, John M. 1988. "Sabotage at Work: The Rational View." *Research in the Sociology of Organizations* 6:101–34.

Jermier, John, Walter Nord, and David Knights. eds. 1994. *Resistance and Power in Organisations.* London: Routledge.

Josefowitz, Natasha. 1983. "Paths to Power in High Technology Organizations." In *The Technological Woman*, edited by Jan Zimmerman. New York: Praeger.

Jurgens, Ulrich, Thomas Malsch, and Knuth Dohse. 1993. *Breaking from Taylorism.* New York: Cambridge University Press.

Kalleberg, Arne, Michael Wallace, and Lawrence Raffalovich. 1984. "Accounting for Labor's Share: Class and Income Distribution in the Printing Industry." *Industrial and Labor Relations Review* 37:386–402.

Kaminski, Michelle, Domenick Bertelli, Melissa Moye, and Joel Yudken. 1996. *Making Change Happen: Six Cases of Unions and Companies Transforming Their Workplaces.* Washington, D.C.: Work and Technology Institute.

Kanter, Rosabeth. 1983. *The Change Masters.* New York: Simon & Schuster.

Katz, Harry C. 1985. *Shifting Gears: Changing Labor Relations in the U.S. Automobile Industry.* Cambridge, Massachusetts: MIT Press.

Keefe, Jeffrey H. 1991. "Numerically Controlled Machine Tools and Workers Skills." *Industrial and Labor Relations Review* 44:503–19.

Kelley, Robin D. G. 1994. *Race Rebels: Culture, Politics, and the Black Working Class.* New York: Free Press.

Kenney, Martin, and Richard Florida. 1993. *Beyond Mass Production: The Japanese System and Its Transfer to the U.S.* Oxford: Oxford University Press.

Kerfoot, D., and David Knights. 1994. "Empowering the Quality Worker: The Seduction and Contradiction of the Total Quality Phenomenon." In *Making Quality Critical*, edited by Adrian Wilkinson and Hugh Willmott. London: Routledge.

Kern, Horst, and Michael Schumann. 1984. "Work and Social Character: Old and New Contours." *Economic and Industrial Democracy* 5:51–71.

Kerr, Clark, John T. Dunlop, Frederick H. Harbison, and Charles A. Myers. 1960. *The Problems of Labor and Management in Economic Growth.* New York: Oxford University Press.

Kidder, Trach. 1981. *Soul of a New Machine.* Boston, Massachusetts: Little, Brown.

Kilborn, Peter. 1994. "College Seniors Find More Jobs, But Modest Pay." *New York Times* 1 May:1.

Kilbourne, Barbara Stanek, Paula England, and Kurt Beron. 1994. "Effects of Individual, Occupational, and Industrial Characteristics of Earnings: Intersections of Race and Gender." *Social Forces* 72:1149–77.

Kilbourne, Barbara Stanek, Paula England, George Farkas, Kurt Beron, and Dorthea Weir. 1994. "Returns to Skill, Compensating Differentials, and Gender Bias: Effects of Occupational Characteristics on the Wages of White Women and Men." *American Journal of Sociology* 100:689–719.

King, Mary C. 1992. "Occupational Segregation by Race and Sex, 1940–1988." *Monthly Labor Review* 115:30–36.

Klein, Heinz, and Philip Kraft. 1994a. "Social Control and Social Contract in Networking: Total Quality Management and the Control of Knowledge Work." In *NetWORKing: Connecting Workers in and between Organization*, edited by A. Clement, P. Kolm, and I. Wagner. Amsterdam: North-Holland.

———. 1994b. "Social Control and Social Contract in NetWORKing: Total Quality Management and the Control of Work in the United States." *Computer Supported Cooperative Work* (CSCW) 2:89–108.

Knights, David. 1995. "Hanging Out the Dirty Washing: Labour Process Theory in the Age of Deconstruction." Paper to 13th International Labour Process Conference. Blackpool, April.

———. 1990. "Subjectivity, Power and the Labour Process." In *Labour Process Theory*, edited by David Knights and Hugh Willmott. London: Macmillan.

Knights, David, and Hugh Willmott, eds. 1990. *Labour Process Theory.* London: Macmillan.

———. 1989. "Power and Subjectivity at Work: From Degradation to Subjugation in Social Relations." *Sociology* 23:535–58.

Kochan, Thomas A., Harry C. Katz, and Robert B. McKersie. 1986. *The Transformation of American Industrial Relations*. New York: Basic Books.

Kornbluh, Joyce L. 1964. *Rebel Voices: An IWW Anthology*. Ann Arbor, Michigan: University of Michigan Press.

Kraft, Philip. 1979. "The Industrialization of Computer Programming." In *Case Studies on the Labor Process*, edited by Andrew Zimbalist. New York: Monthly Review Press.

———. 1977. *Programmers and Managers: The Routinization of Computer Programming in the United States*. New York: Springer Verlag.

Kraft, Philip, and Steven Dubnoff. 1986. "Job Content, Fragmentation, and Control in Computer Software Work." *Industrial Relations* 25:184–96.

Kraft, Philip, and Duane P. Truex. 1994. "Organizational Emergence and the 'Postmodern' Enterprise." In *Transforming Organizations with Information Technology*, edited by Richard Baskerville et al. Amsterdam: North-Holland.

Kunda, Gideon. 1992. *Engineering Culture: Control and Commitment in a High-Tech Corporation*. Philadelphia, Pennsylvania: Temple University Press.

Kusterer, Ken. 1978. *Know-How on the Job: The Important Working Knowledge of "Unskilled" Workers*. Boulder, Colorado: Westview Press.

Laclau, Ernesto, and Chantal Mouffe. 1985. *Hegemony and Socialist Strategy: Towards a Radical Democratic Politics*. New York: Verso.

LaFever, Mortier W. 1924. "Workers, Machinery, and Production in the Automobile Industry." *Monthly Labor Review* 19:1–26.

Lane, Christel. 1994. "Is Germany Following the British Path? A Comparative Analysis of Stability and Change." *Industrial Relations Journal* 25:187–98.

———. 1989. *Management and Labour in Europe: The Industrial Enterprise in Germany, Britain and France*. Aldershot: Edward Elgar.

———. 1987. "Capitalism or Culture? A Comparative Analysis of the Position in the Labour Process and Labour Market of Lower White-Collar Workers in the Financial Services Sector of Britain and the Federal Republic of Germany." *Work, Employment, and Society* 1:57–83.

Larson, Magali S. 1980. "Proletarianization and Educational Labor." *Theory and Society* 9:131–76.

Layder, Derek. 1993. *New Strategies in Social Research: An Introduction and Guide*. Cambridge, Massachusetts: Polity Press.

Lazonick, William. 1991. *Business Organization and the Myth of the Market Economy*. New York: Cambridge University Press.

Leidner, Robin. 1993. *Fast Food, Fast Talk*. Berkeley, California: University of California Press.

Lewis, David. 1976. *The Public Image of Henry Ford*. Detroit, Michigan: Wayne State University Press.

Lippert, John. 1978. "Shopfloor Politics at Fleetwood." *Radical America* 12:53–69.

Littler, Craig R. 1990. "The Labor Process Debate: A Theoretical Review 1974–1988."In *Labor Process Theory*, edited by David Knights and Hugh Willmott. London: Macmillan.

———. 1982. *The Development of the Labour Process in Capitalist Societies*. London: Heinemann.

Lynd, Robert S., and Helen Merrell Lynd. 1929. *Middletown: A Study in Contemporary American Culture*. New York: Harcourt, Brace.

Lyotard, Jean-Francois. 1987. "The Post-modern Condition." In *After Philosophy: End or Transformation?*, edited by Kenneth Baynes, James Bhoman, and Thomas McCarthy. Cambridge, Massachusetts: MIT Press.

MacMinn, Strother, and Michael Lamm. 1985. "A History of American Automobile Design, 1930–1950." In *Detroit Style: Automotive Form, 1925–1950*, 52–101. Detroit, Michigan: Detroit Institute of Arts.

McArdle, L., et al. 1994. "Total Quality Management and Participation: Employee Involvement or the Enhancement of Exploitation?" In *Making Quality Critical*, edited by Adrian Wilkinson and Hugh Willmont. London: Routledge.

McCabe, D., and David Knights. 1995. "TQM Reaches the Subjectivity That Other Management Initiatives Cannot." Paper to 13th International Labour Process Conference. Blackpool, April.

McCann, Michael W. 1994. *Rights at Work: Pay Equity Reform and the Politics of Legal Mobilization*. Chicago, Illinois: University of Chicago Press.

McKinlay, Alan, and Phil Taylor. 1996. "Power, Surveillance and Resistance: Inside the 'Factory of the Future.'" In *The New Workplace and Trade Unionism*, edited by Peter Ackers, Chris Smith, and Paul Smith. London: Routledge.

McLellan, John. 1975. *Bodies Beautiful: A History of Car Styling and Craftsmanship*. Newton Abbot: David & Charles.

McNally, David. 1995. "Language, History, and Class Struggle." *Monthly Review* 47:13–31.

Machung, Anne. 1984. "Word Processing: Forward for Business, Backward for Women." In *My Troubles Are Going to Have Trouble with Me*, edited by Karen Sacks and Dorothy Remy. New Brunswick, New Jersey: Rutgers University Press.

March, James A., and Herbert Simon. 1958. *Organizations*. New York: Wiley.

Marginson, Paul, P. K. Edwards, R. Martin, John Purcell, and K. Sisson. 1988. *Beyond the Workplace*. Oxford: Blackwell.

Martella, Maureen. 1991. *Just a Temp: Expectations and Experiences of Women Clerical Temporary Workers*. Washington, D.C.: U.S. Department of Labor Women's Bureau.

Marx, Karl. [1852] 1978. *The Eighteenth Brumaire of Louis Bonaparte*. Peking: Foreign Languages Press.

———. [1867] 1976. *Capital* vol. I. New York: Vintage Books.

———. [1848] 1975a. "Manifesto of the Communist Party." In *Collected Works*, edited by Karl Marx and Frederick Engels, 6:477–519. New York: International Publishers.

———. [1844] 1975b. "Economic and Philosophical Manuscripts of 1844." In *Collected Works*, edited by Karl Marx and Frederick Engels, 3:229–346. New York: International Publishers.

———. [1857] 1973. *Grundrisse*. New York: Vintage.

———. [1867] 1967. *Capital*. Vol. 1. New York: International Publishers.

Mathews, J. 1993. "Organisational Innovation: Competing Models of Productive Efficiency." Paper to the 5th APROS International Conference. Honolulu, Hawaii.

Meikle, Jeffrey L. 1979. *Twentieth Century Limited: Industrial Design in America, 1925–1939*. Philadelphia: Temple University Press.

Meiksins, Peter. 1994. "Labor and Monopoly Capital for the 1990s: A Review and Critique of the Labor Process Debate." *Monthly Review* 46:45–59.

———. 1988. "The 'Revolt of the Engineers' Reconsidered." *Technology and Culture* 29:219–46.

———. 1984. "Scientific Management and Class Relations: A Dissenting View." *Theory and Society* 13:177–209.

Meyer, Stephan. 1981. *The Five Dollar Day: Labor Management and Social Control in the Ford Motor Company, 1908–1921*. Albany, New York: SUNY Press.

Miles, Dione. 1986. *Something in Common*. Detroit, Michigan: Wayne State University Press.

Milkman, Ruth. 1991. *California's Factors: Labor Relations and Economic Globalization*. Los Angeles: Institute of Industrial Relations, University of California.

———. 1987. *Gender at Work: The Dynamics of Job Segregation by Sex During World War II*. Urbana, Illinois: University of Illinois Press.

Miller, Peter, and Timothy O'Leary. 1987. "Accounting and the Construction of the Governable Person." *Accounting, Organization and Society* 13:235–65.

Mintzberg, Henry. 1979. *The Structuring of Organizations*. Englewood Cliffs, New Jersey: Prentice-Hall.

Moberg, David. 1978. "No More Junk: Lordstown Workers and the Demand for Quality." *Insurgent Sociologist* 8:63–69.

Montgomery, David. 1979. *Workers' Control in America.* New York: Cambridge University Press.

Moody, Kim. 1988. *An Injury to All: The Decline of American Unionism.* London: Verso.

Moseley, Fred. 1991. *The Falling Rate of Profit in the Postwar United States Economy.* New York: St. Martin's Press.

———. 1986. "The Intensity of Labor and the Productivity Slowdown." *Science and Society* 50:210–18.

Mossberg, Walter, and Laurence O'Donnell. 1971. "End of the Affair." *Wall Street Journal* 30 March:A17.

Mueller, Frank. 1994. "Societal Effect, Organization Effect, and Globalization." *Organization Studies* 15:407–28.

Munro, R. 1994. "Governing the New Province of Quality: Autonomy, Accounting, and the Dissemination of Accountability." In *Making Quality Critical*, edited by Adrian Wilkinson and Hugh Willmott. London: Routledge.

Murakami, T. 1994. "Teamwork and Trade Union Workplace Representation in the German and British Car Industry." Paper presented to the 12th International Labour Process Conference. Aston University.

Murphree, Mary C. 1984. "Brave New Office: The Changing World of the Legal Secretary." In *My Troubles Are Going to Have Trouble with Me*, edited by Karen Sacks and Dorothy Remy. New Brunswick, New Jersey: Rutgers University Press.

National Association of Temporary Services. 1992. *Report on the Temporary Help Services Industry.* DRI/McGraw Hill.

National Research Council. 1986. *Computer Chips and Paper Clips.* Vol. 1. Washington, D.C.: National Academy Press.

Negrey, Cynthia. 1993. *Gender, Time, and Reduced Work.* Albany, New York: SUNY Press.

Nevins, Allan, and Frank E. Hill. 1954. *Ford: The Times, the Man, the Company.* New York: Scribner.

Newton, T. 1994. "Re-socialising the Subject? A Re-reading of Grey's 'Career' as a Project of the Self." *Working Paper Series.* Department of Business Studies: University of Edinburgh.

Nine to Five, Working Women Educational Fund. 1992. *High Performance Office Work: Improving Jobs and Productivity.* Cleveland, Ohio: 9 to 5.

Nissen, Bruce, and P. Seybold. 1994. "Labor and Monopoly Capital in the Labor Education Context." *Monthly Review* 46:36–44.

Norsworthy, J. R., and Craig A. Zabala. 1985. "Worker Attitudes, Worker Behavior, and Productivity in the U.S. Automobile Industry, 1959–1976." *Industrial and Labor Relations Review* 38:544–57.

Noyelle, Thierry. 1987. *Beyond Industrial Dualism*. Boulder, Colorado: Westview Press.

O'Connor, James. 1984. *Accumulation Crisis*. New York: Basil Blackwell.

———. 1973. *The Fiscal Crisis of the State*. New York: St. Martin's Press.

O'Doherty, D. 1994. "Institutional Withdrawal? Anxiety and Conflict in the Emerging Banking Labour Process." Paper presented to 12th *International Labour Process Conference*, Aston.

O'Neill, June, and Solomon Polachek. 1993. "Why the Gender Gap in Wages Narrowed in the 1980s." *Journal of Labor Economics* 11:205–28.

Odiorne, George S. 1965. *Management by Objectives: A System of Managerial Leadership*. New York: Pitman Publication Corp.

Oliver, George. 1981. *Cars and Coachbuilding*. London: Sotheby Parke Bernet.

Olssen, Erik, and Jeremy Brecher. 1992. "The Power of Shop Culture: The Labour Process in the New Zealand Railway Workshops, 1890–1930." *International Review of Social History* 37: 350–75.

Osterman, Paul. 1995. "Skill, Training, and Work Organization in American Establishments." *Industrial Relations* 34:125–46.

———. 1992. "Internal Labor Markets in a Changing Environment: Models and Evidence." In *Research Frontiers in Industrial Relations and Human Resources*, edited by David Lewin, Olivia S. Mitchell, and Peter D. Sherer. Madison, Wisconsin: Industrial Relations Research Association.

Ouchi, William. 1981. *Theory Z: How American Business Can Meet the Japanese Challenge*. New York: Avon Books.

Parcel, Toby L. 1989. "Comparable Worth, Occupational Labor Markets and Occupational Earnings: Results from the 1980 Census." In *Pay Equity, Empirical Inquiries*, edited by Robert T. Michael, Heidi I. Hartmann, and Brigid O'Farrells. Washington, D.C.: National Academy Press.

Parker, Mike. 1993. "Industrial Relations Myth and Shop-floor Reality: The 'Team' Concept in the Auto Industry." In *Industrial Democracy in America: The Ambiguous Promise*, edited by Nelson Lichtenstein and Howell John Harris. New York: Cambridge University Press.

Parker, Mike, and Jane Slaughter. 1994. "Management by Stress: The Team Concept in the U.S. Auto Industry." *Science as Culture* 8:27–58.

———. 1988. *Choosing Sides: Unions and the Team Concept*. Boston, Massachusetts: South End Press.

Parker, Robert E. 1994. *Flesh Peddlers and Warm Bodies: The Temporary Help Industry and Its Workers*. New Brunswick, New Jersey: Rutgers University Press.

Pascale, Richard, and Anthony Athos. 1982. *The Art of Japanese Management*. London: Allen Lane.

Penn, Roger. 1984. *Skilled Workers in the Class Structure*. New York: Cambridge University Press.

Perrow, Charles. 1986. *Complex Organizations: A Critical Essay.* 3rd ed. New York: Free Press.

Peters, Tom. 1992. *Liberation Management: Necessary Disorganization for the Nanosecond Nineties.* New York: Knopf.

Petersen, Trond, and Laurie A. Morgan. 1995. "Separate and Unequal: Occupation-Establishment Sex Segregation and the Wage Gap." *American Journal of Sociology* 101:329–65.

Peterson, Richard R. 1989. "Firm Size, Occupational Segregation, and the Effects of Family Status on Women's Wages." *Social Forces* 68: 397–414.

Phillips, Anne, and Barbara Taylor. 1980. "Sex and Skills." *Feminist Review* 6:79–88.

Pine, Joseph B. 1993. *Mass Customization: The New Frontier in Business Competition.* Boston, Massachusetts: Harvard Business School Press.

Piore, Michael J., and Charles F. Sabel. 1984. *The Second Industrial Divide.* New York: Basic Books.

Piven, Francis Fox, and Richard Cloward. 1982. *The New Class War: Regan's Attack on the Welfare State and Its Consequences.* New York: Patheon Books.

Pollert, Anna. 1996. "'Teamwork' on the Assembly Line: Contradiction and Dynamics of Union Resilience." In *The New Workplace and Trade Unionism,* edited by Peter Ackers, Chris Smith, and Paul Smith. London: Routledge.

———. 1991. *Farewell to Flexibility?* Oxford: Basil Blackwell.

Porter, Michael. 1990. *The Competitive Advantage of Nations.* New York: Free Press.

———. 1985. *Competitive Advantage: Creating and Sustaining Superior Performance.* New York: Free Press.

Postone, Moishe. 1993. *Time, Labor, and Social Domination: A Reinterpretation of Marx's Critical Theory.* New York: Cambridge University Press.

Poulantzas, Nicos. 1975. *Classes in Contemporary Capitalism.* London: Verso.

Prechel, Harland. 1994. "Economic Crisis and the Centralization of Control over the Managerial Process: Corporate Restructuring and Neo-Fordist Decision Making." *American Sociological Review* 59:723–45.

Pretzer, William S. 1986. "The Ambiguity of Streamlining: Symbolism, Ideology, and Cultural Mediator." In *Streamlining America.* Dearborn, Michigan: Henry Ford Museum and Greenfield Village.

Rae, John B. 1984. *The American Automobile Industry.* Boston, Massachusetts: Twayne.

Raffalovich, Lawrence, Michael Wallace, and Kevin Leicht. 1992. "Macroeconomic Structure and Labor's Share of Income." *American Sociological Review* 57:243–58.

Ramsay, Harvie. 1991. "Reinventing the Wheel? A Review of the Development and Performance of Employee Involvement." *Human Resource Management Journal* 1:1–22.

Reich, Robert B. 1991. *The Work of Nations: Preparing Ourselves for 21st-century Capitalism*. New York: Knopf.

Reskin, Barbara F. 1994. "Segregating Workers: Occupational Differences by Race, Ethnicity, and Sex." Industrial Relations Research Association Proceedings of the Forty-Sixth Annual Meeting. Madison, Wisconsin: Industrial Relations Research Association.

———. 1993. "Sex Segregation in the Workplace." *Annual Review of Sociology* 19:241–70.

Reskin, Barbara F., and Naomi R. Cassirer. 1994. "Segregating Workers: Occupational Segregation by Sex, Race, and Ethnicity." Washington, D.C.: Paper presented before the American Sociological Association.

Reskin, Barbara F., and Irene Padavic. 1994. *Women and Men at Work*. Thousand Oaks, California: Pine Forge Press.

Reskin, Barbara F., and Patricia A. Roos. 1990. *Job Queues, Gender Queues: Explaining Women's Inroads into Male Occupations*. Philadelphia, Pennsylvania: Temple University Press.

Rifkin, Jeremy. 1995. *The End of Work*. New York: Putnam.

Ritzer, George. 1993. *The MacDonaldization of Society*. London: Pine Forge Press.

Robertson, David, et al. 1993. *The CAMI Report: Lean Production in a Unionized Auto Plant*. Willowdale, Ontario: CAW-Canada Research Department

Roethlisberger, Fritz J., and William J. Dickson, with the collaboration of H. A. Wright. 1946. *Management and the Worker*. Cambridge, Massachusetts: Harvard University Press.

Rogers, Jackie Krasas. 1995a. "Just a Temp: Experience and Structure of Alienation in Temporary Clerical Employment." *Work and Occupations* 22:137–66.

———. 1995b. "It's Only Temporary? The Reproduction of Gender and Race Inequalities in Temporary Clerical Employment." Unpublished doctoral dissertation. Los Angeles: University of Southern California.

———. 1994. "Lawyers for Rent: The Gendering of Temporary Employment for Lawyers." Paper presented at the 1994 Meetings of the American Sociological Association, Los Angeles.

Rogers, Jackie Krasas, and Kevin D. Henson. 1997. "'Hey, Why Don't You Wear a Shorter Skirt?' Structural Vulnerability and the Organization of Sexual Harassment in Temporary Clerical Employment." *Gender & Society* 11:2:215–37.

Roos, Patricia. 1990. "Hot Metal to Electronic Composition: Gender, Technology and Social Change." In *Job Queues, Gender Queues*, edited by

Barbara Reskin and Patricia Roos. Philadelphia, Pennsylvania: Temple University Press.

Rose, M. 1985. "Universalism, Culturalism and the Aix Group." *European Sociological Review* 1:65–83.

Rose, Nikolas. 1990. *Governing the Soul: The Shaping of the Private Self.* London: Routledge.

Roseneau, Paula Marie. 1992. *Post-Modernism and the Social Sciences.* Princeton, New Jersey: Princeton University Press.

Rosenzweig, Roy. 1983. *Eight Hours for What We Will: Workers and Leisure in an Industrial City, 1870–1920.* New York: Cambridge University Press.

Rothschild, Emma. 1973. *Paradise Lost: The Decline of the Auto-Industrial Age.* New York: Vintage.

Russo, John. 1990. "Lordstown, Ohio Strike of 1972." In *Labor Conflict in the United States,* edited by Ronald Filippelli. New York: Garland Publishing.

Sabel, Charles. 1982. *Work and Politics: The Division of Labor in Industry.* New York: Cambridge University Press.

Salerno, Salvatore. 1989. *Red November, Black November: Culture and Community in the Industrial Workers of the World.* Albany, New York: SUNY Press.

Sandberg, A., ed. 1995. *Enriching Production.* Aldershot: Avebury.

Sassen-Koob, S. 1984. "The New Labor Demand in Global Cities." In *Cities in Transformation,* edited by Michael P. Smith. Beverly Hills, California: Sage.

Sayer, Andrew. 1989. "Post Fordism in Question." *International Journal of Urban and Regional Research* 13:666–95.

Schipper, Edward J. 1921. "Closed Body Production Costs Minimized in Essex Coach." *Automotive Industries* 45:956–57.

Schor, Juliette. 1991. *The Overworked American.* New York: Basic Books.

Scott, James C. 1990. *Domination and the Arts of Resistance: Hidden Transcripts.* New Haven, Connecticut: Yale University Press.

Segal, Lewis M., and Daniel G. Sullivan. 1995. "The Temporary Labor Force." *Economic Perspectives* 2:2–19.

Sewell, Graham, and Barry Wilkinson. 1992a. "Someone to Watch Over Me: Surveillance, Discipline and the Just-in-Time Labour Process." *Sociology* 26:271–89.

———. 1992b. "Empowerment or Emasculation? Shopfloor Surveillance in a Total Quality Organisation." In *Reassessing Human Resource Management,* edited by Paul Blyton and Peter Turnbull. London: Sage Publications.

Sewell, William, Jr. 1996. "Three Temporalities: Toward an Eventful Sociology." In *The Historic Turn in the Human Sciences,* edited by Terrence J. McDonald. Ann Arbor, Michigan: University of Michigan Press.

Shaiken, Harley. 1994. *Work Transformed*. Lexington, Massachusetts: Lexington Books.

———. 1984. *Work Transformed: Automation and Labor in the Computer Age*. New York: Holt, Rinehart, and Winston.

Shaiken, Harley, Steven Lopez, and Isaac Mankita. 1997. "Two Routes to Team Production: Saturn and Chrysler Compared." *Industrial Relations* 36:17–45.

Shakow, Don M., Julie Graham, and Katherine D. Gibson. 1992. "Industrial Restructuring in the U.S. Economy: A Value Analysis." *Capital and Class* 47:35–66.

Simon, Herbert A. 1976. *Administrative Behavior*. 3rd ed. New York: Free Press.

Simons, Robert. 1995. *Levers of Control: How Managers Use Control Systems to Drive Strategic Renewal*. Boston, Massachusetts: Harvard Business School Press.

Sloan, Alfred P., Jr. 1972. *My Years with General Motors*. Garden City, New York: Anchor.

Smart, Barry. 1985. *Michel Foucault*. London: Routledge.

Smith, Chris. 1996a. "Harry Braverman (1920–1976)." In *International Encyclopedia of Business and Management*, edited by M. Warner. London: Routledge.

———. 1996b. "Japan, The Hybrid Factory and Cross-National Organisational Theory." Special Issue 'Vernetzung und Vereinnahmung-Arbeitzwischen Internationlisierung und neuen Manaegmentkonzepten' *Austrian Journal of Sociology* (forthcoming).

———. 1987. *Technical Workers*. London: Macmillan.

Smith, Chris, David Knights, and Hugh Willmont, eds. 1996. *White-Collar Work: The Non-Manual Labour Process*. London: Macmillan.

Smith, Chris, and Peter Meiksins. 1995. "System, Society, and Dominance Effects in Cross-National Organizational Analysis." *Work, Employment, and Society* 9:241–67.

Smith, Chris, and Paul Thompson. 1992. "When Harry Met Sally . . . and Hugh and David and Andy: A Reflection on Ten Years of the Labour Process Conference." Paper for the 10th *International Labour Process Conference*, Aston.

Smith, Chris, and Hugh Willmott. 1995. "The New Middle Class and the Labour Process." In *White-Collar Work*, edited by Chris Smith, David Knights, and Hugh Willmott. London: Macmillan.

Smith, Tony. 1994. "Flexible Production and Capital Wage Relations in Manufacturing." *Capital and Class* 53:39–63.

Smith, Vicki. 1994. "Braverman's Legacy: The Labor Process Tradition at 20." *Work and Occupations* 21:403–21.

———. 1993. "Flexibility in Work and Employment: The Impact on Women." *Research in the Sociology of Organizations*. Greenwich, Connecticut: JAI Press.

———. 1990. *Managing in the Corporate Interest*. Berkeley, California: University of California Press.

Sorensen, Elaine. 1989a. "Measuring the Effect of Occupational Sex and Race Composition on Earnings." In *Pay Equity, Empirical Inquiries*, edited by Robert T. Michael, Heidi I. Hartmann, and Brigid O'Farrells. Washington, D.C.: National Academy Press.

———. 1989b. "The Crowding Hypothesis and Comparable Worth." *Journal of Human Resources* 25:55–89.

Sorge, Arndt. 1991. "Strategic Fit and the Societal Effect: Interpreting Cross-National Comparisons of Technology, Organization and Human Resources." *Organization Studies* 12:161–90.

Special Task Force. 1973. *Work in America*. Cambridge: The MIT Press.

Spenner, Kenneth. 1983. "Deciphering Prometheus: Temporal Changes in Work." American Sociological Review 48:824-37.

———. 1979. "Temporal Changes in Work Content." *American Sociological Review* 44:968–75.

Stalk, George, and Thomas M. Hout. 1990. *Competing Against Time: How Time-Based Competition Is Reshaping Global Markets*. New York: Free Press.

Stark, David. 1980. "Class Struggle and the Transformation of the Labor Process." *Theory and Society* 9:89–130.

Steiger, Thomas L., and Barbara Reskin. 1990. "Baking and Baking Off: Deskilling and the Changing Sex Makeup of Bakers." In *Job Queues, Gender Queues*, edited by Barbara Reskin and Patricia Roos. Philadelphia, Pennsylvania: Temple University Press.

Steiger, Thomas L., and Mark Wardell. 1995. "Gender and Employment in the Services Sector." *Social Problems* 42:91–123.

———. 1992. "The Labor Reserve and the Skill Debate." *Sociological Quarterly* 33:413–33.

Steinberg, Ronnie J. 1992. "Cultural Lag and Gender Bias in the Hay System of Job Evaluation." *Work and Occupations* 19:387–423.

Stepan-Norris, Judith, and Maurice Zeitlin. 1991. "'Red' Unions and Bourgeois Contracts? The Effects of Political Leadership on the 'Political Leadership' on the 'Political Regime of Production.'" *American Journal of Sociology* 96:1151–1200.

Stephenson, Carol. 1996. "The Different Experience of Trade Unionism in Two Japanese Transplants." In *The New Workplace and Trade Unionism*, edited by Peter Ackers, Chris Smith, and Paul Smith. London: Routledge.

Straussman, Jeffrey D. 1978. *The Limits of Technocratic Politics*. New Brunswick, New Jersey: Transaction Books.

Stroeber, Myra, and Carolyn Arnold. 1987. "Integrated Circuits/Segregated Labor: Women in Computer-related Occupations and High-tech Industries." In *Computer Chips and Paper Clips*, edited by Heidi Hartmann. Vol. 2. Washington, D.C.: National Academy Press.

Swidler, Ann. 1986. "Culture in Action: Symbols and Strategies." *American Sociological Review* 51:273–86.

Szymanski, Sharon. 1989. "Unrequited Skilled: The Effects of Technology on Clerical Work." Ph.D. dissertation, New York: New School for Social Research.

Tanner, Julian, Scott Davies, and Bill O'Grady. 1992. "Immanence Changes Everything: A Critical Comment on the Labour Process and Class Consciousness." *Sociology* 26:439–53.

Taylor, Frederick. 1913. *The Principles of Scientific Management*. New York: Harper & Brothers.

Terkel, Studs. 1975. *Working*. New York: Avon.

———. 1974. "Gary Bryner, President, Lordstown Local, UAW." In *Working*, edited by Studs Terkel. New York: Pantheon.

Thomas, Robert J. 1994. *What Machines Can't Do: Politics and Technology in the Industrial Enterprise*. Berkeley, California: University of California Press.

Thompson, Heather Ann. 1995. "Auto Workers, Dissent, and the UAW: Detroit and Lordstown." In *Autowork*, edited by Robert Asher and Ronald Edsforth. Albany, New York: SUNY Press.

Thompson, Paul. 1990. "Crawling from the Wreckage: The Labour Process and the Politics of Production." In *Labour Process Theory*, edited by David Knights and Hugh Willmott. London: Macmillan.

———. 1989. *The Nature of Work*. 2nd. London: Macmillan.

Thompson, Paul, Terry Wallace, Jorg Flecker, and Roland Ahlstrand. 1995. "It Ain't What You Do It's the Way That You Do It: Production Organisation and Skill Utilisation in Commercial Vehicles." *Work, Employment, and Society* 9:719–42.

Tilly, Charles. 1995. "Globalization Threatens Labor's Rights." *International Labor and Working Class History* 47:1–23.

Toffler, Alvin. 1990. *Powershift: Knowledge, Wealth, and Violence at the Edge of the 21st Century*. New York: Bantam Books.

Tomaskovic-Devey, Donald. 1993. "The Gender and Race Composition of Jobs and the Male/Female, White/Black Pay Gaps." *Social Forces* 72:45–76.

Treiman, Donald J. and Heidi I. Hartmann. 1981. *Women, Work, and Wages*. Washington, D.C.: National Academy Press.

Townley, Barbara. 1993. "Performance Appraisal and the Emergence of Management." *Journal of Management Studies* 30:221–38.

Tuckman, A. 1994. "Ideology, Quality, and TQM." In *Making Quality Critical*, edited by Adrian Wilkinson and Hugh Willmott. London: Routledge.

Turnbull, Peter. 1988. "The Limits to Japanisation—Just-in-Time, Labour Relations and the U.K. Automotive Industry." *New Technology, Work, and Employment* 3:7–20.

Turner, Brian J., Domenick Bertelli, and Michelle Kaminski. 1996. "What Works and What Doesn't in Workplace Transformations: Lessons from the Cases and the Model—Findings & Conclusions." In *Making Change Happen: Six Cases of Unions and Companies Transforming Their Workplaces*, edited by Michelle Kaminski, Domenick Bertelli, Melissa Moye, and Joel Yudken. Washington, D.C.: Work and Technology Institute.

Turner, L., and P. Auer. 1994. "A Diversity of New Work Organization: Human-Centred, Lean and In-Between." *Industrielle Beziehungen* 1:39–61.

Uchitelle, Louis. 1994. "New Economy Dashes Old Notions of Growth." *New York Times* 27 November, B1.

Udy, Stanley J., Jr. 1970. *Work in Traditional and Modern Society*. Englewood Cliffs, New Jersey: Prentice-Hall, Inc.

U.S. Bureau of the Census. 1992. *Statistical Abstract of the United States 113th edition*. U.S. Bureau of the Census. Washington, D.C.: U.S. Government Printing Office.

———. 1992a. Money Income of Families and Persons in the United States: 1991. Current Population Reports, Series P-60, No. 180 (August). Washington, D.C.: U.S. Government Printing Office.

———. 1992b. Detailed Occupation and Other Characteristics from the EEO File for the United States. 1990 Census of Population Supplementary Reports, 1990 CP-S-1-1 (October). Washington, D.C.: U.S. Government Printing Office.

———. 1991. *Statistical Abstract of the United States 1991*. Washington, D.C.: U.S. Government Printing Office.

———. 1982. *Statistical Abstract of the United States 103rd edition*. U.S. Bureau of the Census. Washington, D.C.: U.S. Government Printing Office.

———. 1972. *Statistical Abstract of the United States 93rd edition*. U.S. Bureau of the Census. Washington, D.C.: U.S. Government Printing Office.

———. 1963. *Statistical Abstract of the United States 84th edition*. U.S. Bureau of the Census. Washington, D.C.: U.S. Government Printing Office.

U.S. Bureau of Labor Statistics. 1995. Employment and Earnings (January).

———. 1993. Employment and Earnings 40 (January). Washington, D.C.: U.S. Department of Labor.

———. 1992. Employment and Earnings 39 (January). Washington, D.C.: U.S. Department of Labor.

————. 1991. Employment and Earnings 38 (January). Washington, D.C.: U.S. Department of Labor.

————. 1972. *Handbook of Labor Statistics*, 1972. Washington, D.C.: U.S. Government Printing Office.

————. Various years. *Analysis of Work Stoppages*. U.S. Government Printing Office.

————. Yearly. Household Annual Averages—Table 39.

U.S. Department of Commerce. 1990. *Annual Survey of Manufactures*. Washington, D.C.: U.S. Government Printing Office.

————. 1980. *Annual Survey of Manufactures*. Washington, D.C.: U.S. Government Printing Office.

————. 1970. *Annual Survey of Manufactures*. Washington, D.C.: U.S. Government Printing Office.

————. 1960. *Annual Survey of Manufactures*. Washington, D.C.: U.S. Government Printing Office

————. 1950. *Annual Survey of Manufactures*. Washington, D.C.: U.S. Government Printing Office.

U.S. Department of Commerce. 1993. *National Income and Product Accounts of the United States Volume 1, 1929–58*. Economics and Statistics Administration. Washington, D.C.: U.S. Government Printing Office.

————. 1993. *National Income and Product Accounts of the United States Volume 2, 1959–88*. Economics and Statistics Administration. Washington, D.C.: U.S. Government Printing Office.

U.S. Department of Commerce. 1972. "Occupation by Industry." Special Reports PC(2)-7C in *1970 U.S. Census of Population*, Bureau of the Census. Washington, D.C.: U.S. Government Printing Office.

————. 1962. "Occupation by Industry." Special Report P-E No. 1C in *1950 U.S. CENSUS of Population*, Bureau of the Census. Washington, D.C.: U.S. Government Printing Office.

————. 1954. "Occupation by Industry." Special Report P-E No. 1C in *1950 U.S. CENSUS of Population*, Bureau of the Census. Washington, D.C.: U.S. Government Printing Office.

U.S. Department of Commerce. 1953. *Statistical Abstract of the United States 74th edition.*

U.S. Department of Commerce. 1993. *Survey of Current Business*. Economics and Statistics Administration. Washington, D.C.: U.S. Government Printing Office.

Useem, Michael. 1990. "Business Restructuring, Management Control and Corporate Organization." *Theory and Society* 19:681–707.

Van der Pijl, Kees. 1984. *The Making of an Atlantic Ruling Class*. London: Verso.

Van Raaphorst, Donna L. 1988. *Union Maids Not Wanted: Organizing Domestic Workers, 1870–1940*. New York: Praeger.

Vallas, Steven P., and John P. Beck. 1996. "The Transformation of Work Revisited: The Limits of Flexibility in American Manufacturing." *Social Problems* 43:339–61.

Vogel, Ezra. 1979. *Japan as Number One: Lessons for America*. Cambridge, Massachusetts: Harvard University Press.

Wajceman, Janet. 1991. "Patriarchy, Technology, and Conceptions of Skill." *Work and Occupations* 18:29–45.

Walby, Sylvia. 1989. "Flexibility and the Changing Sexual Division of Labour." In *The Transformation of Work? Skill, Flexibility, and The Labour Process*, edited by Stephen Wood. London: Unwin & Hyman.

Wallace, Michael. 1979. "Conflict Regulation in the Industrial Sphere: An Indirect Test of Dahrendorf's Theory." *Sociological Focus* 12:229–38.

Wallerstein, Immanuel. 1995. "Response: Declining States, Declining Rights?" *International Labor and Working Class History* 47:24–27.

Wardell, Mark. 1992. "Changing Organizational Forms: From the Bottom Up." In *Rethinking Organization: New Directions in Organization Theory and Analysis*, edited by Michael Reed and Michael Hughes. London: Sage Publications.

———. 1990. "Labour and Labour Process." In *Labour Process Theory*, edited by David Knights and Hugh Willmott. London: Macmillan.

Warner, Malcolm. 1994. "Japanese Culture, Western Management: Taylorism and Human Resources in Japan." *Organization Studies* 15:509–33.

Webb, Janette. 1996. "Vocabularies of Motive and the 'New' Management." *Work, Employment, and Society* 10:251–71.

Weber, Max. 1947. *The Theory of Social and Economic Organization*. Translated by Talcott Parsons and A. M. Henderson. New York: The Free Press.

Webster, Frank, and Kevin Robbins. 1993. "I'll Be Watching You: Comment on Sewell and Wilkinson." *Sociology* 27:243–52.

———. 1989. "Plan and Control: Towards a Cultural History of the Information Society." *Theory and Society* 18:323–52.

Weinbaum, Batya, and Amy Bridges. 1976. "The Other Side of the Paycheck: Monopoly Capital and the Structure of Consumption." *Monthly Review* 28:1–9.

Weller, Ken. 1974. *The Lordstown Struggle and the Real Crisis in Production*. Solidarity Pamphlet #45. London: Solidarity.

West, Jackie. 1990. "Gender and the Labor Process." In *Labour Process Theory*, edited by David Knights and Hugh Willmott. London: Macmillan.

Westwood, Sallie. 1985. *All Day, Every Day: Factory and Family in the Making of Women's Lives*. Urbana, Illinois: University of Illinois Press.

Wickens, P. D. 1993. "Lean Production and Beyond: The System, Its Critics and the Future." *Human Resource Management Journal* 3:75–89.

Wilkinson, Adrian, and Hugh Willmott. 1994. "Introduction." In *Making Quality Critical*, edited by Adrian Wilkinson and Hugh Willmott. London: Routledge.

Wilkinson, B. 1996. "Culture, Institutions, and Business in East Asia." *Organization Studies* 17.

Williams, K., C. Haslam, and J. Williams. 1987. "The End of Mass Production?" *Economy and Society* 16:405–38.

Willmott, Hugh. 1995. "From Braverman to Schizophrenia: The Diseased Condition of Subjectivity in Labour Process Theory." Paper presented to 13th International Labour Process Conference. Blackpool, April.

———. 1993a. "Strength Is Ignorance, Slavery Is Freedom: Managing Culture in Modern Organisations." *Journal of Management Studies* 30:515–52.

———. 1993b. "Managing the Academics: Commodification and Control in the Development of University Education in the UK." Unpublished paper.

———. 1990. "Subjectivity and the Dialectics of Praxis: Opening up the Core of Labour Process Analysis." In *Labour Process Theory*, edited by David Knights and Hugh Willmott. London: Macmillan.

Womack, James P., Daniel T. Jones, and Daniel Roos. 1990. *The Machine That Changed the World*. New York: Rawson Associates.

Wood, Stephen. 1993. "The Production Model." Background paper prepared for the Lean Workplace Conference (Canadian Autoworkers Union), Port Elgin, Ontario, Canada (September).

———. 1982. "Introduction." In *The Degradation of Work? Skill, Deskilling, and the Labour Process*, edited by Stephen Wood. London: Hutchinson & Co. Ltd.

Wood, Stephen, and M. T. Albanese. 1995. "Can We Speak of Human Resource Management on the Shop Floor?" *Journal of Management Studies* 3:215–47.

Wright, Erik O. 1985. *Classes*. London: Verso.

Wright, Patrick J. 1979. *On a Clear Day You Can See General Motors*. Grosse Pointe, Michigan: Wright Enterprises.

Yuthas, Kristi, and Tony Tinker. 1994. *Paradise Regained? Myth, Milton, and Management Accounting*. Typescript.

Zabala, Craig A. 1995. "Sabotage in an Automobile Assembly Plant: Worker Voice on the Shopfloor." In *Autowork*, edited by Robert Asher and Ronald Edsforth. Albany, New York: SUNY Press.

Zetka, James R., Jr. 1995a. *Militancy, Market Dynamics, and Workplace Authority: The Struggle over Labor Process Outcomes in the U.S. Automobile Industry: 1946 to 1973*. Albany, New York: SUNY Press.

———. 1995b. "Union Homogenization and the Organizational Foundations of Plantwide Militancy in the U.S. Automobile Industry, 1959-1979." *Social Forces* 73:789–810.

Zimbalist, Andrew. ed. 1979. *Case Studies on the Labor Process*. New York: Monthly Review Press.

Zolberg, Aristide. 1995. "Response: Working Class Dissolution." *International Labor and Working Class History* 47:28–38.

Zuboff, Shoshana. 1988. *In the Age of the Smart Machine: The Future of Work and Power*. New York: Basic Books.

———. 1982. "New Worlds of Computer-Mediated Work." *Harvard Business Review* 60:142–52.

About the Authors

Beverly Burris is Professor of Sociology at the University of New Mexico. She is the author of *No Room at the Top: Underemployment and Alienation in the Corporation* (Praeger, 1983) and *Technocracy at Work* (SUNY Press, 1993). The later is a retheorization of workplace organization and how it has been transformed by computerization and related socioeconomic developments during the post-World War II period. She has published articles in the areas of theory, work and organizations, and gender in such journals as *Social Problems*, *Social Science Quarterly*, and *Organization Studies*. Presently, her work focuses on the effects of computerization on everyday life.

Larry D. Christiansen is a doctoral candidate in the Department of Sociology at Florida State University. His major interests include political economy and social organization, with special emphasis on labor history/labor process, social movements, and historical-comparative sociology. He received the Braverman Award, given by the Labor Studies Division of the Society for the Study of Social Problems, in 1995; and he recently received a National Science Foundation Dissertation Enhancement Grant to support his work on the National Domestic Workers Union of America.

David Gartman is a Professor of Sociology at the University of South Alabama. He is the author of *Auto Slavery: The Development of the Labor Process in the American Automobile Industry* and *Auto Opium: A Social History of American Automobile Design*. He is currently working on a book on the influence of auto design on modern and postmodern architecture.

James Geschwender is a Professor of Sociology and Department Chair at the State University of New York–Binghamton. He began his career conducting research in the areas of industrial and occupational sociology broadly defined (the sociology of industrial society). Over the course of time his work increasingly shifted in the direction of the study of social inequality and stratification.

265

This began with a focus on the historical development of societal systems of racial stratification as exemplified by the case of African-Americans. This concern gradually broadened to include historical studies of Asians and Portuguese in Hawaii. It soon became evident that it was not possible to understand inequality and stratification without a thorough comprehension of the role played by gender and the manner in which the social construction of race, ethnicity, and gender are all intertwined and differ according to class position.

Joan Greenbaum is professor of Computer Information Systems at LaGuardia College of City University of New York (CUNY). She is author of numerous articles and books, including her most recent book, *Windows on the Workplace* (Monthly Review Press, 1995). During the past several years she has been Visiting Professor of Informatics at the University of Oslo. Her research focuses on issues of participatory design of computer systems with special attention on the need to bridge the gap between technical people and people who are using systems.

Larry W. Isaac received his Ph.D. from Indiana University in 1979. He is currently Professor of Sociology at Florida State University. His research on social movements/state politics, labor studies, and historical methods for analyzing social change have appeared in such publications as the *American Sociological Review, American Journal of Sociology, Research in Social Movements, Conflict & Change, International Journal of Comparative Sociology, Historical Methods, Sociological Methods & Research*, and various anthologies. He is the recipient of the ASA Comparative-Historical Sociology Section "Best Recent Article Award" (now, the "Barrigton Moore Award") for his paper (co-authored with Larry Griffin), "Ahistoricism in Time-Series Analyses of Historical Process: Critique, Redirection, and Illustrations from U.S. Labor History" appearing in the *American Sociological Review*. He has also received an ASA/ NSF "Advancement of the Discipline Award" for his work on social-historical methods. He is currently involved in research projects on organized labor and labor militancy since World War II, the social organization of repressive collective violence, and methods for analyzing historical processes of social change.

Phil Kraft is a Professor of Sociology at the State University of New York–Binghamton. He has studied the organization of computer-intensive occupations and is currently working with Richard Sharpe on a study of global software production.

Peter Meiskskins is Associate Professor and Chair of the Department of Sociology at Cleveland State University. He is co-author of *Engineering*

Labour: Technical Workers in Comparative Perspective (Verso, 1996) with Chris Smith and of numerous articles on technical work, the labor process and theories of class. He is currently working with Peter Whalley on a project (funded by the Sloan Foundation) on part-time work among technical professionals and on a history of the Curtis-Wright Cadettes, a group of women engineers trained during World War II.

Jackie Krasas Rogers is an assistant professor of Labor Studies and Industrial Relations at The Pennsylvania State University. Her interests include gender and racial inequity, specifically with regard to work and employment. She is especially interested in the meaning of recent changes in the workplace for women and people of color. Her forthcoming book is entitled, *It's Only Temporary?* She has published and presented work on many aspects of temporary employment, including temporary (contract) attorneys, sexual harassment, and organizing temporary workers. Her current research studies substitute teachers and the work-family nexus.

Chris Smith is Lecturer of Industrial Relation in the Aston Business School, the University of Aston. He has been as active participant in the Labour Process Conference, having co-organized conferences and edited volumes of papers from the conference. He is co-author of *White Collar Workers, Trade Unions and Class* (with Peter Armstrong, Bob Carter, and Theo Nichols), *Innovations in Work Organisation: The Cadbury Experience* (with John Child and Michael Rowlinson), and *Engineering Labour: Technical Workers in Comparative Perspective* (with Peter Meiksins). He is author of *Technical Worker: Class, Labour and Trade Unionism*.

Thomas L. Steiger is Associate Professor of Sociology and Women's Studies at Indiana State University. He has teaching and research interests in the areas of the labor process, political economy, and gender stratification. He is currently researching effects of the historic shift of women into the paid labor force on occupational sex segregation.

Paul Thompson is Professor of Management at Edinurgh University. He is a co-organizer of the Labour Process Conference in the United Kingdom, and has published widely, including *The Nature of Work: An Introduction to Debates on the Labour Process*, and *Work Organisations* (with David McHugh). During 1997 he was Visiting Principal Fellow at the Department of Management, University of Wollongong, Australia. He is a long-time activist on the left and is currently editor of *Renewal: A Journal of New Labour Politics*.

Mark Wardell is Associate Professor and Head of Labor Studies and Industrial Relations and Associate Professor of Sociology at The Pennsylvania State

University. He has published a variety of articles in the areas of sociological theory, as well as the labor process and the organization of work. His works have appeared in journals such as *Social Problems, Theory and Society, Accounting, Organisations & Society*, and *The Sociological Quarterly*. His current research interests include analyses of workplace restructuring.

Index

269

Product: competitive, 21; cultural
connotations in, 100–101;
decomposition of, 25; defining, 82;
designs, 125, 126–127;
development, 21; differentiation,
104, 107, 108, 125; mix scheduling,
127; output, 24; policy, 101;
proliferation, 105; quality, 24;
standardization, 82, 99, 100, 105,
107; stigmatized, 100, 101;
streamlining, 102; styling, 95, 101,
102; unit costs, 24; value of, 191;
variations, 25, 127, 206

Production; administrative costs of, 21;
alienated processes, 94; "American
System" of, 20; automated, 38, 45,
80, 81, 83; capitalist, 20, 44, 93;
centralized, 96; commodity, 20, 217,
223; computer-based, 19, 45;
control of, 9, 218; coordination of,
105, 218; costs, 43, 105, 147n12,
190; craft, 32, 98–99, 100; cycle
time, 25; decentralized, 127;
defining, 192; designs, 21, 98;
differentiated, 107; direct, 26;
disruption of, 96; division of
monetary rewards, 190, 192;
economic imperatives of, 95;
elements of, 4; flexible, 107, 199,
206, 207; fragmentation of, 100;
global, 26, 229; goals, 31tab;
imperatives, 98; increasing, 80;
innovation-mediated, 226, 230n4;
intensification, 120;
internationalization of, 50;
investment in, 192; Japanese, 108,
109, 209, 229; labor-intensive, 21;
lean, 10, 24, 108, 206, 208, 209, 226,
230n4; mass, 33n6, 93, 94, 95–98,
96, 97, 98–103, 103, 107, 108, 125,
132; mechanized, 81; modular, 207;
new concepts, 206; objective, 93;
organization of, 93, 219; pace, 106;
parts-sharing in, 105, 106; physical,
6; relations of, 178, 217;
reorganization of, 127; rigidification

of, 100; as social activity, 27, 34n18;
social means of, 4; social
organization of, 134;
standardization, 125; standards, 25;
stoppages, 96, 106; surplus labor,
218; surplus value, 118; system
design, 24, 26; targets, 121; team-
based, 219; technical means of, 4;
technocratic reorganization of,
38–42; traditional, 17–18;
transformation of, 37, 50;
transnational, 222–223, 224; volume
of, 99; workers, 18, 19, 20, 25, 198,
202

Profit: distribution process, 144; falling,
95, 105, 191; pursuit of, 4, 14;
slowing, 123, 125; "squeeze," 196

Public sector: competition in, 209;
employment in, 229; privatization
in, 18; Taylorism and, 43

Quality circles, 108, 209
Quit rates, 126

Race: contingent employment and, 54;
expertise and, 49; exploitation and,
176; labor process and, 6, 65–68;
labor value and, 199, 200;
management bias and, 10; new
configurations, 38; segregation, 39,
48; strikes and, 138, 141;
technocracy and, 47–50

Rationality, bounded, 22, 28

Rationalization: limits of, 32;
management, 220; Taylorist, 25;
technocratic, 44; work, 34n18, 80,
86

Regulations: bureaucratic, 48;
governmental, 6, 9, 10; workplace
activity, 4

Relations: authority, 217;
authority/command, 217;
capital/labor, 196; circulation, 144;
class, 38, 44, 45, 47, 117, 221;
competitive, 211;
conception/execution, 38, 44, 50,

DATE DUE